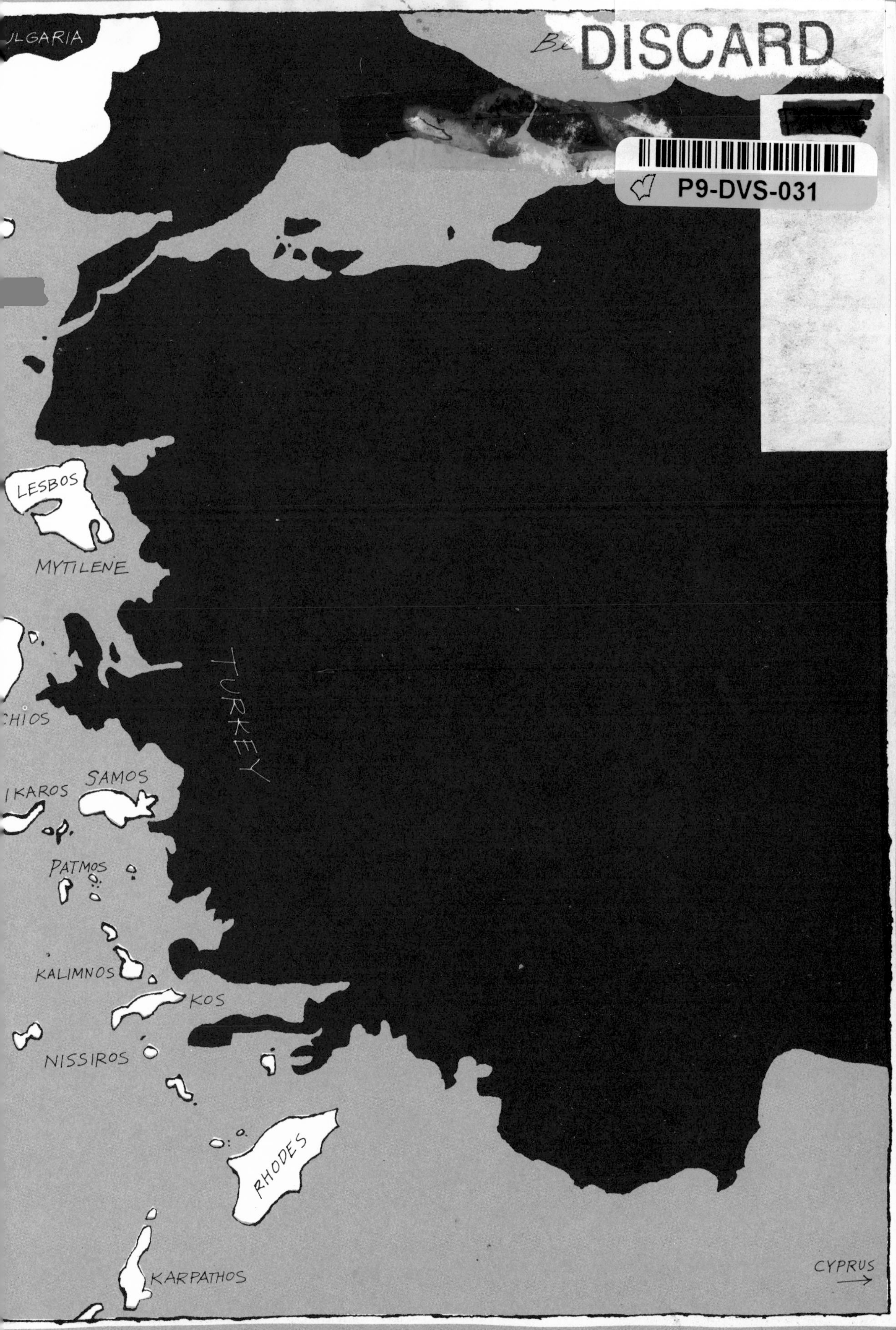

BULGARIA

DISCARD

P9-DVS-031

LESBOS

MYTILENE

TURKEY

CHIOS

IKAROS SAMOS

PATMOS

KALIMNOS

KOS

NISSIROS

RHODES

KARPATHOS

CYPRUS →

THE REGIONAL
CUISINES OF GREECE

The Regional

by The Recipe Clu[b]

Cuisines of Greece

of St. Paul's Greek Orthodox Church

Authors of *The Art of Greek Cookery*

WASH DRAWINGS BY EARL THOLLANDER

Doubleday & Company, Inc.
Garden City, New York

The authors would like to express their gratitude to Helen P. Hayes for her assistance in preparing the first set of sketches for this book. In addition, Mr. Thollander, the artist, would like to thank Walt Barnes for his help in locating Greek material that aided him immeasurably in preparing the final illustrations.

Library of Congress Cataloging in Publication Data

Hempstead, N.Y. St. Paul's Greek Orthodox Church.
    Recipe Club.
    The regional cuisines of Greece.

    Includes index.
    1. Cookery, Greek.   I. Title.
TX723.5.G8H45   1981   641.59495
ISBN: 0-385-15680-4
Library of Congress Catalog Card Number 79-6038

THE RECIPE CLUB
OF ST. PAUL'S GREEK ORTHODOX CHURCH

Katherine R. Boulukos, Chairperson
Tina Barbatsuly
Lydia S. Baris
Nina Bendo
Irene Carnavos
Sandy Cidis
Carol Efthimiou
Mary Livadas
Theodora Lourekas
Helen Manis
Mary Mormanis
Helen Pappas
Athena Philippides
Dora Prieston
Maria Prois
Irene Skeados
Epiphany Touris
Ethel Wiley
Dede Yale

*The present members of the Club would like to acknowledge
the help of the following past members:*

Georgia Arapakis
Helen Calfo
Bella Carpou
Mary Djinis
Helen P. Hayes
Kay Poulos

Contents

A Note on Using This Book: Whenever an asterisk (°) follows the name of a recipe, that recipe appears elsewhere in the book. Consult Index for page numbers.

Introduction

More than twenty years ago a group of women from St. Paul's Greek Orthodox Church in Hempstead, Long Island, decided that a novel way to raise money for their church would be to gather together some of the many wonderful Greek recipes they, and their mothers and grandmothers, had been using for generations, and publish them in book form. The result of their efforts, subsequently published by Doubleday as *The Art of Greek Cookery*, went on to become a bestseller among cookbooks, and over the years has introduced thousands upon thousands of readers to the marvels of Greek cooking.

The success of *The Art of Greek Cookery* was particularly remarkable in that it stemmed from nowhere. Its publication predates the American gastronomic revolution; in fact, the entire field of ethnic cooking was pretty much unexplored at the time. This situation obviously has changed dramatically, especially over the last decade, but the Recipe Club of St. Paul's Church feels (and felt all along) that neither *The Art of Greek Cookery*, despite its excellence and success as a basic introduction, nor its subsequent imitators, exhausts the range of Greek cuisine. Thus, almost from the day of publication of the first book, the Recipe Club began assembling the recipes that have found their way into this volume.

As the work of selecting (and discarding) recipes proceeded, it became obvious to us that volume two would differ from volume one in a number of ways. Perhaps most important, the recipes here are on the whole more sophisticated (though not necessarily more complex) than those in *The Art of Greek Cookery*, a development fostered by the greater sophistication of American cooks in general, and by the greater availability in this country of Greek products such as *Phyllo* and the various Greek cheeses. As we explored our recipe files, it also became evident that many of the recipes we were considering for inclusion here had deep roots in specific localities of Greece. Hence our title, *The Regional Cuisines of Greece*, and the inclusion of point of origin designations for the majority of recipes. Finally, we have endeavored throughout the book to look forward without losing authenticity. In many instances, recipes have been subtly altered to facilitate the use of blenders and food processors; we frequently recommend substitutes for ingredients that might be difficult to find in this country; and the number of recipes that lend themselves to advance preparation and freezing has been dramatically increased and all are designated as such.

Some things, however, don't change. As in the first volume, we have indicated Lenten recipes (an important factor in Greek cooking and a boon to vegetarians and anyone wishing to cut down on the consumption of animal protein), and have included in the appendix a selection of Greek menus (based, of course, on the recipes in the book) for a variety of occasions. Above all, our intent has remained the same: to preserve the heritage of Greek cooking, to make it known to as many Greeks and non-Greeks as possible, and in the process to aid our beloved St. Paul's Church. We seem to have accomplished these goals with *The Art of Greek Cookery* and hope that our second effort will find equal favor among our friends and readers.

KATHERINE R. BOULUKOS
Chairperson, Recipe Club
1981

THE REGIONAL
CUISINES OF GREECE

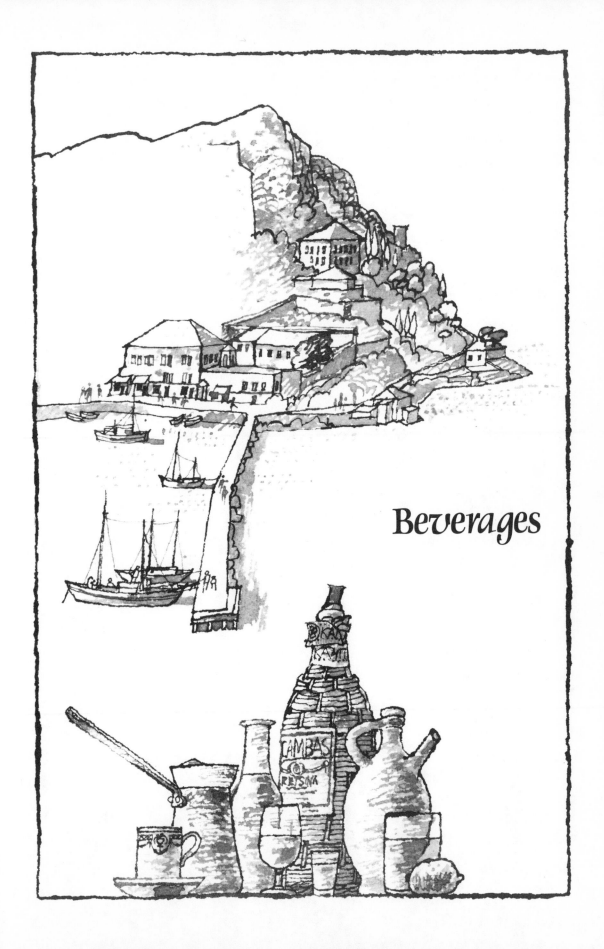

Beverages

GREEK WINES AND SPIRITS

Cultivation of the vine is an ancient activity in Greece, dating back, according to some archeologists, to around 400 B.C. In a country blessed by a constant sun and endowed with vast expanses of chalky, volcanic ash terrain ideal for grape-growing, it is no wonder that Dionysus, the god of wine, was revered in ancient times. Though overshadowed by the quality of French wines, the products of Greek vintners have long held their own in the world marketplace. It was, in fact, to Greece (and America) that France turned to replenish her vineyards when they were devastated by the Phylloxera epidemic of the late nineteenth century. Greek vintners responded with vast new plantings to replace the French losses and for years exported heavily to France and other European countries.

Over the last two decades, the Greek wine industry has expanded rapidly and is making impressive inroads in the growing American market, so much so that with very little effort it is possible to sample and enjoy in America a representative variety from Greece's wine-producing regions at relatively modest prices.

The Wine Regions of Greece

The history-rich peninsula of the Peloponnese is the country's largest vine-growing area, accounting for as much as one third of total production. The beautiful, sloping mountains of the region gave birth to a classic dry white wine, named *Santa Helena*, as well as to a sweet white Muscat and the world-famous *Mavrodaphne*, a dark, velvety dessert wine best sipped at room temperature.

The Attic plain, stretching south of Athens down to Sounion, is the second largest wine producer of Greece and the greatest source of domestically consumed table wines. *Roditys*, the popular rosé, and the dry *Hymmettus* white (grown near famed Mount Hymettus) are two of Attica's best-known products.

Famous for its sweet Muscat, the island of Samos is unique in Greek viniculture in that its vineyards and their products are protected by government-controlled place of origin designations, similar to the French *appellation contrôlée*. In other words, no wine not grown on Samos may take the name, nor may Samos wine be blended with any other.

Other areas contributing to Greece's wine production are Macedonia, a heavy producer of robust table wines; the Island of Rhodes, known for its dry white *Lindos* wine; the Island of Santorini, whose volcanic soil and sun-parched slopes produce wines of high alcoholic content; Crete, another maker of big robust table wines; Cyprus, source of the renowned *Commanderie St. John* dessert wine; and Cephalonia, one of the chief wine producers among the Ionian islands, and the home of a famous dry white wine called *Robola*.

Retsina

No discourse on Greek wines is complete without at least a mention of the unique pine-resin flavored wine known as *Retsina*. The term *Retsina* is a generic name that applies to any wine (usually white or rosé) that has been flavored with pine resin, a practice that dates back to ancient times when resin (or sometimes pitch) was used as a preservative. Resinated wines do not improve with age and should always be drunk cold. Though admittedly an acquired taste, *Retsina* is so indigenous a Greek product, that no traveller in the country should leave without at least having tasted it. Who knows, you might discover in yourself a born *retsina* aficionado, not a bad thing to be considering the low prices of the wine.

Greek Wines Readily Available in the U.S.

A reputable brand name on a bottle of wine is one way of ensuring the quality of the wine within. Fortunately, three outstanding Greek houses export their line of products to the United States. They are *Cambas*, *Achaia Clauss*, and *Botrys*. More recently two large co-operatives of viticulturists have begun exporting wines to the United States under the brand names of *Marko* and *Patraiki*. In addition, some brand names found on locally available Greek wines are indicative of place of origin, such as KEO, for wines from Cyprus, and *Samos*, for wines from that storied island.

The following is a listing of the varieties and types of Greek wines currently being exported to the United States, with capsule descriptions:

WHITE (serve well chilled)

    St. Helena—an aristocratic dry wine, best reserved for special occasions

    Demestica—a light, clean, very fine wine; one of Greece's best-sellers

    Mantina—a well-balanced, full-bodied wine

    Robola—Cephalonia's delicate, dry white wine

    Aphrodite—a fine, vintage wine from Cyprus

    Hymettus—another popular dry wine, from the mountain area that also produces Greece's best honey

    Retsina—the resin-flavored wine of the people (for more about Retsina, see above).

ROSÉ (serve chilled)

    Roditys—a light, dry, very popular all-purpose wine

    Kokkineli—a full-bodied, resin-flavored wine, closely related to Retsina

    Rosella—a more robust version of Roditys from Cyprus.

RED (serve at room temperature)

    Castel Danielis—a vintage wine of great quality and depth

    Pendeli—a dry, full-bodied, estate-grown wine from the southern slope of Mt. Pendeli

    Mont Ambelos—a big dry wine with a smooth finish

    Othello—a subtle, velvety wine from Cyprus.

DESSERT WINES

Greece's sweet wines have long been ranked among the world's best. The most important and famous are: Mavrodaphne; Commanderie St. John, a KEO wine from Cyprus; and Muscat from Samos.

Liqueurs and Brandies

Though never a large producer of spirits, Greece is nonetheless the source of a small number of distinctively-flavored, high-quality liqueurs and brandies. In fact the best of Greece's brandies are at no disadvantage when compared with the finest products of other European distillers. Among the most famous and frequently exported Greek spirits are the following:

Metaxa (5 and 7 stars)—a world renowned, highly praised brandy with a unique and wonderfully palatable flavor. 92-proof Metaxa has a warm, rich color and is perfect for sipping slowly from a warmed snifter in order to better savor its aroma. Though Greeks prefer it neat, Metaxa is great in mixed drinks or on the rocks with a twist of lemon. A superb *Grande Fine* grade is also available, but in limited quantities.

Achaia Clauss—Metaxa's major competitor, Clauss' 7-star, 92-proof brandy was little known outside Greece until fairly recently, though this situation is changing rapidly. The same distiller also produces a lower proof brandy-based liqueur marketed under the name Grecian Gold.

Cambas—the third big name in Greek brandies. Since 1882, this distiller has been successfully producing four distinct grades of brandies, ranging from the popular 10-year-old Cambas Brandy to the unique Brandy Extra, a 60-year-old conversation piece for the connoisseur.

KEO—a popular 12-year-old brandy made from the famous grapes of Cyprus.

Botrys—a newcomer on the American market, this firm produces superb 25- and 50-year old brandies equal to the finest cognacs of France.

Ouzo

Think of Greek wines, and *Retsina* will probably come to mind; think of Greek liqueurs, and very few will not immediately think of *Ouzo*, the colorless, licorice-flavored liqueur that seems to be ubiquitous in Greece. Distilled from choice grape extracts and aromatic plants and seeds cultivated in Greece (the flavor of anise predominates, as it does in the French version known as Pernod), *Ouzo* is usually served with water (which turns it cloudy) or on the rocks and is a superb cooler for hot weather. The Greeks of course drink it year round and many take it straight. Beloved of tourists and the native sidewalk-cafe crowd, *Ouzo* is becoming increasingly popular in the United States as an aperitif. Most Greek distilleries have an

Ouzo label; these differ very little one from the other, except in proof. Of course, the higher the proof, the better the drink.

Many consider *Ouzo* to be a man's drink. If this is the case, then *Mastiha* is its feminine counterpart. A soft, slightly sweet, anise/flavored liqueur, *Mastiha* is made from the aromatic gum extracted from a tree that grows exclusively on the island of Chios. *Mastiha* is best drunk neat.

Mixed Drinks

American-style cocktails and mixed drinks are not very popular in Greece. High-proof liqueurs and brandies are usually taken neat, or at most with a little water or on the rocks. Nonetheless, with a little imagination you can create a number of quite delightful concoctions based on Greek spirits, particularly Metaxa and Clauss 7-star brandies. The following are only a few of the possibilities (all recipes, with the exception of Ouzo Punch, are for single servings):

"The Golden Age"—⅔ Metaxa, ⅓ Ouzo, 3 drops aromatic bitters. Shake well and serve over shaved ice.

"The Golden Greek"—Simply pour 2 ounces of Metaxa over ice and add a lemon twist.

"Greek Coffee"—⅓ Metaxa or Clauss 7-Star, ⅓ Triple Sec or Cointreau, ⅓ cold black coffee. Shake well with ice and strain into a cocktail glass or demitasse cup.

"Greek Honeymoon"—Spread a tablespoon of bitter orange marmalade on the bottom of an old-fashioned glass. Add 2 ice cubes and 2 ounces of Metaxa; stir well.

"Helen of Troy"—⅓ each of Metaxa, Vodka, and orange juice. Shake well with ice and serve straight up, or with shaved ice.

"Metaxa Cocktail"—Combine the juice of ½ lemon, 2 ounces of Metaxa, and 1 tablespoon sugar. Shake well, and pour into a cocktail glass. Add an ice cube, if desired, stir, and serve.

"Ouzo Punch"—In a large punch bowl with plenty of ice, mix 1 cup Ouzo, 4 cups orange juice, 1 32-ounce bottle of club soda, ¼ cup fresh mint leaves, and 1 pint fresh strawberries (sliced). (Makes about 18 4-ounce servings.)

"The Queen's Choice"—Pour a jigger of Metaxa over an ice cube in a large wine glass. Fill the glass with Champagne.

A WORD ON COFFEE

Dark, rich, finely ground Greek coffee *(Kafedaki)* is traditionally brewed in a long-handled, cylindrical pot known as a *briki* (though a small, deep saucepan will do as well). *Briki* pots come in 2, 4, or 6 demitasse cup sizes and are available in Greek specialty shops. Greek coffee cannot be made in larger quantities because the *kaimaki* (the "cream," or the essence, of the coffee that settles on the bottom of the cup) tends to lose its proper consistency otherwise.

Greek coffee is usually served plain, moderately sweet or very sweet; below, we give a general recipe that will serve for all three levels of sweetness. Reaching a consensus on how to brew *Kafedaki*, however, was no mean feat since every Greek has his or her own way of doing it.

Plain *(Sketos)*
½ cup water
1 tablespoon Greek coffee

Medium *(Metrios)*
1 teaspoon sugar
½ cup water
1 tablespoon Greek coffee

Sweet *(Glyko)*
2 teaspoons sugar
½ cup water
1 tablespoon Greek coffee

Place the sugar (if used) and water in the *briki* or saucepan and stir until sugar dissolves. Bring to a boil. Remove pot from the heat and add the coffee; stir well. Return pot to a low flame. As soon as the coffee starts rising to the rim of the coffeepot (just below the boiling point), remove the pot from the heat and pour a little coffee into each of four demitasse cups. This step is very important, since the first rise forms the *kaimaki* or cream of the coffee. Return the pot to the heat and allow the coffee to rise to the rim a second time. Again pour a little coffee into each cup, being very careful not to disturb the *kaimaki* on the bottom of the cups. Serve the coffee hot. Since the grounds are served in the cup along with the brewed coffee, you must let the coffee stand for a few seconds to allow the grounds to settle. Sip the coffee carefully without disturbing the *kaimaki*. Accompany with a glass of cold water.

Note: A *kafetzou* is a fortune-teller who specializes in reading the future from the grounds left in a coffee cup. When you finish your coffee, leave a little liquid in the cup, invert the cup on the saucer and let it dry upside down for a few seconds. The designs made by the coffee grounds will give a clear picture of your fate to any passing *kafetzou*.

Appetizers

To us, the word appetizer (in Greek, *Mezedakia*) brings to mind a little restaurant on Mt. Lykabettos, overlooking all of Athens. Here the view, the wine, and the food combine to create unforgettable memories. What could be better than a bottle of wine or perhaps some *Ouzo* on the rocks, accompanied by an assortment of Greek olives and *feta* cheese, spiced meatballs *(Keftedakia)*, flaming cheese *(Saganaki)*, the traditional *tarama* dip, and *phyllo* puffs filled with an array of tempting delights. The list of hot and cold appetizers could go on and on as you will see in this chapter.

HOT APPETIZERS

ARTICHOKE COCKTAIL BALLS ⤴ KARPATHOS

Anginares Keftedes

3 (10-ounce) packages frozen artichoke
    hearts, or 6 fresh artichokes
3 eggs
¼ teaspoon salt
Pepper to taste
1 clove garlic, crushed
4 scallions, minced (include some of the
    green tops)
¼ cup minced dill or parsley
¼ cup grated *kefalotiri* or Parmesan
    cheese
1 cup fine bread crumbs
1 cup oil for frying

Cook frozen artichokes according to package directions, or prepare fresh artichokes as indicated below. Cut the artichokes into small pieces. Add eggs, seasonings, scallions, and dill and mix well. Shape into balls and roll in the bread crumbs. Fry in hot oil, turning frequently, until golden brown. Drain on paper towels. Serve hot. May be served with Garlic Sauce *(Skordalia).*° YIELD: 24–30 balls.

PREPARATION OF FRESH ARTICHOKES

To prepare fresh artichokes for cooking, break off stems and trim any ragged edges. Remove all but the inner cone of petals (this is the artichoke's heart); open up the inner cone of petals to reveal the choke. Remove the choke with a spoon and discard the remaining petals. Rub all over with a lemon half and boil in 1 quart of water, to which 2 tablespoons lemon juice and 1½ teaspoons salt have been added, for 30 to 40 minutes, or until tender. Proceed with recipe.

ARTICHOKE PUFFS
Bourekakia me Anginares

1 (10-ounce) package frozen artichoke
    hearts
1 small onion, finely minced
4 tablespoons margarine
1 tablespoon finely minced fresh dill
¼ cup grated *kefalotiri* or Parmesan
    cheese
½ cup thick Béchamel Sauce° (optional)
½ pound *phyllo* pastry
¼ pound melted butter for brushing
    phyllo

Let the artichokes thaw and drain them well. Cut in small pieces. In a small saucepan, sauté the onion in the margarine. Add the dill and artichoke pieces and sauté for 3 to 5 minutes. Simmer until all the liquid is absorbed. Remove from heat and add the grated cheese and Béchamel Sauce, if used. Put in refrigerator for at least an hour to cool.

Preheat oven to 350°F. Prepare triangular artichoke puffs according to directions and diagram 2 in How to Work with *Phyllo* (page 211). Use 1 teaspoon filling for each puff. Place puffs on ungreased cookie sheets. Bake for 15 minutes, or until golden brown. YIELD: 40 pieces.

Note: This recipe may be prepared ahead of time and frozen, unbaked. When ready to use, bake without prior thawing but double the cooking time.

✳ ARTICHOKE TRIANGLES
Bourekakia me Anginares

3 (10-ounce) packages frozen artichoke
    hearts
1 medium onion, finely minced
¼ pound butter
1 tablespoon finely minced fresh dill, or
    1 teaspoon dried dill
⅓ cup grated *kefalotiri* cheese
Salt and pepper to taste
1 pound *phyllo* pastry
½ pound melted butter for brushing
    phyllo

Preheat oven to 350°F. Boil artichokes according to package directions. Drain thoroughly, let cool, and squeeze until artichokes are thoroughly dry. Dice the artichokes. Melt the butter. Add the onion and fry until golden. Add dill and artichokes. Brown thoroughly until all liquid is absorbed. Remove from heat and add the cheese, salt, and pepper. Fold *bourekakia* according to directions in How to Work with *Phyllo* (page 211). Use 1 teaspoon filling per triangle. Bake for 15 to 20 minutes, or until golden brown. Serve warm. YIELD: 70–80 pieces.

Note: This recipe may be prepared ahead of time and frozen, unbaked. When ready to use, bake without prior thawing but double the cooking time.

BROILED SAUSAGES
Loukaniko Meze

↜ CHIOS

1 pound Greek sausages
1 fresh lemon

Greek sausages have an unusual orange and cumin flavor, quite unlike that of hot pepper-type sausages. These sausages may be purchased at Greek specialty shops. Or, if you prefer homemade Greek sausages, see *The Art of Greek Cookery*, page 41.

Preheat broiler. Cut sausages in ¾-inch-thick slices. Broil for 3 minutes on each side. Sprinkle with lemon juice and serve warm. YIELD: 2 dozen pieces.

CHEESE TOAST

Psomakia me Tyri

2 eggs
½ cup grated *kefalotiri* cheese
½ cup grated *feta* cheese
½ cup *kefalograviera* cheese or *kasseri* cheese
½ cup fresh *mizithra* cheese or ricotta cheese
1 teaspoon finely minced dill, mint, or parsley
Dash of pepper
½ pound butter for frying
1 pound sliced white bread, trimmed

Beat the eggs. Add the cheeses, dill, and pepper and mix well. Spread the mixture on each slice of bread and then cut diagonally. Refrigerate slices for 15 minutes. Sauté the refrigerated slices in butter until golden brown, turning once. Drain on paper towels and serve hot. YIELD: 36–40 pieces.

Note: Prepared slices may also be broiled for 3 minutes, or until golden. Omit butter.

CHEESE TRIANGLES

Trigona me Tyri

½ pound *feta* cheese
½ pound soft *mizithra* or ricotta cheese
1 tablespoon minced parsley, dill or chives
9 slices thin sandwich bread, trimmed

Preheat oven to 450°F. Blend cheeses and herbs and spread mixture on each slice of bread. Bake for 10 to 15 minutes, or until cheese melts. Cut each slice diagonally into 4 triangles. Serve warm. YIELD: 36 pieces.

CHICK-PEA TARTS

Kaparmades

PASTRY:

4 cups flour
2 teaspoons baking powder
2 teaspoons salt
1 cup oil
1 egg, beaten
¾ cup warm milk

FILLING:

1 (20-ounce) can chick-peas
1 medium onion, chopped
2 tablespoons butter
1 egg, beaten
2 tablespoons minced parsley
Salt and pepper to taste
Dash of dried oregano
2 tablespoons *kefalotiri* or Parmesan cheese
Oil for deep-fat frying

Make the pastry by mixing the flour, baking powder, salt, oil, egg, and milk to form a soft dough. Roll out dough to a thickness of ⅛ inch and cut into 2-inch rounds.

Prepare the filling by draining and mashing the chick-peas (reserve the liquid). Sauté the onion in the butter until soft and golden; add to the chick-peas. Add the beaten egg, parsley, salt, pepper, oregano, and cheese. Add enough reserved liquid to form a soft mixture. Add filling to each round, fold over, and seal. Deep fry in hot oil until pastry is golden brown. YIELD: 50–60 pieces.

CHICKEN LIVER TRIANGLES

Bourekakia me Sikotakia

1 pound chicken livers
2 onions, finely minced
½ cup butter
½ cup *kefalotiri* or Parmesan cheese
Dash of nutmeg
2 tablespoons cognac
Salt and pepper to taste
½ pound *phyllo* pastry
¼ pound melted butter for brushing
    phyllo

Preheat oven to 350°F.

Melt the butter and add the onions and sauté until the onion is soft. Add chicken livers and continue cooking until they are browned. Remove from heat and add cheese, nutmeg, cognac, and salt and pepper.

Prepare stuffed *phyllo* triangles according to directions in How to Work with *Phyllo* (page 211). Use 1 teaspoon filling per triangle. Place triangles on ungreased baking sheets and bake for 15 to 20 minutes, or until golden brown. YIELD: 30 pieces.

Note: This recipe may be prepared ahead of time and frozen, unbaked. When ready to use, bake without prior thawing, but double the cooking time.

CHICKEN *PHYLLO* ROLLS

KITHIRA

Kotopetakia

1 (4-pound) whole chicken
½ lemon
1 quart water
2 pounds onions, peeled and halved
3 stalks celery
2–3 tablespoons minced parsley
1 teaspoon salt
1½ teaspoons pepper
½ pound butter
2 tablespoons fresh minced dill
½ cup grated *kasseri* cheese
2 eggs
1 pound *phyllo* pastry
½ pound melted butter for brushing
    phyllo

Clean the chicken; rub inside and outside with ½ lemon. Place chicken in a deep pot with 1 quart water. Add the onions, celery, parsley, salt, ½ teaspoon pepper and bring to a boil. Lower heat and simmer for 1 hour, or until the meat comes easily off the bones. After chicken cools remove skin and bones and shred meat. Drain broth (which may be saved for another use) but reserve celery and onion. Mash the celery and onion together and combine with the shredded chicken. Melt ½ pound butter in a pan, add chicken-onion mixture and sauté for 2 to 3 minutes. Add dill and sauté for 1 minute. Add cheese and 1 teaspoon pepper. Cool completely. After mixture is cool add the eggs and blend thoroughly.

Preheat oven to 350°F.

Prepare stuffed *phyllo* rolls according to directions in How to Work with *Phyllo* (page 211). Use 1 teaspoon filling for each roll. Place rolls seam side down on an ungreased cookie sheet. Bake for 20 minutes, or until golden. Serve warm. YIELD: 75 pieces.

Note: This recipe freezes well.

COCKTAIL MEAT BALLS WITH CHEESE CENTERS

Keftedakia me Tyri

1 recipe Meat Balls II°, using
    approximately 1 pound ground
    round (or see *The Art of Greek
    Cookery*, page 40, or use your
    favorite meat ball recipe).
½ pound *kasseri* cheese
½ pound *feta* cheese
Oil for deep frying

Cut the cheeses into ¾-inch cubes. Roll meat around each cube forming a meat ball, making sure the cheese is completely covered. Fry as in meat ball recipe or bake in a 350°F. oven until brown. YIELD: 2–3 dozen meat balls.

COCKTAIL SHISH KEBAB

Souvlakia Meze

1 (8–10 pound) leg of lamb, boned and
    trimmed

MARINADE:

  I 1 cup olive oil
      1 teaspoon ground cumin
      1 teaspoon dried oregano
      2 bay leaves, crushed
      Salt and pepper to taste

  II 1 cup chopped green peppers
      2 onions, chopped
      4 ounces tomato purée

  III ¼ cup port wine
      ¼ cup vinegar
      ¼ cup fresh lemon juice

This is the traditional *Souvlakia* recipe adapted as an appetizer.

Cut leg of lamb into 1-inch cubes. Combine olive oil, cumin, oregano, bay leaves, salt, and pepper to make marinade. Add lamb cubes and marinate overnight in refrigerator. On the following day add green peppers, onions, and tomato purée to the marinade. Marinate for several hours or overnight. Add wine, vinegar, and lemon juice to the marinade and refrigerate for several hours or overnight. (The longer the ingredients are allowed to marinate the better the recipe will taste.)

Preheat oven to 375°F.

When ready to serve, thread the meat only on small, 5- or 6-inch long wooden skewers. Bake for 12 to 15 minutes, turning frequently, until nicely browned. Serve the *Souvlakia* on the skewers. YIELD: about 2 dozen skewers.

COCKTAIL *SOUZOUKAKIA* WITH LEMON SAUCE   ⌁ KITHIRA

Souzoukakia Lemonata

1 pound ground round steak
½ teaspoon ground cumin
¼ cup bread crumbs
1 clove garlic, minced
1 egg
Salt and pepper to taste
¼ pound butter
Juice of 1 lemon
¼ cup water

Combine the meat, cumin, bread crumbs, garlic, egg, salt, and pepper. Shape 1 teaspoon of the meat mixture at a time into oval or oblong shapes (wetting your hands to facilitate handling). Fry in butter over medium heat, turning frequently. Combine lemon juice and water and pour over the *Souzoukakia*. YIELD: 2 dozen pieces.

Note: Instead of frying the *Souzoukakia*, they may be placed in a single layer in a pan and brushed with oil. Broil on both sides until brown. Top with lemon sauce. They may be used as an entrée over rice.

CRAB MEAT WRAPPED IN *PHYLLO*

Kavouri Bourekakia

1 small onion, peeled and chopped
5 tablespoons butter
2 tablespoons flour
2 cups lukewarm milk
1 tablespoon minced parsley
1 tablespoon minced dill
½ cup chopped mushrooms
2 hard-cooked eggs, chopped
1 teaspoon sherry
Dash of dried basil
Salt to taste
1½ pounds lump crab meat, picked over
½ cup fine bread crumbs
½ pound *phyllo* pastry
¾ cup melted butter for brushing *phyllo*

Sauté onion in butter until wilted. Add the flour and mix. Add milk slowly, stirring constantly, until mixture is creamy. Remove from heat. Add remaining ingredients except the *phyllo* pastry and melted butter. If the consistency is too thin add more bread crumbs. If too thick, add more milk.

Preheat oven to 350°F.

Prepare stuffed *phyllo* rolls according to directions in How to Work with *Phyllo* (page 211). Use 1 teaspoon filling per roll. Place rolls seam side down on an ungreased cookie sheet. Brush top of roll with melted butter. Bake for 30 to 35 minutes, or until golden. YIELD: 72 rolls.

Note: This recipe may be prepared ahead of time and frozen, unbaked. When ready to use, bake without prior thawing but increase the cooking time by about 15 minutes.

EGGPLANT BALLS

Melitzanokeftedes

2 medium eggplants
1 large onion, finely minced
¼ cup minced parsley
½ cup grated *kefalotiri* or Parmesan
    cheese
2 eggs
Salt and pepper to taste
1 cup plain bread crumbs
Vegetable oil for frying

Preheat oven to 450°F.

Bake the eggplants for about 30 minutes. Remove skins, drain in colander, and remove seeds. Add the onion, parsley, cheese. eggs, and salt and pepper and mix well. Shape into 1-inch balls. Roll in the bread crumbs and fry in the oil until golden. Serve warm. YIELD: 5 dozen balls.

FETA CHEESE PUFFS

Sou me Feta

PASTRY:

1 cup water
½ pound butter
1 cup sifted flour
4 eggs

FILLING:

½ pound *feta* cheese
5 tablespoons butter

Preheat oven to 400°F.

Heat water and butter to a rolling boil. Stir in the sifted flour all at once. Stir over low heat until the mixture leaves the sides of the pan and forms a ball (approximately 1 minute). Remove from the heat and beat in the eggs, one at a time, until the mixture is smooth and glossy. Drop by half teaspoonsful onto an ungreased cookie sheet. Bake for 10 minutes, lower oven temperature to 350°F. and bake for 20 minutes, until puffed, dry, and golden brown. Allow to cool slowly in a draft-free place. Mash together the cheese and butter. Slit sides of puffs, remove any excess soft dough and fill with the cheese mixture. YIELD: approximately 75 puffs.

Note: These puffs may be filled and frozen. When ready to use, simply thaw and serve at room temperature.

FETA CHEESE ROUNDS

Feta Roula

½ pound butter, softened
½ pound *feta* cheese, crumbled finely
2 cups flour
1 (4¾-ounce) package slivered almonds or pignolias (pine nuts)

Preheat oven to 350°F.

Cream butter until very light and fluffy. Gradually beat in the crumbled *feta* cheese. Gradually blend in the flour to make a soft dough. Shape the dough into 1½-inch rounds (¼ inch thick). Decorate the center of each with an almond sliver. Put on baking sheets and bake for 15 minutes. Serve warm. YIELD: 6–7 dozen rounds.

Note: This recipe may be prepared and frozen before baking. Double baking time.

FLAMING GREEK CHEESE

Tyri tis Floghas

½ pound *kasseri* cheese
2 tablespoons brandy
Juice of ½ lemon
4 slices thin bread, trimmed, toasted, and quartered

This and the following two recipes are very popular throughout Greece. Tasty and eye appealing, they are also quick and easy to prepare.

Cut the cheese into ¼-inch-thick slices. Place in an ovenproof dish and broil for approximately 5 minutes, or until the cheese is soft and the surface bubbles slightly. Heat the brandy, flame it, and pour it over cheese. Squeeze the lemon over the cheese. Spread on thin slices of toast. YIELD: 16 pieces.

FRIED *FETA* CHEESE

Saganaki Feta

½ pound *feta* cheese
1 egg, beaten
¼ pound butter
Juice of ½ lemon
Pepper to taste
Toast rounds or crackers as needed

Cut the cheese into ¼-inch-thick slices. Dip the cheese slices into the beaten egg. Melt the butter in a frying pan until lightly browned and fry the cheese slices until golden, turning once. Use a spatula to remove them from the pan. Sprinkle with lemon juice and pepper and serve immediately on toasted bread or crackers. YIELD: about 15 pieces.

SAGANAKI CHEESE

Saganaki

1 pound hard cheese, such as *kasseri*,
    kefalotiri, *haloumi*, or *feta*
¼ pound butter
Juice of 1 lemon

Slice the cheese into ¾–1-inch-thick cubes. Fry in hot butter for 3 minutes on each side. Sprinkle with lemon juice. Serve hot. YIELD: 20–24 pieces.

Note: Cheese may be broiled instead of fried. Spread cheese in an ovenproof dish. Broil approximately 3 minutes without turning and serve hot.

FRIED ARTICHOKE HEARTS

⚓ MYTILENE

Tiganites Anginares Meze

2 eggs, lightly beaten
Salt and pepper to taste
½ cup flour
3 tablespoons *kasseri* cheese, grated
Vegetable oil for frying
1 (15½-ounce) can artichoke hearts,
    drained

Combine eggs, flour, salt, pepper, and grated cheese. Heat vegetable oil. Dip artichoke hearts in batter and fry until golden brown. Serve warm. YIELD: 8–10 pieces.

FRIED CHICK-PEA BALLS

⚓ MYTILENE

Revithokeftedes

1 (20-ounce) can chick-peas
1 medium onion, minced
2 tablespoons butter
1 egg, beaten
2 tablespoons minced parsley
Salt and pepper to taste
Dash of dried oregano
2 tablespoons grated sharp cheese, such
    as *kefalotiri*
Flour
Oil for frying
Sesame Seed Sauce (see following)

Drain and mash the chick-peas (reserve the liquid). Sauté the onion in butter until soft and golden; add to chick-peas. Blend in the beaten egg, parsley, salt, pepper, oregano, and grated cheese. Add enough reserved chick-pea liquid to form soft mixture. Shape mixture into small balls. Roll in flour and fry until golden. YIELD: about 24 pieces.

Note: The balls may be made larger and served as an entrée.

SESAME SEED SAUCE
Tahini Saltsa

2–3 cloves garlic, crushed
½ cup *tahini* (sesame seed paste)
Juice of 2 lemons
⅛ cup cold water (approximate)
½ teaspoon ground cumin
Salt to taste

Beat the garlic into the *tahini*, then gradually beat in the lemon juice and enough cold water to make a smooth creamy dressing. Add cumin and salt. YIELD: 1½ cups dressing.

Note: May be served alone as a dip with crackers.

FRIED EGGPLANT
Melitzanes Tiganites

❧ NAXOS

1 large eggplant, peeled and cut into 1-inch cubes
Flour as needed
1 egg, lightly beaten
Hot oil for frying
Garlic salt

Roll eggplant cubes in flour, then dip in egg, and roll in flour again. Deep fry until golden brown. Sprinkle with garlic salt. Serve hot on toothpicks. YIELD: about 2 dozen.

(Lenten)

FRIED MUSHROOMS
Manitaria Tiganita

❧ KARPATHOS

1 pound fresh mushrooms
Salt and pepper to taste
½ cup flour
Oil for frying
Juice of 1 lemon

Clean the mushrooms and remove stems if you wish. Sprinkle wet mushrooms with salt and pepper; drain well. Coat the mushrooms with flour and deep fry in oil. Drain on paper towels. Sprinkle with lemon juice. Serve hot. YIELD: 20–25 pieces.

FRIED MUSSELS
Midia Tiganita

2 quarts mussels
2 eggs
Salt and pepper to taste
½ cup flour
Oil for frying

Clean, beard, and steam mussels in about ½ cup water for 10 to 15 minutes or until shells open (see page 35 for Preparation of Fresh Mussels). Remove mussels from shells and set aside. Discard shells. Beat eggs and add salt and pepper. Add flour to make a thick batter. Stir mussels into the batter. Heat the oil and deep fry the mussels by dropping one teaspoon of batter into the hot oil, making certain that one mussel is in each teaspoon of batter. Fry until golden brown. Drain on paper towels. May be served with Garlic Sauce *(Skordalia)*° or oil and lemon dressing.

FRIED SMELTS
Marithes Tiganites

2 pounds smelts (about 3 dozen)
Salt to taste
Flour for coating
1 cup olive oil
Juice of 1 lemon

The tiny smelt (*Marithes* in Greek) is plentiful in Greek waters and makes an extremely popular seaside summer snack. Caught in large nets close to shore, they are then deep fried and eaten whole much as Americans consume French fries or potato chips.

Clean, wash, and drain the smelts. Sprinkle with salt. Coat with flour. Heat 1 cup olive oil in a large frying pan. Fry the smelts until golden brown and crisp on both sides. Sprinkle with lemon juice and serve hot. Serves 6.

(Lenten)
FRIED SNAILS
Saligaria Tiganita

2 pounds large fresh snails, or 1 (12-ounce) can snails
Flour for coating
Oil for deep frying
Salt and pepper to taste
Juice of 1 lemon

Prepare fresh snails according to the directions given below or remove canned snails from their shells and drain. Dip snails in flour and deep fry them in hot oil until golden brown. Drain on paper towels. Sprinkle with salt, pepper, and lemon juice. Serve warm. YIELD: 24 pieces.

PREPARATION OF FRESH SNAILS

Fresh snails may be purchased in many fish markets, supermarkets, and Greek specialty stores.

Wash the snails thoroughly under cold running water. Place them in a heavy skillet with a little water, cover and weight down the lid. Let stand overnight. The next day rinse snails repeatedly in cold water until they come out of their shells. If some of them don't come out, see if they are alive by poking them with a sharp knife at the opening of their shell. If they do not move they are dead and should be discarded. Place the snails in a colander, pour boiling water over them, and proceed with the recipe.

FRIED SNAILS WITH VINEGAR
Tiganita Saligaria me Xide

1 pound snails
⅓ cup olive oil
¼ cup red wine vinegar

Follow directions for preparing snails in the preceding recipe. In a deep, heavy pan, heat olive oil almost to the boiling point. Add the snails and fry for 10 minutes, turning carefully with tongs to avoid spattering the oil. Pour in the red wine vinegar. Remove from heat and stir constantly for a few minutes. Remove the snails to individual plates and serve hot with a little of the remaining sauce as an appetizer or first course. Serves 8–10.

LAMB ROLLS

Bourekakia me Arni

2 pounds ground lamb
2 tablespoons butter
½ cup red wine
1 cup raisins
½ cup pignolias (pine nuts)
2 teaspoons ground cinnamon
1 teaspoon ground nutmeg
1 pound *phyllo* pastry
½ pound melted butter for brushing
    phyllo

Preheat oven to 350°F.

Sauté the ground lamb in the 2 tablespoons butter over medium heat until browned. Add wine, raisins, pignolias, and spices; stir until liquids are absorbed. Cool. If chopped meat mixture is lumpy, purée to a smooth consistency in a blender. Prepare *bourekakia* according to directions in How to Work with *Phyllo* (page 211). Use 1 teaspoon filling for each roll. Place rolls seam side down on an ungreased cookie sheet. Butter tops and bake for 30 minutes, or until golden brown. Do not overcook. Transfer to a serving tray and serve warm. YIELD: 60 pieces.

Note: Bourekakia may be prepared ahead of time and frozen, unbaked. When ready to use, bake, without prior thawing, for about 45 minutes.

LAMB TRIANGLES

                                                                                      ❧ SPETSA

Arni Bourekia

3 pounds leg of lamb, boned
Salt and pepper to taste
2 tablespoons oregano
½ cup fine-quality olive oil
½ cup lemon juice
½ cup water
½ pound *kefalotiri* cheese
1 pound *phyllo* pastry
¾ pound melted butter for brushing
    phyllo

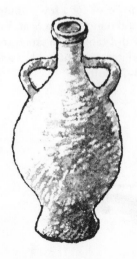

Preheat oven to 350°F.

Dry lamb with paper towels, cut into ½- to ¾-inch cubes and season with salt and pepper. Put meat in a pan and sprinkle with the oregano. Add the oil, lemon juice, and water. Roast until the liquid has been absorbed, about 45 minutes to 1 hour. Remove from oven and partially cool. Cut the cheese into small cubes and add to the meat; mix well.

Cut the *phyllo* into strips about 2½ inches wide, stack them on top of each other and cover so they do not dry out. Take 1 strip at a time and brush it with the melted butter. Fold *Bourekia* according to directions in How to Work with *Phyllo* (page 211). Use 1 tablespoon of filling for each triangle. Brush the surface with butter and place *Bourekia* on a buttered baking sheet, seam down so they do not open during baking. Bake for 15 minutes, or until golden. Serve hot. YIELD: about 36 pieces.

Note: This recipe may be prepared in advance and frozen before final baking. To serve, bake without prior thawing, for about 30 minutes.

MARINATED LAMB LIVER

Sikoti Marinato

1 pound lamb liver
Salt and pepper to taste
1 teaspoon garlic powder
1 teaspoon dried oregano
¼ cup plus 2 tablespoons lemon juice
½ cup wine vinegar
½ cup flour or as needed
1 cup olive oil for frying

Cut the lamb liver into bite-size pieces. Mix with the seasonings, ¼ cup lemon juice, and vinegar. Marinate overnight. Dip liver pieces in flour and sauté in olive oil. Sprinkle with remaining lemon juice. Serve hot. YIELD: about 15 pieces.

Note: Liver may also be skewered and broiled.

MEAT PUFFS

Sou me Kema

PASTRY:

1 cup water
½ pound butter
1 cup sifted flour
4 eggs

FILLING:

1 pound ground sirloin steak
1 onion, chopped
Salt and pepper to taste
⅛ teaspoon ground cinnamon

SAUCE:

3 tablespoons butter
4 tablespoons flour
½ cup scalded milk or cream
¾ cup chicken stock
1 egg, beaten
½ teaspoon ground nutmeg
Salt and pepper to taste
Grated *kefalotiri* cheese

Preheat oven to 400°F.

Heat water and butter to a rolling boil. Stir in the sifted flour all at once. Stir over low heat until the mixture leaves sides of the pan and forms a ball (approximately 1 minute). Remove from the heat. Beat in the eggs, one at a time, until the mixture is smooth and glossy. Drop scant teaspoons of batter on a greased cookie sheet and bake for 10 minutes. Lower the oven temperature to 350°F. and bake for 20 minutes. Combine sirloin and onion and sauté in a large frying pan until brown. Season with salt, pepper, and cinnamon. To make the sauce, melt the butter in a saucepan and add the flour, stirring until smooth. Remove from the heat and gradually stir in milk and chicken stock. Return to heat and cook, stirring constantly, until sauce is smooth and thickened. Add beaten egg and nutmeg. Reduce heat and cook for a few minutes longer. Stir in salt and pepper and remove from heat. Fill puffs with meat mixture; top with 1 tablespoon sauce and grated cheese. Bake for 10 minutes, or until bubbly and golden. Serve warm. YIELD: 60–75 puffs.

MEAT ROLLS WITH PIGNOLIA NUTS

Bourekakia me Kreas kai Koukounaria

4 tablespoons butter
1 pound ground beef (preferably round)
1 medium onion, finely minced
½ cup tomato sauce
½ cup water
¼ cup white wine
¼ teaspoon ground cumin
Salt and pepper to taste
½ cup pignolias (pine nuts)
¼ cup grated *kasseri* cheese
½ pound *phyllo* pastry
¼ pound melted butter for brushing
    phyllo

Preheat oven to 350°F.

Melt the 4 tablespoons of butter in a heavy frying pan. Add the ground beef and onion; brown well, stirring constantly. When the meat has lost its redness, add the tomato sauce, water, wine, cumin, and salt and pepper. Simmer until all the liquid is absorbed. Remove from the heat and add the pignolias and cheese; stir well and set aside to cool. Prepare stuffed *phyllo* rolls according to directions in How to Work with *Phyllo* (page 211). Use 1 tablespoon of filling for each roll. Place rolls seam side down on an ungreased cookie sheet. Bake for 15 to 20 minutes, or until golden brown. Serve warm. YIELD: 40–50 pieces.

Note: Rolls may be prepared ahead of time and frozen, unbaked. When ready to use, bake without prior thawing for about 30 minutes.

MUSHROOM TRIANGLES I

⚓ KARPATHOS

Bourekakia me Manitaria

3 pounds fresh mushrooms
1 medium onion, finely minced
¼ pound butter
½ cup *kefalotiri* cheese, grated
Salt and pepper to taste
1 pound *phyllo* pastry
½ pound melted butter for brushing
    phyllo

Preheat oven to 350°F.

Clean mushrooms thoroughly and chop finely. Sauté onion in butter until soft and golden. Add mushrooms to onions and toss. Cook until all liquid from mushrooms is absorbed. Remove from heat and add cheese. Fold *Bourekakia* according to directions in How to Work with *Phyllo* (page 211). Use 1 teaspoon of filling for each triangle. Bake for 15 to 20 minutes, or until golden brown. Serve warm. YIELD: 70–80 pieces.

Note: Triangles may be prepared ahead of time and frozen, unbaked. When ready to use, bake without prior thawing for 30 minutes.

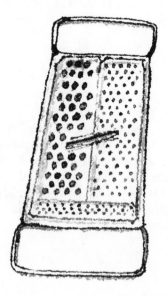

MUSHROOM TRIANGLES II
Bourekakia me Manitaria

½ pound fresh mushrooms, finely
    chopped
3 shallots, finely minced, or 2 scallions,
    finely minced
¼ cup butter
1 (3-ounce) package cream cheese
1 egg
1 teaspoon salt
¼ teaspoon pepper
½ pound *phyllo* pastry
¼ pound melted butter for brushing
    phyllo

Preheat oven to 350°F.

Melt ¼ cup butter in a heavy skillet. Add the mushrooms and shallots and sauté over medium heat until soft and beginning to brown. Put in mixing bowl and add the cream cheese, egg, salt, and pepper, stirring well to mix. Fold *Bourekakia* according to directions in How to Work with *Phyllo* (page 211). Use 1 teaspoon of filling for each triangle. Bake for 15 to 20 minutes, or until golden brown. Serve warm. YIELD: 40 pieces.

Note: Triangles may be prepared ahead of time and frozen, unbaked. When ready to use, bake without prior thawing for 30 minutes.

ONION PUFFS
Bourekakia me Kremedia

1½ pounds (about 3 large) white onions
1 teaspoon oregano
1 teaspoon salt
½ teaspoon pepper
½ cup olive or vegetable oil
½ pound melted butter for brushing
    phyllo
½ pound *phyllo* pastry

Preheat oven to 350°F.

Peel and chop the onions coarsely. Add oregano, salt, and pepper and sauté in oil until tender. Strain well. Prepare *phyllo* by cutting the sheets in 1½-inch strips crosswise (10 strips per sheet). Cover the *phyllo* with a damp cloth to keep it from drying out. Place ½ teaspoon of the onion mixture on the corner of the *phyllo* strip and fold the *phyllo* into a small triangle. Place the triangles on an ungreased baking sheet. Butter tops of the triangles and bake until light golden brown. Serve warm. YIELD: 106 pieces.

Note: This recipe may be prepared ahead of time and frozen, unbaked. When ready to use, bake without prior thawing but increase baking time by 15 minutes.

POTATO BALLS
Patato Keftedes

1 pound potatoes, peeled and boiled
¼ pound *feta* cheese, or ½ cup grated
    cheese, such as *kefalotiri*
1 tablespoon minced parsley
1 small onion, minced
1 clove garlic, crushed
2 eggs, separated
Salt and pepper to taste
1 teaspoon lemon juice
Dry bread crumbs
Oil for deep frying

With electric beater, beat potatoes until smooth. Mash the *feta* cheese with a fork and add to the potatoes along with the parsley, onion, garlic, egg yolks, and salt and pepper. Add the lemon juice and blend well. Shape into tiny balls. Dip in slightly beaten egg whites and roll in the bread crumbs. Deep fry in oil until golden. YIELD: about 2 dozen.

PUMPKIN BALLS

Kolokithokeftedes

1 small pumpkin
½ cup grated onion
2 tablespoons minced parsley
1 tablespoon ground cumin
2 cups bread crumbs
4 eggs
4 cloves garlic, crushed
Salt and pepper to taste
2 cups flour
1 cup vegetable oil for frying

Peel, clean, and seed the pumpkin. Grate pumpkin (there should be about 2½ cups). Place in a colander to drain for 30 minutes; squeeze out any excess moisture. Combine all the ingredients except the flour and oil and blend well. Shape into balls (large for use as an entrée, bite size for use as an appetizer) and roll in flour. Fry until golden brown. Drain on paper towels. Serve warm. YIELD: about 40 balls.

SAUERKRAUT "PIE"

Armiopeta

3 cups flour
1 teaspoon salt
1 cup warm water
3 tablespoons olive oil
½ pound butter, melted, plus
1 heaping tablespoon butter or
shortening, melted

FILLING:

24 ounces canned sauerkraut
3 cups water
6 eggs, beaten
4 tablespoons butter
Salt to taste

This unique variation of the well known *spanakopeta* and *tyropeta* is a famous specialty of Kastoria in northern Greece.

Preheat oven to 375°F.

Sift the flour and salt into a bowl. Add water and oil and mix and knead for 15 minutes, using more flour if necessary to keep dough from sticking. Divide dough in half. Cover one half with a damp towel; divide the other half into 10 balls. On a floured table, roll each ball into circles 6 inches in diameter. Butter and stack the circles on a plate. Fold the edges up to form a ball and refrigerate until butter hardens, about 1 hour. Repeat the procedure with the remaining dough. Cook the sauerkraut in the water for 1½ hours. Drain well. Add the eggs, butter, and salt. Roll the first cold ball out on floured table to a rectangle two inches larger all around than an 11- x 17-inch pan or equivalent. Butter the pan and line with the pastry rectangle. Pour in the filling. Roll out the second dough ball to the same size as the first, and place on top of filling. This top crust should be very loose and wrinkly. Fold the bottom edge over the top, roll, and seal by fluting. Brush melted butter over the pie and bake for 1 hour. Allow to cool before cutting. YIELD: 36 pieces.

Note: This pie may be served as an appetizer, as a vegetable side dish, or as a brunch entrée. The Kastorians, as a rule, serve it at the end of their meal.

SESAME CHEESE RINGS

Koulourakia me Tyri

1½ cups all-purpose flour, sifted
1 cup *kefalotiri* cheese, grated
½ cup butter or margarine
3 tablespoons milk
1 egg, slightly beaten
Sesame seeds

Combine flour and cheese. Cut in butter. Stir in milk and mix well. Divide the dough into 24 pieces. Roll each piece into a 5-inch-long strip. Shape the strips into rings and place on an ungreased cookie sheet. Brush tops of pastries with slightly beaten egg and sprinkle with sesame seeds. Bake in a 350°F. oven for 25 minutes, or until lightly browned. Serve warm. YIELD: 2 dozen rings.

SHRIMP TRIANGLES

Bourekakia me Garides

2 onions, chopped
4 tablespoons butter, melted
1 pound raw shrimp, cleaned and
    chopped
¼ cup minced parsley
Salt and pepper to taste
1 egg
¼ cup grated *kefalotiri* cheese
½ pound *phyllo* pastry
¼ pound melted butter for brushing
    phyllo

Brown the onions in the 4 tablespoons of butter. Add shrimp, parsley, and salt and pepper. Sauté briefly until the shrimp turns pink. Cool. Beat the egg and add the grated cheese to it, and blend into the shrimp mixture. Prepare the triangles according to directions in How to Work with *Phyllo* (page 211). Use 1 teaspoon of filling for each triangle. Bake in a 350°F. oven for 20 minutes, or until golden. Serve warm. YIELD: 36–40 pieces.

Note: These may be frozen before baking. To serve, put frozen directly into a preheated oven for 20 to 25 minutes, or until golden.

SPINACH BALLS

Spanakokeftedes

3 pounds fresh spinach
3 eggs
3 tablespoons butter
1 large onion, chopped
1 cup *kefalotiri* cheese or Parmesan
    cheese
½ cup *feta* cheese, crumbled
½ cup minced dill
Salt and pepper to taste
1 cup bread crumbs
Hot oil for frying

Wash and pick over the spinach, removing the stems. Parboil for 5 to 6 minutes. Drain well, pressing the water out with the back of a spoon. Chop. Mix all ingredients together, except the bread crumbs and oil. Shape the mixture into ½-inch balls. Roll in bread crumbs and deep fry in hot oil and drain on paper towels. Serve warm. YIELD: 24 balls.

Note: 3 (10-ounce) packages of frozen chopped spinach may be used in place of the fresh spinach. It is not necessary to precook the frozen spinach. Simply thaw, drain well, and proceed with the recipe.

STUFFED MUSHROOMS
Manitaria Gemista

1 pound sweet Greek sausage
36 mushroom caps (about 2 pounds)
1 lemon

Wipe mushrooms with a damp towel. Slice the sausage into 36 pieces. Stuff each mushroom cap with a slice of sausage. Broil until the sausage is thoroughly cooked and lightly browned. Sprinkle with lemon juice. Serve warm. YIELD: 36 pieces.

Variation: Bake in a 400°F. oven for 20 to 25 minutes.

TRIPLE CHEESE BARS
Almira Biskota

⌁ PAROS

DOUGH:
¼ pound butter
¼ pound cream cheese
1 cup flour

FILLING:
3 tablespoons butter
3 tablespoons flour
1½ cups milk
1 teaspoon salt
¼ teaspoon pepper
1 pound *feta* cheese
1 cup grated *kasseri* cheese
1 (8-ounce) package cottage cheese, or ½
    pound fresh *mizithra* (see note)
6 eggs, beaten

Preheat oven to 350°F.

Combine ¼ pound butter, cream cheese, and flour to form a soft dough. Refrigerate until firm, approximately 1 hour. Put dough in a 9- x 12-inch pan and flatten into a thin layer. Melt the 3 tablespoons of butter and add the flour, milk, salt, and pepper. Stir to combine into a thick cream sauce. Add the *feta* and all the other ingredients. Pour the filling into the prepared pan. Bake for 30 minutes. Cut into squares. Serve warm. YIELD: 3 dozen bars.

Note: Since fresh *mizithra* is not readily available, cottage cheese or ricotta may be substituted in its place.

VEAL BALLS
Keftedes Vithelo

⌁ PIRAEUS

1 cup fresh bread crumbs or croutons
½ cup water
½ cup red wine
1 small onion, minced
1 pound ground veal
1 tablespoon vegetable oil
2 teaspoons salt
¼ teaspoon pepper
1 tablespoon minced parsley or mint
½ cup dry bread crumbs for coating
5 tablespoons butter

Soak fresh bread crumbs in water and wine; stir with a fork until smooth. Add the onion, veal, oil, and seasonings. Shape into small balls. Coat with the bread crumbs and allow to dry, about 15 minutes. Sauté in hot butter over moderate heat until evenly browned. YIELD: 25 veal balls.

Variation: Reduce salt to 1 teaspoon and add 3 tablespoons grated cheese, such as *kefalotiri.*

COLD APPETIZERS

BRAIN DIP
Miala

1 pair lamb brains
2 medium onions, finely minced
5 tablespoons olive oil
2 eggs, well beaten
Minced dill to taste
1 or 2 cloves garlic, crushed
2 tablespoons lemon juice
Salt and pepper to taste

Prepare brains according to directions given below. Sauté onions in 3 tablespoons of the olive oil until wilted. Lower heat. Mash brains with a fork until completely pulverized. Quickly add to the onions, stirring constantly. Add 2 more tablespoons of olive oil to soften the mixture, and continue stirring until brains, onions, and oil are completely blended. Keep mixture over low heat and add eggs, stirring constantly until completely absorbed. Remove from heat. Add garlic, dill, lemon juice, and salt and pepper; mix thoroughly. Serve hot or cold garnished with freshly chopped dill. YIELD: 1 cup.

PREPARATION OF BRAINS

Brains
1 onion, quartered

Wash brains gently. Cover them with water and soak for 15 minutes. Remove membranes and veins, then rinse brains under cold water. Place brains in boiling water. Add the onion and simmer for 25 minutes. Remove from the water and drain. The brains are ready to be used as desired.

BRAINS WITH DILL SAUCE
Miala me Anitho

1 pound lamb or calf brains
4 teaspoons vinegar
1 egg, beaten
2 onions, chopped
1 clove garlic, chopped
1½ tablespoons olive oil
½ teaspoon dried oregano
½ teaspoon minced dill
1 tablespoon lemon juice
Salt and pepper to taste

An excellent appetizer, as well as a good luncheon or first course recipe.

Soak the brains in lukewarm water. Add salt and vinegar to a pot of boiling water. Boil the brains for 15 to 20 minutes. Drain and remove the membranes. Mash the brains with a fork, add the beaten egg and blend. In a separate pan, sauté the chopped onions and garlic in the oil until wilted. Blend into the brains. Add oregano, dill, lemon juice, and salt and pepper. If the mixture is too dry, blend in a little more olive oil. Serve slightly warm with toast or rice. Serves 3–4.

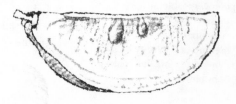

CHEESE PIE

Tiropeta me Meli

PASTRY:

1½ cups sifted flour
¼ teaspoon salt
½ cup butter
1 egg, well beaten

FILLING:

½ pound *feta* cheese, crumbled
½ pound *mizithra*, ricotta, or farmer's
    cheese
½ pound *kasseri* cheese, grated
½ cup honey
¼ teaspoon ground cinnamon
5 eggs

This unusual brunch dish features three different cheeses.

Sift together the flour and salt. Cut in the butter until the mixture resembles coarse meal. Blend in the egg. Knead with the fingers until well blended and chill for one hour. Roll out between sheets of wax paper, then press into a 10-inch quiche pan. Chill for 30 minutes. Preheat oven to 450°F. Bake the shell for 10 minutes. Remove shell and reduce oven temperature to 325°F. Prepare the filling while the crust bakes. Combine the cheeses, honey, and cinnamon; beat to blend well. Beat in eggs, one at a time. Add cheese mixture to partially baked crust, return to oven, and bake for 50 minutes, or until a knife inserted in the center comes out clean. Cool and chill before serving. Serves 8.

CHICKEN LIVER PÂTÉ

Pate me Sikotakia tis Kotas

2 cups fresh chicken livers
1 medium onion, chopped
¾ cup mayonnaise, preferably
    homemade
1 tablespoon brandy
1 hard cooked egg, chopped
Salt and pepper to taste

Put chicken livers and water to cover in a large saucepan and simmer for 10 to 15 minutes. Drain, cool, and chop finely. Add the onion to liver and transfer to the bowl of an electric mixer. Add the mayonnaise, brandy, egg, and salt and pepper. Beat for 10 minutes, or until fluffy. Butter a 2-cup mold. Fill with the pâté mixture and refrigerate for several hours, or overnight. Remove from the refrigerator ½ hour before unmolding. (If necessary, place hot towels around the mold to help loosen the pâté.) Decorate the pâté with black olives, if desired. Serves 12.

CHICKEN WALNUT SPREAD

Kota me Karithia Alima

1 cup finely chopped cooked chicken
    breast
¾ cup chopped walnuts
¼ teaspoon salt
½ teaspoon paprika
1 tablespoon finely minced scallion
2 tablespoons *kaimaki* (see note) or sour
    cream
2 tablespoons mayonnaise

Combine all the ingredients in a bowl. Blend together until well mixed. Chill for 2 hours. Serve on crackers, as a filling for cream puffs, or in finger sandwiches. YIELD: 2 cups.

Note: Kaimaki is a milk product similar to sour cream. It is sold all over Greece in special dairy stores called *galatopolia.*

(Lenten)

CHICK-PEA AND *TAHINI* DIP
Revithia me Tahini Alima

1 (12-ounce) can chick-peas, drained
2–3 teaspoons *tahini* (see note)
⅓ cup water
Juice of 1 lemon
¼ cup olive oil
2 cloves garlic, finely minced
½ teaspoon ground coriander (optional)
½ teaspoon ground cumin (optional)
Salt and pepper to taste
Minced parsley

Chop the chick-peas by hand or pulverize them in a blender or food processor. Put the *tahini* and water in a small bowl and beat by hand until dissolved, using a whisk or fork. Add the *tahini* mixture, a teaspoonful at a time, to the chick-peas, alternating with equal quantities of lemon juice and olive oil. When all has been added, add the garlic, spices, and 1 tablespoon parsley. Beat for a minute or so until well blended; then taste for seasonings and adjust if necessary. Chill overnight. Serve at room temperature, sprinkled with additional chopped parsley if desired. YIELD: 2 cups.

Note: Tahini, or sesame seed paste, is available in gourmet shops, Greek and Middle Eastern food stores, and health food stores. See Appendix for list of Greek food stores and distributors.

CUCUMBER AND YOGURT DIP
Tzatziki

2 cups plain yogurt
2 cucumbers
1 clove garlic, crushed
1 tablespoon vinegar
2 tablespoons olive oil
Salt and pepper to taste

This dip is extremely popular throughout Greece and is almost always included in the assorted appetizers served in restaurants and *tavernas.*

Put yogurt in a cheesecloth-lined sieve in a bowl. Drain overnight in the refrigerator. When ready to prepare, peel and chop cucumbers very finely and drain well. Add garlic, vinegar, olive oil, and salt and pepper to the cucumber and mix well. Add yogurt and blend. Serve with toast points or crackers. YIELD: 2 cups.

Note: This mixture may be prepared using a food processor.

CUMIN STICKS
Koulourakia me Kimino

KARPATHOS

2 cups flour
1 teaspoon salt
⅛ teaspoon powdered mustard
½ cup grated *kefalotiri* cheese
½ pound melted butter or margarine
1 egg yolk
2 tablespoons *Ouzo*
4 tablespoons water
1 egg white for brushing Cumin Sticks
2 teaspoons cumin seeds

Preheat oven to 350°F.

Blend together the flour, salt, mustard, and cheese. Add the melted butter, egg yolk, *Ouzo,* and water to form a soft dough. Roll out the dough to a thickness of ¼ inch and cut into 3- x ½-inch strips, or cut into various shapes with a cookie cutter. Place on a greased cookie sheet. Brush with egg white and sprinkle with cumin seeds. Bake for 15 minutes. YIELD: 4–5 dozen.

(Lenten)

EGGPLANT SPREAD

Melitzanosalata

2–3 large eggplants
1 onion, peeled
1 cup cold water
Salt and pepper to taste
Lemon juice or vinegar to taste
1 cup olive oil, as needed

Preheat oven to 350°F.

Wash the eggplants and put into a pan (or wrap in aluminum foil), and bake for 1½ hours, or until soft. Soak the onion in the cold water to remove some of its acidity. Remove the skins and seeds from the cooked eggplants. Set to drain in a colander for about 5 minutes, squeezing the liquid from the eggplant. Mash the pulp thoroughly. Drain the onion well, grate it finely, and add it to the eggplant. Add salt and pepper and beat. Add the lemon juice alternately with the oil, beating all the while, until the mixture is thick. Serve in a bowl with crackers. YIELD: 2 cups.

FETA DIP

Feta Meze

½ pound *feta* cheese
2 tablespoons olive oil
8 tablespoons milk
1 cup chopped walnuts
Dash of cayenne pepper
1 teaspoon paprika

↵ ZAKINTHOS

Feta is the best known Greek cheese. The following two recipes use this tasty cheese in new and interesting ways.

Soak the *feta* in cold water in the refrigerator overnight. Break the *feta* into chunks. Put 1 tablespoon oil and 4 tablespoons milk in a blender. Add half of the *feta* and half of the walnuts. Blend to a smooth consistency. Empty the blender container and repeat with the rest of the oil, milk, *feta,* and walnuts. Combine the two batches in a large bowl, add the cayenne, blend, and refrigerate. Before serving, sprinkle with paprika, and serve with crackers. YIELD: 2 cups.

Variation: Add ½ cup red caviar to the dip.

FETA MOLD

Feta se Kaloupi

½ pound *feta* cheese
½ cup sweet butter, softened
12 black olives, pitted
1 small onion, very finely minced
1 red or green pepper, finely minced
Garnish: celery sticks, carrot sticks,
    pepper strips

↵ CHIOS

Blend the cheese and the butter to the consistency of whipped cream using an electric mixer or food processor. Stir in olives, onion, and pepper and pack mixture solidly into an oiled mold. Refrigerate until firm. When ready to serve, unmold in the center of a large platter. Garnish with celery sticks, carrot sticks, and pepper strips. Serve with crackers.

(Lenten)

FISH ROE SPREAD

Taramosalata

4 tablespoons *tarama* (see note)
8 slices white bread
¾ cup olive oil
4 tablespoons lemon juice
1 teaspoon grated onion

Taramosalata, the famous Greek fish roe spread, is considered the "poor man's caviar." The secret of its success lies in mashing together the fish roe and the bread to form a paste, *before* the lemon juice, olive oil, and onion are added. Although a blender can be used to mash the roe with the bread, the best way to prepare it is by hand with a mortar and pestle.

Place the *tarama* in a mortar and pound it until the roe splits. Remove the crust from the slices of bread and moisten the bread with water; squeeze out any excess water. Add the bread to the *tarama* in the mortar and continue to pound until they are completely blended, about 5 minutes. Put this mixture in a mixing bowl and beat with an electric mixer, adding small amounts of olive oil alternately with lemon juice. Beat for 5 minutes. Add the onion and mix well. Serve in a bowl surrounded by crackers or thinly sliced bread. Keep refrigerated. YIELD: 1½ cups.

Note: Tarama (fish roe) is is available in gourmet shops, Greek and Middle Eastern food stores. See Appendix for list of Greek food stores and distributors.

MOLDED FISH ROE SALAD

Taramosalata Sti Forma

2 tablespoons unflavored gelatin
¼ cup cold water
2 cups boiling water
1 (4-ounce) jar *tarama*
1 cup mayonnaise
1 tablespoon lemon juice
1 cup fresh bread crumbs
Dash of cayenne pepper
½ cup grated onion
Dash of salt
1 (4-ounce) can pimiento
4 black olives, pitted
1 (8-ounce) package cream cheese

GARNISH:

2 cups chopped parsley
Whole olives
Pickles

Chill a metal fish mold in the freezer. Sprinkle the gelatin over the cold water to soften it. Add 2 cups boiling water and stir until the gelatin dissolves. Put in the refrigerator to cool, about 5 minutes. (Do not allow the gelatin to set.)

Blend the *tarama*, mayonnaise, lemon juice, bread crumbs, pepper, onion, and salt in a blender or electric mixer. Mix 1 cup of the gelatin liquid into the *tarama* mixture and put in refrigerator. Cut the olives into slices and the pimientos into narrow strips. Pour ¼ cup of the gelatin liquid into a fish mold and tip it to spread into all the crevices. Arrange slices of olives and pimiento as scales, eyes, tail, etc. Return mold to the freezer for 15 minutes. Pour ¼ cup more of the gelatin mixture into the decorated mold and return to the freezer. Beat or blend cream cheese and add remaining ½ cup gelatin liquid to beaten cheese. Set aside to cool in the refrigerator for 15 minutes. Do not let it jell completely. Spread cheese mixture over the bottom and sides of the mold. Return to the freezer for 15 minutes to set. Fill the mold with the *tarama* mixture. Refrigerate to set for 4 hours, or overnight. Chill serving platter in the refrigerator also.

To serve, dip mold in hot water. Place serving platter over mold and turn mold over quickly. Garnish with chopped parsley, olives, pickles, and any other vegetables desired. Serve with bread or crackers. Serves 12–16.

(Lenten)

MARINATED ARTICHOKES

Anginares Lathoxitho

16 artichoke hearts, cooked and drained
    (see note)
½ cup olive oil
2 tablespoons lemon juice
½ teaspoon salt
1 teaspoon prepared mustard
Fresh parsley
1 tablespoon finely minced fresh dill, or
    1 teaspoon dried dill

Cut the artichoke hearts in halves or in quarters. Combine the lemon juice and salt and gradually beat in the oil. Blend in the mustard. Pour this marinade over the artichokes and marinate overnight. Arrange the artichokes on bed of fresh parsley and sprinkle with dill. Serves 8–10.

Note: Fresh, frozen, or canned artichoke hearts may be used. If fresh, see Index for method of preparation and parboil. If frozen, cook according to package directions, cool, and proceed with recipe.

(Lenten)

MARINATED CELERY

Selino Lathoxitho

1 head celery
½ cup olive oil
Juice of 1½ lemons
2 tablespoons chopped fennel leaves
1–2 sprigs thyme, minced
2 sprigs parsley, minced
1 small bay leaf
Salt and pepper to taste
½ cup water
Lemon slices and fennel leaves for
    garnish (optional)

Scrub the celery stalks, scraping only the tough ones. Using a sharp knife, cut the stalks diagonally into 1½-inch lengths (cut the wider pieces in half lengthwise). Combine the oil, lemon juice, herbs, salt and pepper, and water in a pan. Bring to a boil, drop in the celery and add enough water to barely cover the celery. Cover and simmer for 15 minutes, or until the celery is tender but still crisp (do not overcook). Remove from the heat and cool in the marinade. Store, marinade and all, in a glass jar in the refrigerator. Serve garnished with lemon slices and fennel leaves. YIELD: approximately 1 quart.

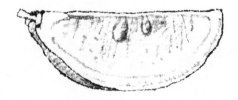

(Lenten)

MARINATED MUSHROOMS
Manitaria se Lathoxitho

1 pound small mushroom caps, fresh or
    canned (about 36 caps)
1 clove garlic
½ cup olive oil
½ cup red wine vinegar
1 teaspoon dried oregano
½ teaspoon salt
¼ teaspoon pepper

Clean the mushrooms if fresh. Mash the garlic and combine with the olive oil, vinegar and seasonings. Put the mushrooms in a covered jar, pour in the marinade, cover, and refrigerate. Marinate for 2 days or longer. YIELD: 36 pieces.

MELON WITH *OUZO*
Peponi me Ouzo

1 large cantaloupe or 2 small ones
½ cup sugar
1 cup *ouzo*
Rind of 1 lime (optional)

Halve the cantaloupe; remove the seeds and filaments. Either remove the pulp with a melon baller or peel the halves and slice. Put melon in a glass bowl and add the sugar and *ouzo*. Let stand for at least 3 hours, turning fruit occasionally. Grate lime rind over the fruit, if desired. Serves 6–8.

(Lenten)

MARINATED OLIVES
Elies Lathoxitho

1 pound large black or green olives
    (about 1 quart)
3 stalks celery from center of head,
    finely chopped
3 cloves garlic, finely minced
1 lemon, cut in pieces
1 cup olive oil
½ cup wine vinegar
2 tablespoons oregano

This is an old family recipe developed to give American olives a Greek flavor. Use *kalamatas* if they are available, for they are especially good prepared this way.

Drain the olives and slit each one with a knife to allow the marinade to penetrate. (This is not necessary for *kalamatas*, which have a natural slit.) Combine the olives with all the other ingredients and pack in jars. If the liquid does not completely cover the olives add water to cover. Seal and marinate for 2 to 3 weeks before serving. Shake the jars every few days. The olives will keep well in this marinade for 6 months.

(Lenten)

MARINATED MUSSELS

⌇ KITHIRA

Midia se Lathoxitho

2 quarts mussels
1 large onion
1 tablespoon vinegar
¼ cup olive oil
Sliced white bread

Clean and beard the mussels (see note). Steam the mussels in ½ cup water for 10 to 15 minutes, or until the shells open (discard those that don't). Remove mussels from shells and place in a jar. Combine onion, vinegar, and olive oil in blender and purée. Pour marinade over mussels. Refrigerate for several hours, or overnight. Serve cold with soft white bread cut into squares or triangles.

PREPARATION OF FRESH MUSSELS

To clean mussels place under cool (not cold) running water to remove surface dirt. Using a dull knife, scrape the shells very well to remove all clinging weeds and sand. Pull off the "beard" (a hairy-looking tuft projecting outside of the shells at the point where they are joined together) and scrub shells very well with a hard brush under cool (not cold) running water.

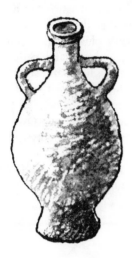

(Lenten)

MUSSELS WITH MUSTARD

⌇ KITHIRA

Midia me Moustartha

2 dozen mussels
2 tablespoons olive oil

Sauce:
½ tablespoon lemon juice
2 tablespoons mussel broth
1 tablespoon olive oil
1 tablespoon prepared mustard

Clean, beard, and scrub mussels thoroughly (see above). Steam mussels in about 2 cups water just until shells open, about 3 to 5 minutes, and reserve the broth. Remove mussels from the shells and place them in a jar. Strain the broth through a cheesecloth and add it to the mussels. Add enough additional water (if necessary) to cover the mussels. Add 2 tablespoons olive oil and refrigerate. When ready to serve, drain mussels, reserving 2 tablespoons of the mussel broth. Prepare sauce by alternately adding lemon juice, mussel broth, and olive oil to the mustard, beating after each addition, until all ingredients are used and mixture is thickened. Pour sauce over mussels and serve cold. YIELD: 24 pieces.

Note: Canned mussels may be used in place of fresh

(Lenten)

MUSSELS PILAF WITH PIGNOLIA NUTS

Midia Pilafi me Koukounaria   ✢ ANDROS

2 dozen mussels
2 cups water
1 (2½-ounce) package pignolias (pine
   nuts)
3 tablespoons olive oil
½ cup chopped onion
2 cups broth from steamed mussels
¼ cup dried currants
½ cup raw long-grain white rice
1 teaspoon salt
¼ teaspoon pepper
½ cup white wine
2 tablespoons minced parsley

Preheat oven to 350°F. Clean, beard, and scrub mussels thoroughly (see page 35). Steam mussels in 2 cups water just until shells open, about 3 to 5 minutes. Drain mussels, reserving broth, and arrange in a single layer in shallow baking dish. Discard any mussels that do not open. Place pignolias in a 9- x 9- x 1¾-inch baking pan and toast in the oven for 5 minutes. In a medium saucepan, heat the oil, add the onion and sauté until golden. Add 2 cups mussel broth (or the reserved broth plus sufficient water to equal 2 cups), currants, rice, and salt and pepper and bring to a boil. Cover, reduce the heat, and simmer, for 10 to 15 minutes, or until all liquid is absorbed. Remove from heat. Add the toasted pignolias, wine, and parsley and mix well. Place a tablespoon of the mixture in each mussel shell. Bake, uncovered, for 10 minutes, or until hot. Serves 8.

Note: Mussels may be prepared several hours ahead. Refrigerate unbaked mussels until ready to bake.

(Lenten)

MUSSELS WITH VEGETABLES

Midia Lathera

2 large onions, diced
½ cup olive or salad oil
3 medium carrots, diced
1 medium potato, diced
3 cloves garlic, minced (optional)
1 teaspoon sugar
Salt to taste
1 large tomato, peeled, cored, and
   chopped
2 (8-ounce) cans shelled mussels (reserve
   liquid)
1 cup chopped parsley
1 tablespoon lemon juice

Sauté the onions in oil in a deep frying pan over medium heat, stirring constantly, until wilted. Add the carrots and sauté for 3 minutes. Add potato, garlic, sugar, salt, liquid from cans of mussels, and tomato. Cover and cook over medium heat until vegetables are tender and almost all the liquid is absorbed. Add the mussels, parsley, and lemon juice and mix well. Remove from the heat and cool. Serve at room temperature with assorted crackers. Serves 6–8.

(Lenten)

OCTOPUS SAUTÉED IN WINE VINEGAR

⚓ SIPHNOS

Oktapodi me Xidi

3 pounds fresh octopus, skinned
4 tablespoons olive oil
3 large onions, sliced lengthwise
½ cup wine vinegar
Pinch of salt and pepper
1 bay leaf

Pound the octopus (use tentacles only) to tenderize it and cut into cubes. Heat the oil in a large skillet, add the octopus and sauté for 2 minutes. Add the onions and cook for 2 minutes. Add the wine vinegar, salt and pepper, and bay leaf. Cover and cook over low heat for 1 hour, or until tender enough to cut with a fork. Serve hot or cold. Serves 6.

OLIVE SPREAD

⚓ MYTILENE

Eliovoutiro

½ pound *kalamata* olives
1 cup butter, softened
⅛ teaspoon pepper
2 tablespoons minced scallions
2 tablespoons minced parsley

Pit the olives and purée in a blender, or chop very finely. In a mixing bowl, cream the butter with the olive paste. Blend in the pepper, scallions, and parsley. Chill. Serve with assorted crackers or toast points. YIELD: 1 cup.

SARDINES AND EGGS APPETIZER

⚓ PAROS

Sardelles me Avga

2 (3¾-ounce) cans skinless and boneless
    sardines
12 hard-cooked eggs
2 tablespoons lemon juice
2 tablespoons soft butter
Parsley for garnish

Mash the sardines. Separate the eggs and mash the yolks. Combine with sardines and season with lemon juice and butter. Garnish with chopped egg whites and parsley. Serve with assorted crackers or toast points. YIELD: 1 cup.

(Lenten)

STUFFED ARTICHOKES

⚓ CEPHALONIA

Anginares Yemistes

1 (15½-ounce) can artichoke hearts
⅔ cup *Taramosalata*°
Juice of 1½ lemons
¼ teaspoon dried thyme
½ pound small shrimp, cooked and
    peeled

Drain artichoke hearts. Push aside leaves from center to make a well. Mix *Taramosalata* with lemon juice and thyme. Place one shrimp in each artichoke heart. Fill with *Taramosalata* mixture. Garnish with shrimp. Chill. YIELD: 8–10 pieces.

Variation: Crab meat salad or shrimp salad may be substituted for *Taramosalata*.

MEATLESS STUFFED GRAPE LEAVES

Dolmades Politikes

2½ cups olive or salad oil
2½–3 pounds onions, diced
1 tablespoon salt
1 cup rice
1 teaspoon dried mint, or ½ cup minced
    parsley
1 teaspoon sugar
Pepper to taste
Juice of 2 lemons
1 (8-ounce) jar grape leaves

Greece is an arid and relatively poor country. Thus, its inhabitants have always looked for ways to make the most of what was available to them. The use of grape leaves in Greek cuisine is a case in point. Since vineyards are plentiful throughout the country, grape leaves provide the basic ingredient for several inexpensive, but nutritious, meals. This Lenten recipe is suitable for parties because it can be prepared ahead of time and served cold.

Heat 1½ cups of the oil in a large saucepan, add the onions and salt and cook, stirring, until the onions are wilted. Allow the onions to cool. Add rice, mint leaves, sugar, pepper, juice of 1 lemon, and salt to taste. Mix well. Rinse the grape leaves well, making sure to remove all of the brine. Cut stems off the leaves; arrange leaves dull side up in piles. Line the bottom of a Dutch oven or a large casserole with smaller or broken leaves. Put 1 tablespoon or more (depending on size of leaf) of rice and onion filling on each leaf (see diagram). Fold sides in toward the middle, then roll into small oblong shapes. (Do not roll too tightly so that rice will have room to expand.) Place *Dolmades* in the Dutch oven, point side of leaf down. Add remaining 1 cup oil and all liquid from onion filling. Cover with a heavy plate and add water to the level of the plate. Bring to a boil, lower the flame, and simmer for at least 1 hour or until the rice is tender. Sprinkle with the juice of the second lemon. Serve at room temperature. YIELD: 36 *Dolmades*.

Note: Do not skimp on the amount of chopped onions, even though it seems there should be more rice for all those onions. It is precisely this ratio that makes these *Dolmades* superior and worth the extra chopping.

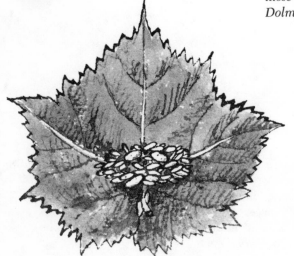

HOW TO FREEZE FRESH GRAPE LEAVES

Select young, tender grape leaves from the ends of the vines. (Grape vines grow wild in many parts of the United States.) Trim the stems and wash the leaves thoroughly in cold water. Bring water to a boil in a very large pot. Add the leaves and blanch for about 5 minutes. Remove the leaves from the pot, drain well and rinse in cold water. Layer the leaves dull side down in stacks of about 30 leaves each (enough for 1 pound of ground meat). Center each stack on a square of plastic wrap and roll the leaves and plastic wrap into cigar-shaped rolls, squeezing excess water from the leaves as you proceed. Place each roll in a plastic bag and freeze. To use, place frozen rolls (still wrapped in plastic) in warm water until thawed. Fresh grape leaves may stay in the freezer indefinitely and leftover leaves may be refrozen.

Soups

To the non-Greek world, soups and Greece equals *Avgolemono,* the famous (and delicious) egg- and lemon-flavored chicken soup; in reality, however, the range of Greek soups is much wider than that. From the rich barley soups of northern mainland Greece to the exquisite Mussel Soup with Wine and the hearty *Kakavia* of the islands (actually a Greek version of the French Bouillabaisse), soups of all kinds are an important part of the Greek diet. The emphasis on seafood soups is not surprising in a land teeming with the bounty of the sea.

BARLEY SOUP WITH LAMB

Kreatosoupa me Krithari

3 pounds lamb shoulder, cut into cubes
½ cup pearl barley
12 cups water
1 tablespoon salt
1 tablespoon minced dill
1 tablespoon minced parsley
¼ teaspoon pepper
1 cup sliced carrots
1 cup sliced leeks
¾ cup sliced celery
Juice of 1 lemon

Simmer meat and barley in water for 1½ hours. Add the remaining ingredients, except the lemon juice, and simmer for 30 minutes more. Remove meat from the bones and dice; discard the bones. Return the meat to the soup, add lemon juice, and stir. Serves 6.

Note: This soup is also good with *Avgolemono* Sauce°.

FISH SOUP WITH TOMATOES

↯ PATMOS

Psarosoupa me Ntomata

3 pounds whole fish (bass, cod, blackfish, or any other oily fish)
Salt and pepper to taste
2–3 medium carrots, sliced
2–3 medium onions, sliced
2–3 stalks celery, sliced
3 quarts water
1 (2-pound) can whole tomatoes, drained
¾ cup oil
6 tablespoons raw rice (optional)

Clean and dress fish. Season lightly with salt and pepper and set aside to drain. Put the carrots, onions, and celery into a large pot. Add the water and bring to a boil. Add the whole tomatoes, pierced in several places with a fork, and cook for 45 minutes. Add the fish and oil and simmer for 20–30 minutes, or until the fish flakes easily (do not overcook). Remove the fish to a warm tureen, handling it carefully to avoid breaking. Strain the soup and return it to the heat. Add the rice, stirring until the soup starts to simmer. Lower heat and simmer for 20 minutes, or until the rice is tender. Transfer soup to the tureen and serve hot. Serves 6–8.

KAKAVIA
Kakavia

4–6 pounds whole fish suitable for
   boiling, such as striped bass, sea
   bass, or red snapper
½ cup olive oil
4 large onions, chopped
2 stalks celery, cubed
3 cloves garlic, sliced
2 leeks, sliced
3 large carrots, pared and cubed
2 tablespoons salt
1 teaspoon pepper
Juice of 1 lemon
1 (1-pound) can plum tomatoes with
   liquid
6 cups water
1 cup white wine
3 bay leaves
½ teaspoon dried thyme
1 tablespoon minced parsley
1 (2-pound) lobster, cut into serving-size
   pieces (include shells)
12 clams, scrubbed
12 shrimp, shelled and deveined
12 mussels, scrubbed, bearded, and
   cleaned

What the French call bouillabaisse, the Greeks call "Kakavia," a name with an interesting derivation. When fisherman gathered on the beach after their daily catch, they would make a huge fire and place all the fish they could not sell into a large kettle or "kakavia." Hence, the name of this hearty fish soup which is still a favorite main meal among Greek islanders. The following is an adaptation of the traditional recipe.

Prepare fish by cleaning and cutting into small pieces. Heat the oil in a large pot. Sauté the onions, celery, garlic, and leeks over medium heat for 5 minutes. Add the remaining ingredients except the seafood and bring to a boil. Reduce heat and cover. Cook for 15 minutes. Add the fish and cook for 15 minutes. Add shellfish and simmer for 10 minutes, or until clams and mussels open. Remove the fish from the pot and clean it, removing skin and bones; discard the shells from the shellfish. Return fish and shellfish to the pot and reheat briefly. Serve in deep bowls with crusty garlic bread. Serves 12.

LAMBS FEET SOUP

❧ MYTILENE

Patscha

4 lamb hoofs (see note) and shanks
2 stalks celery, finely chopped
1 onion, sliced
3 cloves garlic, crushed
Salt and pepper to taste
½ cup rice (optional)
3 eggs
Juice of 2 lemons

This traditional Easter soup can also be made with pigs feet and without *Avgolemono* Sauce. In its more authentic version *Patscha* is, frankly, an acquired taste.

Clean hoofs and shanks well and put in a large pot. Add enough water to cover and add the celery, onion, garlic, and salt and pepper. Boil for 1 hour. Remove the hoofs and shanks from the pot and strain the broth. Return the broth to the pot. Separate the skins of the hoofs and shanks from the bones and cut the meat into small pieces; add to the broth. Add the rice and simmer for 20 minutes, or until the rice is tender. Prepare an *Avgolemono* Sauce by beating the eggs until creamy and adding the lemon juice and again beating until thick. Add the sauce to the hot (but not boiling) soup. Serve hot. Serves 6–8.

Note: Lamb hoofs may be obtained at Easter time in Greek meat markets. They are sold skinned and ready to use.

MOCK *MAGERITSA*

Apli Mageritsa

3 pounds lamb shoulder
2 pounds lamb bones
2 stalks celery
1 carrot, scraped
2 small onions, peeled
Salt and pepper to taste, or salt and 8
    peppercorns
12 cups water
8 scallions, finely minced
1 bunch dill, finely minced
½ cup rice
4 eggs
Juice of 2 lemons

The traditional *Mageritsa* recipe calls for lamb tripe, lungs, and heart. The following simplified recipe substitutes more readily available ingredients.

Simmer the meat and bones, celery, carrot, onions, and salt and pepper in the water for 2 hours. Strain broth and reserve. Remove meat from bones and dice. Add meat, scallions, dill, and rice to broth and simmer for 20 minutes, or until the rice is tender. Strain again and use broth to prepare an *Avgolemono* Sauce. In a blender, beat the eggs thoroughly. Slowly add the lemon juice and hot broth and continue beating. If there is more liquid than the blender will hold, empty half of the egg mixture into a saucepan and continue beating in the blender, slowly adding the rest of the liquid. Mix all the sauce together in the saucepan, add the meat and reheat over a low flame. Serves 6–8.

MUSSEL SOUP WITH WINE   ↲ IOS

Midia Soupa me Krasi

3 tablespoons butter
3 scallions, minced
1 clove garlic, minced
1 stalk celery, chopped
1 bay leaf
½ teaspoon dried thyme
¾ cup white wine
2 pounds mussels, cleaned, bearded, and
    scrubbed
2 cups water
1½ cups light cream
Salt and pepper to taste

Melt the butter in a frying pan and sauté the scallions, garlic, and celery until wilted. In a saucepan simmer the bay leaf and thyme in the wine. Put the mussels in another pot with the water and steam until they open. Remove mussels from their shells and chop. Strain the mussel broth and combine all the ingredients. Serve warm. Serves 4.

(Lenten)

TAHINI SOUP

Tahinosoupa

2 quarts water
Salt
1 cup rice
6 ounces *tahini* (sesame seed paste)
½ cup cold water
Juice of 1 or 2 lemons
1 teaspoon tomato paste (optional)

Bring salted water to a boil, add the rice, and cook for 20 minutes. While rice is cooking, mix *tahini* in a bowl with ½ cup cold water and add the lemon juice. Mix well. Slowly add 1 or 2 full ladles of the rice water to the *tahini*. Remove the rice from the heat and pour all the *tahini* mixture into it. Add tomato paste. Serves 6.

YOGURT SOUP WITH BARLEY

↯ SAMOS

Yiaourtosoupa me Krithari

⅛ cup pearl barley
3 tablespoons butter
¼ cup finely minced onion
6 eggs
3 tablespoons flour
3 cups chicken broth
3 cups plain yogurt
2 sprigs fresh dill, minced
½ teaspoon ground coriander
2 sprigs parsley, minced
¼ teaspoon dried thyme
Salt to taste
Juice of ½ lemon
Paprika or 1 cucumber

Cook the barley until tender according to package directions. As the barley cooks, heat the butter in a small skillet and sauté the onion until translucent. Drain the cooked barley well and transfer it to a bowl. (The barley grains should not clump together.) Add the onion to the drained barley. In a separate mixing bowl, beat the eggs lightly. Beat in the flour a little at a time. Beat the broth and yogurt together and when thoroughly blended stir into the eggs. To this mixture add the barley and onion, dill, coriander, parsley, and thyme. Pour the soup into a large saucepan and cook, stirring constantly, over low heat until it is piping hot but not boiling or else it will curdle. Add salt to taste and lemon juice. Serve hot with a sprinkling of paprika, or chill and serve cold with a garnish of cold, thin cucumber slices. Serves 8.

COLD *AVGOLEMONO* SOUP

↯ CRETE

Kria Avgolemono Soupa

4 eggs
Juice of 2 lemons
4 cups (32 ounces) chicken broth with
    rice, preferably homemade
1 pint heavy cream

In a large bowl, beat the eggs, gradually adding the lemon juice. Heat the chicken broth in a large saucepan. Slowly add the hot broth to the egg sauce, beating vigorously. Return the soup to the heat and stir until thickened. (Do not allow the soup to boil). Cool. Just before serving beat the heavy cream until thick and fold it into the soup. Serve at once. Serves 6.

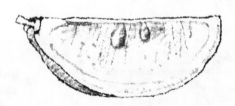

COLD GARLIC SOUP
Kria Skordosoupa

6 cloves garlic, minced
6 slices white bread, trimmed and
    soaked
½ cup olive oil
2 tablespoons wine vinegar
1 tablespoon salt
½–¾ cup minced parsley
3 cups cold water
½ cucumber, roughly chopped

BLENDER METHOD

Place garlic, soaked bread, oil, vinegar, salt, and parsley in a blender (reserving some parsley for garnish). Blend thoroughly. Pour mixture into a bowl, add water and cucumber and mix well. Refrigerate and serve very cold, sprinkled with the remaining parsley. Serves 4–6.

HAND METHOD

Put garlic and salt in a wooden bowl and mash into a paste. Add soaked bread and oil alternately. Work mixture thoroughly. Add vinegar, cucumber, parsley, and water. Mix thoroughly. Refrigerate and serve very cold. Serves 4–6.

SUMMER CUCUMBER SOUP
Kalokerini Soupa me Angourakia

✤ CRETE

3 cups yogurt
1½ cups grated cucumber
¾ cup cold water
1 tablespoon minced dill
3 tablespoons minced chives
½ teaspoon salt
¼ teaspoon pepper
Garlic salt to taste

The Greeks have long had a love affair with yogurt, which is the basis of this delicious and refreshing soup.

Place all the ingredients in a mixing bowl. Stir until well blended. Serve in chilled bowls with garlic bread. Serves 4.

Meats and
Poultry

The rugged terrain of Greece is ideal for the grazing of sheep, which accounts for the preponderance of lamb on the Greek menu. In fact, few cuisines can rival the Greek way with tender baby lamb. Veal is the next most popular meat, though beef, most of which must be imported, is becoming increasingly popular. An unusual, though very popular, recipe from the fertile land of Macedonia combines pork with cabbage and green olives. As in most other countries, chicken is a staple in Greece, where cooks prepare it with *feta*, and *phyllo*, and in combination with the cornucopia of vegetables and spices indigenous to the country.

LAMB

SPINACH-STUFFED LAMB

Arni Gemisto me Spanaki

1 (10-ounce) package frozen spinach, thawed
2 cups fresh bread crumbs
½ cup chopped walnuts or pine nuts
½ cup minced parsley
1 egg, well beaten
2 tablespoons finely minced shallots
1 clove garlic, crushed
1 teaspoon salt
¼ teaspoon pepper
2 pounds breast of lamb, boned

Rosé Wine Sauce:

3 tablespoons butter or margarine
2 tablespoons flour
¾ cup water
¼ cup rosé wine
2 cubes beef bouillon
1 tablespoon minced parsley

This is a simplified version of a traditional recipe.

Preheat oven to 325°F.

Combine the spinach, bread crumbs, nuts, parsley, egg, shallots, garlic, salt, and pepper. Place stuffing mixture on the boned breast; roll the meat and stuffing from the thickest end to the thin end. Tie roll securely with string. Place lamb on rack in a shallow roasting pan. Bake for 2 hours. As lamb bakes, make the wine sauce by melting the butter in a small saucepan. Stir in the flour and cook for 1 minute. Remove from heat and stir in the water, wine, and bouillon. Return to heat; cook, stirring constantly, until smooth. Add the parsley. Remove string from lamb, slice thickly, and arrange with yellow rice on a platter. Serve with the wine sauce. Serves 5–6.

ROLLED STUFFED BREAST OF LAMB

Arnisio Rolo Gemisto

1 (4-pound) lamb breast, boned
Salt and pepper to taste
1 cup butter
½ pound ground veal or beef
½ cup minced scallions
½ cup white wine
1 pound ripe tomatoes, peeled, seeded,
    and chopped
2 tablespoons minced parsley
1 tablespoon minced dill
½ cup toasted bread crumbs
½ cup grated *kasseri* cheese
1 lemon

Preheat oven to 400°F.

Dry the lamb and sprinkle with salt and pepper. Melt one third of the butter in a large pot, add the ground veal and scallions, and brown lightly. Add salt, pepper, and the wine, a little at a time so that it steams as it is added. Add the tomatoes, parsley, and dill and cook over high heat for 15 minutes, or until all the liquid has been absorbed. Remove from the heat and partially cool. Add the bread crumbs and *kasseri* cheese. Spread the mixture on the lamb breast and roll it up carefully. Sew or tie the breast together. Rub the surface of the lamb with lemon and a little more salt and pepper. Put the remaining butter into a baking pan; place the rolled meat in it and roast for 20 to 30 minutes, or until brown on all sides. Lower the oven temperature to 325°F. and roast for 2 hours, or until meat is tender. Cool slightly to make carving easier. Serve with beans and sautéed carrots or other vegetables. Serves 6.

STUFFED CROWN ROAST OF LAMB

Korona Arniou Gemisti

1 (6-pound) crown roast of lamb
2 cloves garlic, peeled and cut into
    slivers
2 tablespoons salt
½ teaspoon pepper
½ lemon
1 small eggplant
2 tablespoons vegetable or olive oil
1 onion, finely minced
1 stalk celery, finely minced
¼ cup minced parsley
1 pound ground lean lamb
¼ teaspoon ground cinnamon
¼ teaspoon ground cardamom
¼ cup raisins
8 Greek olives, pitted and chopped
½ cup chestnuts (cooked and cut into
    small pieces) and/or pignolias (pine
    nuts) or walnuts
1 teaspoon grated lemon rind
1½ cups cooked rice or cooked *orzo*
Kalamata olives for garnish

Preheat oven to 350°F.

Pat the meat dry. Make incisions all over the roast and insert the garlic slivers. Rub with 1 tablespoon salt, pepper, and lemon half. Put in a roasting pan. Peel and cut the eggplant into 1-inch cubes. Sprinkle with 1 tablespoon salt. Let stand for 15 minutes, then rinse and dry on paper towels. Sauté in hot oil until golden on all sides. Add onion and cook until wilted, then add celery and cook until soft. Add parsley and ground meat and sauté, separating with a fork, until golden brown. Add cinnamon, cardamom, raisins, chopped olives, chestnuts, and lemon rind. Add rice and cooked eggplant; mix all ingredients lightly. Season with salt and pepper to taste. Spoon into the roast. Wrap the ends of the bones with aluminum foil. Roast for 1½ hours. Let stand 10 minutes before carving. Remove aluminum foil and decorate the ends of the bones with pitted Greek olives. Serves 8.

BAKED LAMB CHOPS WITH *FETA* CHEESE

Psita Paidakia me Feta

⚓ KOS

4–6 loin or shoulder lamb chops
Salt and pepper to taste
Dried oregano to taste
2 cloves garlic, peeled and cut into
    slivers
4½ tablespoons melted butter
Juice of 1 lemon
½ pound *feta* cheese, cut into squares

Preheat oven to 375°F.

Season chops with salt, pepper, and oregano. Cut slits in the lamb and insert slivers of garlic. Pour mixture of melted butter and lemon juice over the meat. Place each chop on a piece of aluminum foil large enough to cover it completely. On top of each chop place a square of *feta* cheese. Fold aluminum foil carefully to prevent the escape of any juices. Place chops in a roasting pan and bake until meat is done, approximately 2 hours. Serve chops in their foil envelopes on individual plates. Serves 4–6.

BAKED LAMB WITH OLIVES AND CHEESE

Psito Arni me Elies kai Tyri

⚓ TIRI

1 (6–8-pound) leg of lamb
3 tablespoons butter
2 cloves garlic, crushed
Salt and pepper to taste
1 onion, chopped
1 cup dry red wine
1 cup boiling water
1 tablespoon flour
¼ cup cold water
12 small whole potatoes
12 small whole onions
½ cup vegetable oil
¾ pound *kefalotiri* cheese, cut into 8
    ½-inch cubes
12 large black olives

Preheat oven to 325°F.

Rub the lamb with butter, garlic, and salt and pepper. In a covered roasting pan, sear the meat over medium heat until well browned. Add the chopped onion and brown slightly, then add the wine and boiling water. Cover the roaster and bake for 1½ hours. Lift the roast from pan and set aside in a warm place. Pour stock from the roasting pan into a saucepan and skim off the fat. Make a paste of the flour and water and stir it into degreased pan juices. Cook for 5 minutes, stirring, or until the gravy thickens. Wash and peel the potatoes and onions. Heat the oil in a skillet until it sizzles. Fry the vegetables until brown. Make eight slits in the leg of lamb and insert a piece of cheese in each. Pour the thickened stock over the lamb in the roasting pan. Surround the meat with olives, potatoes, and onions. Return to the oven uncovered. Raise the oven temperature to 375°F. and bake for 40 minutes, basting often to keep moist. Serves 6–8.

ROLLED STUFFED LEG OF LAMB

Gemisto Arni me Feta

MARINADE:

¼ cup olive oil
Juice of 1 lemon
¼ cup wine
¼ teaspoon dried thyme, or ½ teaspoon
    dried oregano
1 bay leaf, crushed
2 cloves garlic, crushed
Salt and pepper to taste

1 (7–9-pound) leg of lamb, boned and
    butterflied

STUFFING:

8 scallions
1 bunch parsley
½ bunch dill
3–4 cloves garlic, peeled
¾ pound *feta* cheese

GRAVY:

½ stick butter
½ pound fresh mushrooms
3 tablespoons flour
¾ cup beef broth
1 cup water

Combine all the ingredients for the marinade and pour over the leg of lamb; refrigerate in a covered bowl for several hours, or overnight.

Preheat oven to 350°F.

Finely chop the scallions, parsley, and dill. Mince the garlic and add it to the chopped greens. Put in a bowl until ready to use. When ready to bake the lamb, crumble the *feta* into the chopped herbs and garlic mixture. Flatten the lamb and spread the stuffing in the center. Fold over each side of the lamb envelope style and tie the lamb securely. Pour the marinade over the lamb. Bake for about 2½ hours.

Prepare the gravy by sautéing the mushrooms in the butter. Remove the mushrooms from the pan and set aside. Add the flour to the pan and blend. Combine the beef broth and water, add to pan, and stir over low heat until gravy thickens. Add the reserved mushrooms. Serve the lamb with the gravy. Serves 8.

STUFFED LEG OF LAMB WITH *PASTRUMA*

Gemisto Arni me Pastrouma

1 (4–5-pound) leg of lamb, boned
1 tablespoon olive oil
½ teaspoon dried thyme
1 tablespoon salt
½ tablespoon pepper
8 artichoke hearts, cooked
2 tablespoons butter
10 slices *pastruma* (see note)
1 cup red wine
½ cup water

Preheat oven to 350°F.

Rub the lamb with the olive oil, thyme, salt, and pepper. In a blender or food processor purée the cooked artichoke hearts. Combine the purée with the butter and salt and pepper to taste and heat gently. Spread out the boned leg of lamb and overlap the slices of *pastruma* on it. Spread the artichoke purée over the *pastruma*. Roll up lamb and tie it securely. Roast for 2½ to 3 hours, basting with a mixture of 1 cup wine and ½ cup water. Cool for 15 minutes prior to slicing. Serves 8–10.

Note: Pastruma is meat cured in red pepper. It is sold in Greek and Middle Eastern meat shops.

LAMB PIE WITH *PHYLLO*

Peta me Arni

1½ pounds lean shoulder of lamb, boned
3 tablespoons butter
1 teaspoon salt
½ teaspoon pepper
½ cup finely minced onion
1 cup diced potatoes (cooked until barely
    tender)
¾ cup crumbled *feta* cheese
½ cup cooked rice (optional, if not used
    increase amount of potato by ½ cup)
½ cup chopped celery
¼ cup minced parsley
¼ cup olive oil
½ teaspoon crushed dried mint
½ teaspoon ground cinnamon
12 sheets *phyllo* pastry
¼ pound melted butter for brushing
    phyllo

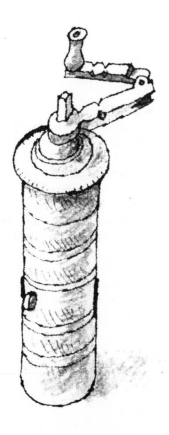

Wipe the lamb with paper towels and cut into ½-inch cubes. Melt 3 tablespoons butter in a large skillet, add the lamb and brown well. (You will probably have to do this in two batches.) Transfer the cubes to a mixing bowl using a slotted spoon and sprinkle with salt and pepper. In the fat remaining in the skillet, sauté the onion until wilted. Toss the onion with the lamb and add the potatoes, *feta* cheese, rice, celery, parsley, olive oil, mint, cinnamon, and salt and pepper to taste.

Preheat oven to 350°F.

Brush the bottom and sides of a baking dish, 11¾- x 7½- x 1¾-inches, with melted butter. Brush 1 *phyllo* sheet with melted butter and place in the pan so that half the sheet hangs over the rim. Arrange 5 more sheets in the pan in the same manner so that the bottom and sides of the pan are entirely covered with overlapping *phyllo*. (Each sheet must be buttered separately; as you work, keep remaining *phyllo* covered with a damp cloth or plastic wrap to prevent drying out.) Spread meat filling evenly over the *phyllo* and fold overhanging edges of *phyllo* over the filling. Butter the remaining *phyllo* sheets and arrange over the filling, folding where necessary to accommodate the pan. Brush the top with the remaining butter and with a sharp knife score it into 12 squares, but do not cut all the way through. (Recipe may be prepared to this point and frozen. To serve, bake unthawed for 1 hour and 15 minutes.) Otherwise, bake for 45 minutes, or until golden. Let stand for 5 minutes, then cut through the squares to separate. Serves 12.

VEAL, BEEF, AND PORK

STUFFED BREAST OF VEAL

Stithos Moshari Paragemiston

1 (3–4-pound) veal breast, boned, with
pocket
Salt and pepper to taste
1 large onion, chopped
1 clove garlic, crushed
3 stalks celery, chopped
1 cup butter
1½ cups bread crumbs
2 tablespoons minced parsley
½ teaspoon dried marjoram
¼ teaspoon dried basil
¼ teaspoon dried thyme
¼ cup flour
2 cups chicken broth
½ cup dry white wine

Sprinkle the inside of the veal pocket with salt and pepper. Lightly sauté the onion, garlic, and celery in ½ cup of the butter. Add the bread crumbs, parsley, herbs, and salt and pepper to taste. Stuff the veal breast with the mixture and skewer to close. Dredge the meat with flour and brown well in the remaining ½ cup butter in a Dutch oven. Add the chicken broth and wine, cover, and simmer for 2 hours, or until tender. Serves 6.

VEAL PIE

Peta Moshariou

CRUST:

1½ cups flour
1 teaspoon garlic salt
1 teaspoon dried oregano
¼ cup grated *kefalotiri* cheese
½ cup butter
4–5 tablespoons cold water

MEAT FILLING:

2 pounds veal, cubed
½ cup flour
¾ cup butter
2 cups tomatoes, whole
1 cup tomato sauce
¼ cup chopped onions
3 teaspoons grated *kefalotiri* cheese
1 tablespoon sugar
½ tablespoon salt
½ tablespoon garlic salt
½ tablespoon dried oregano
¼ tablespoon pepper
1 tablespoon dried basil
¼ cup *kasseri* cheese

Preheat oven to 400°F.

To make the crust, mix the flour with the garlic salt, oregano, and grated cheese. Cut in butter finely. Sprinkle with cold water and stir with a fork until the dough holds together. Roll out two thirds of the dough on a floured surface. Fit into a 9- x 9-inch baking dish. Save the remaining dough for the top.

Dredge the veal with flour and brown in butter. Stir in the remaining ingredients, except for the *kasseri* cheese. Cover and simmer for 30 minutes. Turn into the pastry-lined pan and top with the *kasseri* cheese.

Roll out the remaining dough ⅛ inch thick and cut into 2-inch rounds. Place rounds over cheese, overlapping slightly. Bake for 35 minutes, or until the pastry is golden. Serves 6–8.

SMOTHERED CHOPS

Breezoles me Tomates

4 large thick shoulder chops (veal or
    lamb), approximately ½ pound each
Salt and pepper to taste
2 tablespoons flour
¼ cup vegetable oil
3–5 cloves garlic, finely minced
¼ cup minced parsley
1 cup canned tomatoes
½ cup tomato sauce
3 tablespoons wine vinegar
¼ cup dry white wine

Season the chops with salt and pepper and dredge them in flour. Heat the oil in a skillet and brown the chops on both sides. Combine the garlic and parsley in a small dish. In a bowl blend together the tomatoes, tomato sauce, vinegar, and wine. Spread the garlic and parsley over the chops in the skillet. Pour the tomato mixture over the chops. Cover tightly and simmer for 1 hour. Serves 4.

STEWED STEAK

Sofrito

2½ pounds fully trimmed veal shoulder
    or veal scallopini, cut into ½-inch-
    thick slices
1 cup flour
½ cup olive or vegetable oil
¼ cup vinegar
1½ cups hot water
2–3 cloves garlic, finely minced
1 teaspoon salt
½ teaspoon pepper
½ cup minced parsley

This recipe is an adaptation of the traditional *sofrito* of the island of Corfu.

Coat steak slices with flour. Fry meat in oil until well browned on both sides. Sprinkle meat with vinegar and enough water to barely cover. Add garlic and season with salt and pepper. Cover and simmer gently until meat is tender and liquid is reduced to a thick sauce.

Sprinkle with parsley and serve *sofrito* with mashed potatoes. Serves 4–6.

PITA BREAD STUFFED WITH BEEF

Fetes Vodines se Peta

1 cup plain yogurt
½ cup dry red wine
2 tablespoons olive or cooking oil
1 small clove garlic, minced
½ teaspoon dried oregano, crushed
½ teaspoon salt
Dash of pepper
1 pound sirloin steak
1 tablespoon butter or margarine
4 pita (see note)
3 cups chopped lettuce
1 cup diced, seeded, peeled tomato
1 cup diced, seeded cucumber

Thicken yogurt by placing it in a cheesecloth-lined sieve and allow it to stand overnight in the refrigerator. Next day, combine wine, oil, garlic, oregano, salt, and pepper. Cut steak into strips, 2 inches long by ¼ inch wide. Pour wine marinade over beef strips, and let stand for 1 hour at room temperature. Drain meat strips and cook, in two batches, in hot butter, stirring for 2 to 3 minutes, or until brown on all sides. Serve the meat in a chafing dish or on a hot tray to keep warm. Open one end of the pita to make a pocket. Set out dishes of the lettuce, tomato, cucumber, and yogurt. Allow each person to fill his own sandwich. Serves 4.

Note: In some larger cities, pita may be purchased in ethnic bakeries or even in supermarkets under such names as "Syrian," "Greek," and "Arab" bread.

PORK WITH CELERY
Hirino me Selino

6 pork chops
3 tablespoons oil
2 onions, chopped
3–4 carrots, cut in 2-inch pieces
¾ cup water
1 head celery, cut in 1½-inch pieces

Avgolemono SAUCE:

1 tablespoon cornstarch
3 tablespoons water
2 eggs, separated
3 tablespoons lemon juice

Brown the pork chops in oil. Add the onions and carrots and sauté for 5 minutes. Add the water and cook for 25 minutes. Place the celery on top and continue cooking until tender (about 20 minutes). Add water as needed. To prepare *Avgolemono* Sauce, drain the liquid from the pork-celery pan. Add water or stock to make 1 cup. To this add the cornstarch diluted in 3 tablespoons water; cook until liquid is thick and clear. Beat egg whites until stiff. Add egg yolks and then lemon juice. Continue to beat the egg mixture as you add the hot stock. Pour over the meat and vegetables. Serves 4–6.

Note: Blender method may be used to prepare *Avgolemono* Sauce (see Index).

POULTRY

CHICKEN BREASTS IN *PHYLLO*   ❧ PATMOS
Kotopites

¼ pound butter
1 onion, finely minced
½ pound mushrooms, finely minced
2 tablespoons minced parsley
1 clove garlic, finely minced
1 tablespoon flour
¼ cup dry vermouth or dry white wine
Salt and pepper to taste
2 tablespoons vegetable oil
2 whole chicken breasts, boned and
    halved
8 sheets *phyllo* pastry
1¼ cup melted butter
2 cups bread crumbs
½ pound *feta* cheese

Preheat oven to 350°F.

In a skillet, melt 2 to 3 tablespoons of the butter and sauté onion until golden; remove onion and set aside. Melt 2 to 3 more tablespoons butter and sauté the chopped mushrooms until all juices are absorbed. Add the onions, parsley, and garlic and sauté for 1 minute. Stir in the flour and blend well. Add the vermouth and stir over moderate heat until thickened. Season with salt and pepper to taste. Remove the mushroom mixture and set aside. In the same skillet, melt the remaining butter with the oil and sauté the chicken breasts until lightly browned, about 1 minute on each side. Remove from the heat. Brush one sheet of *phyllo* at a time with the melted butter (keep remaining sheets from drying out by covering with a damp towel or plastic wrap). Sprinkle with bread crumbs, place a second sheet of *phyllo* on top of the first, butter and sprinkle with bread crumbs. Place chicken breast in the lower half of the *phyllo*. Put a quarter of the mushroom mixture and a quarter of the *feta* over the chicken. Fold up the sides of the *phyllo* over the chicken, envelope style. Repeat with remaining breasts. (Recipe may be prepared to this point and frozen. To serve, bake without prior thawing for about 50 minutes.) Butter the chicken rolls well and place seam side down on a baking sheet. Bake for 35 minutes, or until brown. Serves 4.

BAKED CHICKEN BREASTS
Ornithas Psita Stithia

3 whole chicken breasts, boned and
    halved
1 cup plain yogurt
2 tablespoons lemon juice
2 cloves garlic, finely minced
2 teaspoons celery salt
2 teaspoons salt
¼ teaspoon pepper
1 cup dry bread crumbs
½ cup butter

Wipe the chicken breasts well. Combine the yogurt, lemon juice, garlic, celery salt, salt, and pepper. Add the chicken to the yogurt mixture, coating each piece well. Let stand covered overnight in refrigerator.

Preheat oven to 350°F.

Remove chicken from yogurt mixture and roll each piece in bread crumbs, coating evenly. Arrange the chicken in a single layer in a large, shallow, lightly greased baking pan. Melt half the butter; spoon over the chicken. Bake, uncovered, for 45 minutes. Melt and spoon the remaining butter over the chicken. Bake for 10 to 15 minutes, or until chicken is tender and nicely browned. Serves 6.

STUFFED CHICKEN

✣ KITHIRA

Paragemisti Ornitha

½ pound ground lean lamb
⅛ cup cooking oil
1½ cups cooked rice
⅛ cup pignolias (pine nuts), toasted
½ teaspoon salt or more to taste
⅛ teaspoon pepper or more to taste
¼ teaspoon plus dash ground cinnamon
3 dashes of ground nutmeg
½ teaspoon dried thyme
1 (3–3½-pound) chicken

Preheat oven to 375°F.

In a skillet, brown the lamb in 3 tablespoons of the oil. Add rice, pignolias, salt, pepper, and herbs and spices and mix well. Stuff the chicken with the rice mixture. (Do not pack the stuffing.) Skewer neck skin to back, tie legs to tail and tuck in wings. Place on a rack in a shallow baking pan. Sprinkle with additional salt and pepper; brush with a little of the remaining cooking oil. Roast for 1¼ to 1½ hours, or until chicken is golden brown and juices run clear. Brush occasionally with oil. Serves 4.

CHICKEN STUFFED WITH *FETA*

✣ SALONIKA

Kota Gemisti

1 (3½–4-pound) roasting chicken
3 scallions, chopped, including green
    ends
½ pound *feta* cheese, crumbled
1 teaspoon pepper
1 fresh tomato, chopped
½ cup mushrooms, fresh or canned
2 tablespoons minced parsley
Chicken liver from the chicken
2 eggs, lightly beaten
¼ pound butter
1 (8-ounce) can tomato sauce

Preheat oven to 350°F.

Clean chicken and pat dry. Combine scallions, *feta*, pepper, tomato, mushrooms, and parsley. Cut up the chicken liver and add to the mixture. Add the eggs. Season with salt and pepper to taste (taste mixture before adding salt since *feta* tends to be salty). Stuff the chicken and sew opening closed. In a roasting pan, cook chicken in butter until well browned. Pour tomato sauce over chicken and bake, uncovered, for 1 hour. Serve with rice. Serves 4–5.

CHICKEN *PHYLLO* ROLLS

Tilihti Kota se Filo

1 (5–6-pound) chicken
1 large onion, peeled and coarsely
    chopped
1 stalk celery with leaves, coarsely
    chopped
2 carrots, coarsely chopped
Few peppercorns
Salt to taste
1 heart of celery, minced
1 pound butter
3 medium onions, minced
1 cup strong chicken broth
2 tablespoons minced parsley
¼ teaspoon ground nutmeg
Pepper to taste
3 eggs
1 pound *phyllo* pastry

Clean and dry the chicken and put it in a kettle. Add the onion, celery, carrots, peppercorns, and salt. Add cold water to cover well and bring to boil. Reduce the heat and simmer for 1½ hours, or until done. Remove chicken and cool. When chicken is cool, discard the bones and skin. Chop the meat very fine. Cook the heart of celery in ¼ pound of the butter for 5 minutes. Add the onions and cook until the onions are tender but not brown. Add the chopped chicken and chicken broth and cook until all the liquid has been absorbed. Remove mixture from heat and cool. Add the parsley, nutmeg, and salt and pepper to taste. Beat the eggs with a rotary beater until they are frothy. Fold the eggs into the chicken mixture and blend. This mixture is enough for two or three rolls.

Preheat oven to 350°F.

Melt the remaining butter. Brush 5 sheets of *phyllo* pastry one at a time with the remaining butter, melted. Place one sheet on top of the other. Spread the chicken mixture on the pastry and carefully roll up, jelly-roll style. You should be able to make 4–5 rolls. Press each end of the roll so the filling does not escape. (Recipe may be prepared to this point and frozen. To serve, bake without prior thawing for about 1 hour.) Place roll on baking sheet, seam side down. Brush well with butter and bake for 40 minutes, or until pastry is browned and crisp. Let cool slightly; cut into slices and serve warm. Serves 8.

CHICKEN PIE

Kotopita

1 (6-pound) stewing chicken
1 pound onions, thinly sliced
½ cup milk
1 cup grated *kefalotiri* or Parmesan
    cheese
5 eggs
Salt and pepper to taste
½ teaspoon ground nutmeg
¾ pound *phyllo* pastry
½ pound melted butter for brushing
    phyllo

Clean and dry the chicken and put into a pot with enough water to cover. Bring to a boil, removing the froth as it rises. Add the onions and cook for 1½ to 2 hours, or until the chicken is tender. Remove the chicken from the broth and let cool. Continue to cook the onions until they become pulpy. When the chicken is cool, remove the skin and bones and cut the meat into thin strips. Pass the stock through a strainer to purée the onions. Return to the pot and add the chicken strips and milk. Cook for 5 minutes. Remove from heat. Add the cheese and stir well. Beat the eggs lightly with a little salt and pepper and the nutmeg; add to the pot.

Preheat oven to 350°F.

Line the bottom and sides of a 9- x 9- x 2-inch baking dish with half the *phyllo* (there should be some overhang), brushing each sheet with melted butter. (Work with one sheet at a time and keep remainder covered with damp cloth or plastic wrap.) Pour in the filling and fold the overhanging edge of the *phyllo* so as to cover part of the filling; brush well with butter. Cover with remaining *phyllo* sheets, brushed with butter one at a time, as before. Cut through top layers of *phyllo* to score into 8 pieces. Pour any remaining butter over the pie. Bake for 1 hour. Cool for 15 minutes, cut into portions, and serve. Serves 8.

ROAST GOOSE WITH APPLE AND CHESTNUT STUFFING

Psiti Hina me Yemisi

1 (11–13-pound) goose
Salt and pepper to taste
Juice of 3 lemons

STUFFING:

2½ medium onions, chopped
½ cup butter
1½ cups tart apples, peeled, cored, and chopped
½ cup milk
1 teaspoon sugar
2 teaspoons ground cinnamon
¼ cup chopped parsley
½ cup pignolias (pine nuts)
1½ teaspoons salt
¼ teaspoon pepper
3 cups chestnuts, shelled, boiled and chopped (see page 175 for Preparation of Chestnuts)

Preheat oven to 350°F.

Rinse the goose in cold water and pat dry. Season with salt, pepper, and lemon juice. Prick skin all over with sharp fork. To make the stuffing, sauté the onions in butter. Add apple and cook over low heat for 2 minutes. Add milk, sugar, cinnamon, parsley, pignolias, salt, and pepper and simmer for a few minutes. Add chestnuts and mix thoroughly. Let cool before stuffing goose. Fill goose cavity lightly. Roast on a rack in roasting pan allowing 20 to 30 minutes per pound. Remove fat from pan as necessary. Serves 6–8.

RABBIT WITH GARLIC SAUCE

Kouneli me Skordalia

1 small rabbit (about 2½ pounds)
Salt
1 cup wine vinegar
Pepper
½ cup olive oil
½ cup dry white wine
½ cup Garlic Sauce°

Greeks are great hunters and eaters of rabbit. Here is one interesting way they prepare it.

Clean and wash the rabbit and cut into serving pieces. Place in a large bowl; sprinkle with salt and pour vinegar over it. Add enough cold water to cover and allow to stand for several hours. Rinse and dry the rabbit; sprinkle with salt and pepper. Heat the oil in a heavy skillet. Add the rabbit and fry slowly until golden brown on all sides. Add the wine, cover, and cook until the rabbit is tender. Prepare Garlic Sauce and spread over the rabbit before serving. Serves 4.

GROUND MEATS

Greeks have a predilection for ground meat dishes spiced with cinnamon, cumin, garlic, cloves and whatever else is at hand. The variety of such dishes and the ingredients that can be combined are endless. In the countryside, for instance, one might dine on *Manti*, a delectable mixture of ground meat and *pligouri*, a coarse wheat, akin to bulghur. Meat-stuffed vegetables—tomatoes, peppers, squash, or eggplant—are popular throughout Greece, and anyone who has been to a Greek restaurant needs no further introduction to the classic *Moussaka* and *Pastitsio*. Here we present several variations on the traditional recipes, such as *Moussaka* with Artichokes and *Pastitsio* with Eggplant.

ARTICHOKES STUFFED WITH LAMB IN WINE SAUCE
Gemistes Anginares me Saltsa Krasi

4 whole fresh artichokes
1 pound ground lamb
¾ cup chopped onion
2 tablespoons cooking oil
½ cup fine dry bread crumbs
¼ cup snipped parsley
2 eggs, beaten
½ teaspoon salt
¼ teaspoon pepper
¼ teaspoon ground nutmeg
Hot water

WINE SAUCE:

¼ cup white wine
1 tablespoon minced onion
½ cup olive oil
¼ cup vinegar
2 tablespoons snipped parsley
1 tablespoon lemon juice
Salt and pepper to taste

Preheat oven to 375°F.

Wash artichokes and cut off stems close to the base. Cook in boiling salted water for 25 to 30 minutes, or until stalk can be pierced easily with a fork. Drain upside down. Cut off the top third of the leaves with kitchen shears; remove center leaves and chokes. Lightly brown lamb and onion in oil; drain well. Add bread crumbs, parsley, eggs, salt, pepper, and nutmeg and mix well. Spread artichoke leaves slightly apart and fill centers with meat mixture. Place in a 9- x 9- x 2-inch baking dish. Pour hot water around artichokes to depth of 1 inch. Bake, uncovered, for 30 to 35 minutes, or until heated through. Meanwhile, prepare wine sauce by combining the wine and onion in a small saucepan. Let stand for 10 minutes. Add the olive oil, vinegar, parsley, lemon juice, and salt and pepper; mix well. Cook until mixture is heated through, but do not boil. Serve the stuffed artichokes with the wine sauce. Serves 4.

STUFFED TOMATOES WITH LAMB AND *FETA*

Ntomates Gemistes me Arni ke Feta

8 tomatoes
1 medium onion, chopped
¼ pound butter
½ pound ground lamb or beef
½ cup raw rice
1 teaspoon minced mint
1 teaspoon minced dill
Salt and pepper to taste
¼ pound *feta* cheese
¼ cup water

Preheat oven to 350°F.

Slice the tops off the tomatoes and reserve. Remove pulp and seeds; reserve the pulp. Sauté the onion in the butter. Add lamb and cook for 5 minutes. Add rice, mint, dill, reserved tomato pulp, and salt and pepper. Stir to blend. Fill the tomatoes with the lamb mixture and crumble *feta* cheese on top. Replace tomato tops. Put in a casserole with ¼ cup water. Cover and bake for 30 minutes. Serve hot or cold. Serves 8.

LAMB EGGPLANT BALLS

Keftedes me Melitzana

1½ pounds ground lamb
2 cups peeled, chopped eggplant
½ cup chopped onion
1 clove garlic, minced
⅛ cup bread crumbs
1 egg, slightly beaten
1 teaspoon minced parsley
Salt and pepper to taste
½ teaspoon dried dill
Pinch of dried rosemary
½ cup corn or vegetable oil
1 (8-ounce) can tomato sauce

Combine all ingredients except oil and tomato sauce. Shape into 18 balls. In a skillet, brown the balls on all sides in hot oil. Drain off any excess fat. Add tomato sauce to the skillet and simmer covered 30 minutes. Serve warm. Serves 6.

Note: The balls may be made smaller and browned for an exotic and unusual appetizer.

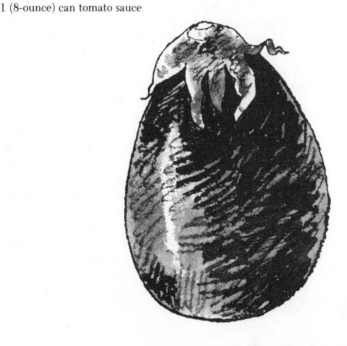

GROUND BEEF AND PEAS CASSEROLE

Kima me Bizelakia

1 pound ground chuck
1 medium onion, chopped
Dash of ground nutmeg
Dash of ground cloves
1 tablespoon butter
2 tablespoons minced parsley
1 (10-ounce) package frozen peas
¼ pound butter
6 tablespoons flour
1½ quarts milk
½ cup grated *kasseri* cheese
Salt and pepper to taste

Preheat oven to 350°F.

Sauté the meat, onion, and spices in butter until the meat has lost its red color. Add the parsley and set aside. Put peas in boiling water, bring back to a boil, and drain. To prepare a Béchamel Sauce, melt the butter in a saucepan, add the flour, and stir to blend. Gradually add the milk, stirring constantly until creamy and smooth. Add the cheese and salt and pepper. In a lightly greased 2-quart casserole, spread first one third of the cream sauce, then half the meat, and half the peas; repeat, ending with cream sauce. Bake for 35 to 40 minutes. Serves 4.

BAKED STUFFED GARDEN VEGETABLES

Kolokithia, Melitzanes, Piperies kai Ntomates Gemistes

2 large zucchini, scrubbed
2 medium eggplants (on the thin side)
4 green peppers
4 large firm tomatoes
2 pounds ground chuck
2 cups parboiled rice, drained
3 eggs
1 large onion, grated
1 (8-ounce) can tomato sauce
¼ cup plus 2 tablespoons vegetable oil
1 (16-ounce) can tomato purée
¼–½ cup chopped fresh mint, or 3 tablespoons dried mint
Salt and pepper to taste
½ cup grated *kefalotiri* or Parmesan cheese

Preheat oven to 350°F.

Depending on the size of the zucchini, cut into 3½-inch high cups. Scoop out the pulp and reserve. Use long narrow eggplants and cut into 3½-inch high cups. Scoop out the pulp, chop, and add to zucchini pulp. Cut a wide circle around stem of peppers and lift off. Core, seed, and wash thoroughly. Cut a thin slice from the top of each tomato, scoop out pulp, and add to the zucchini-eggplant mixture. Parboil the zucchini, eggplant, and green peppers in boiling water for 5 to 10 minutes. Set aside. In large bowl, combine ground meat, parboiled rice, eggs, onion, tomato sauce, ¼ cup vegetable oil, mint, salt and pepper, and vegetable mixture. Mix by hand to blend thoroughly. Stuff prepared vegetables with enough stuffing to form rounded mounds on top of each piece. Add 2 tablespoons of oil and the tomato purée to the bottom of a large baking pan. Cover the stuffed vegetables loosely with aluminum foil and bake for 1 hour, basting frequently with the pan juices. When almost done, remove foil and sprinkle tops with grated cheese. Increase oven temperature to 375°F. or 400°F. and bake for 10 minutes, or until tops are brown.

Note: This recipe may be made the day before and heated before serving.

STUFFED GRAPE LEAVES WITH *AVGOLEMONO* SAUCE

Dolmades Avgolemono

2 (12-ounce) jars grape leaves
2 pounds ground beef
1 pound rice
2 large onions, grated
1 (8-ounce) can tomato sauce
3 eggs
Salt and pepper to taste
⅛ cup crushed mint (chopped fresh
    leaves if available)
½–¾ cup vegetable oil

Avgolemono SAUCE:
Liquid from *Dolmades*
1 cup chicken broth
Juice of 3 lemons
3 eggs

Prepare the grape leaves by rinsing them in cold water several times, until all traces of brine or salt are gone. Thoroughly mix the beef, rice, onion, tomato sauce, eggs, salt and pepper, and mint. If necessary, add a little water. (The consistency of the mixture should not be thick.) To stuff the leaves, place 1 tablespoon of the mixture in the center of the dull side of the leaf (see diagram page 38) and fold outer parts over filling. In a 5-quart casserole, put ½ to ¾ cup vegetable oil. Arrange *Dolmades* on bottom, folded side down, and keep piling them up until meat mixture is all used. (If any leaves are left over, they can be put back into a jar with salt and water for use at another time.) Add enough water to cover the *Dolmades*. Cover and cook over medium heat until rice and leaves are tender, about 30 minutes. Immediately drain the liquid from the pot and into a saucepan. Keep *Dolmades* covered while *Avgolemono* Sauce is being prepared. Keep liquid simmering in the saucepan, and add the chicken broth for extra flavor. Also add more salt, if necessary. In a blender (or with an electric or hand mixer) beat 3 eggs thoroughly. Slowly add the lemon juice and hot liquid, blending continuously as you do so. If there is more liquid than the blender will hold, empty half of egg mixture into a saucepan. Continue beating remaining mixture in the blender, slowly adding the rest of the liquid. Mix all the sauce together in the saucepan, then pour it over the *Dolmades*, shaking pot so that the sauce will permeate. Cover with lid until ready to serve. YIELD: 50–60 pieces.

Variation: Cabbage leaves may be substituted for grape leaves. The method of preparation is basically the same. Remove the core from a medium-size round cabbage. Place whole cabbage in boiling salted water, prying open the leaves with two forks. Boil for 3 to 5 minutes. Drain off hot water and add cold water, until the leaves are cool enough to work with. Cut each leaf in half, if large, and remove or trim heavy center vein. Continue to roll as above, using the same method for cooking. *Avgolemono* Sauce is also poured over the stuffed cabbage.

MEAT PIE

Yianniotiki Kreatopita

1 tablespoon butter
½ cup grated onion
1 pound ground lamb or beef
Salt and pepper to taste
½ teaspoon minced parsley
1 teaspoon ground cinnamon
2 tablespoons tomato sauce
2 cups lamb stock or beef bouillon
4 slices dry toast
2 cups milk
4 eggs
½ cup grated *kefalotiri* cheese
¾ pound *phyllo* pastry
½ pound melted butter for brushing
  phyllo

Preheat oven to 350°F.

Melt 1 tablespoon butter in a large kettle. Add the onion and ground meat and brown well. Drain off the fat, then add salt, pepper, parsley, cinnamon, tomato sauce, and stock. Cover and simmer for 45 minutes. Soak the toast in the milk to soften, then mash to a soft paste and add to meat sauce, blending well. Beat the eggs until thick and creamy, and blend in the cheese. Line the bottom and sides of a 9- x 9- x 2-inch baking dish with half the *phyllo* (there should be some overhang on all sides), brushing the sheets one at a time with melted butter. Spread the meat sauce over the pastry, then cover with the egg and cheese mixture. Fold the overhanging edge of the *phyllo* so as to cover part of the filling. Cover with remaining *phyllo* sheets, brushed with butter one at a time as before. Score top layers of *phyllo* into 8 pieces. Bake for 45 minutes. Remove from oven and let stand for 15 minutes before cutting, then serve immediately. Serves 8.

MANTI WITH *PHYLLO*

Manti me Phyllo

1 medium onion, chopped
2 tablespoons vegetable oil
1½ pounds ground beef
Salt and pepper to taste
1 cup *pligouri* or bulghur wheat
1 cup milk or plain yogurt
¼ cup water
1 pound *phyllo* pastry
¾ pound melted butter for brushing
  phyllo
2 or 3 cups hot beef or chicken broth
2 cups plain yogurt

This regional dish from the north is quite unusual in that it calls for *pligouri*, a coarse wheat, similar to bulghur, that is mixed with ground meat and covered with *phyllo*. *Pligouri* is available in Greek specialty shops.

Preheat oven to 350°F.

Sauté the onion in the oil. Add the ground beef and cook until well browned. Add salt and pepper. Add *pligouri*, milk, and water. Bring to a boil and remove from heat. Cut the *phyllo* into 4-inch squares. Take 4 squares and cover the remainder with a damp cloth or plastic wrap. Brush squares with melted butter and stack on top of each other. Place a heaping teaspoon of the meat mixture in the center of the *phyllo* and pick up the four corners to form a small bag or sack. Press corners together to seal and place sack in a large baking pan. Continue this process until *phyllo* and/or filling are used up.

Do not crowd sacks in the baking pan. Brush the top of each sack with more butter. Bake for 1 hour, or until golden brown. As soon as the pan is removed from the oven, pour boiling hot broth into the center of each sack with a baster (or use a teaspoon). Continue adding broth as long as it can be absorbed. Serve with yogurt on the side. YIELD: 24 servings.

MOCK *MANTI*

Aplo manti

1½ pounds ground meat
1 large onion, minced
2 tablespoons butter
Salt and pepper to taste
½ teaspoon ground cumin
1 teaspoon ground cinnamon
1 cup *pligouri* or bulghur wheat
¼ cup milk or plain yogurt
2 cups beef or chicken broth
2 cups plain yogurt

For the busy cook this "mock" *manti* is a simplified version of the original recipe (see previous recipe), again using the wholesome *pligouri* wheat (available in Greek specialty shops) and yogurt.

Brown the meat and onion in the melted butter. Add salt and pepper, cumin, cinnamon, *pligouri*, milk, and broth. Cover and cook until liquid is absorbed and grain is tender. Serve with yogurt on the side. Serves 6.

MEAT BALLS I

Keftedes

½ cup fine bread crumbs
1 cup milk
¾ cup finely minced onion
¼ pound butter
½ pound ground beef
½ pound lean ground pork
1 egg, well beaten
1 teaspoon salt
¼ teaspoon ground allspice
1 teaspoon ground cinnamon

Soak the bread crumbs in ½ cup milk for 10 minutes. Sauté the onion in 3 tablespoons butter until wilted. Combine the bread crumbs and meats and mix well. Stir in the egg, remaining milk, and seasonings. Add sautéed onion and mix well. Roll into balls. Melt 5 tablespoons of butter in a frying pan and brown balls on all sides. Cover and cook over very low flame until meat is done, approximately 10 minutes. YIELD: 24 meat balls.

Note: If cooked in advance, the meat balls may be reheated by putting them on an ungreased cookie sheet under the broiler for a few minutes.

MEAT BALLS II

Keftedes

1 pound onions, grated
1 tablespoon plus ½ teaspoon salt
1 pound ground beef
Pepper to taste
1 teaspoon dried oregano
½ cup bread crumbs
¼ teaspoon vinegar
¾ cup water
¼ teaspoon dried basil (optional)
1 teaspoon dried mint (optional)
2 cups flour
1 quart corn or vegetable oil for frying

To the onions add 1 tablespoon salt and squeeze together. Put this pulp in a cheesecloth bag and let cold water run through it for 2 minutes. Squeeze the water from the pulp and then place it in a bowl. Add the ground meat, ½ teaspoon salt, pepper to taste, oregano, bread crumbs, vinegar, water, basil and mint. Put the flour on a sheet of wax paper. Take a tablespoonful of the meat mixture and drop on the flour. Roll the meat in the flour into a ball. Flatten each ball to resemble a half dollar. Heat the oil in a deep fryer or a large frying pan. Fry the patties until golden brown. Serve warm or cold with Greek salad. YIELD: 24 balls

Note: This recipe may be served as an appetizer. Use 1 teaspoon rather than 1 tablespoon of meat per ball.

MOUSSAKA WITH ARTICHOKES

Moussaka me Anginares

4 (10-ounce) packages frozen artichoke
    hearts
8 tablespoons butter
2 pounds ground beef
1 onion, grated
1 cup tomato sauce
¼ cup white wine
2 tablespoons ground dill
Salt and pepper to taste
½ cup butter
6 tablespoons flour
1 quart hot milk
2 eggs, lightly beaten
1 cup grated *kefalotiri* cheese
Dash of white pepper
¼ cup bread crumbs

Preheat oven to 350°F.

Drop the artichokes into boiling salted water, return to a boil, and cook for 3 minutes. Drain thoroughly in a colander. Place in a heatproof dish. Melt 6 tablespoons butter until brown. Pour butter over artichokes and set aside. Sauté meat and onion in 2 tablespoons butter until lightly browned. Add tomato sauce, wine, dill, and salt and pepper and simmer for 15 minutes.

Make a Béchamel Sauce by melting ½ cup butter in a saucepan. Add the flour and stir to blend. Gradually add first the milk and then the eggs, stirring constantly. Cook over low heat until sauce is smooth and thickened. Add ½ cup *kefalotiri* cheese and cook for a few minutes longer, stirring constantly. Stir in 1 teaspoon salt and white pepper. Cover tightly and place over hot water to keep warm. Sprinkle the bread crumbs over the bottom of a 9- x 13- x 1¾-inch roasting pan. Over this place half the artichokes, one third of the sauce, and all the meat mixture. Continue layering one third of the sauce, the remaining artichokes, and the final third of the sauce and sprinkle with the remaining cheese. Bake for 35 minutes, or until golden brown. Serves 8–10.

Note: Two 28-ounce cans of artichokes may be substituted for the frozen. Drain canned artichokes in a colander and run cold water over them for 5 minutes to remove salty brine.

GREEN BEANS MOUSSAKA

✤ KOS

Fasolakia Moussaka

3 pounds fresh green beans
½ cup olive oil
6 tablespoons butter
1½ pounds ground meat
1 medium onion, chopped
½ teaspoon ground cinnamon
½ bunch parsley, minced
Salt and pepper to taste
2½ cups milk
1 egg, beaten
4 tablespoons flour
¾ cup grated *kefalotiri* cheese

Preheat oven to 350°F.

In a skillet sauté the beans in the oil until tender. Remove and set aside. Melt 2 tablespoons of the butter in the skillet and brown the meat and onions with the cinnamon and parsley. Add salt and pepper. Prepare a Béchamel Sauce by melting the remaining 4 tablespoons butter in a saucepan over low heat. Add flour and stir to blend. Gradually add first the milk and then the egg, stirring constantly. Cook until the sauce thickens. Add half of the grated cheese. Place alternate layers of beans and meat mixture in a casserole (a 9- x 13-inch pan may also be used). Spread sauce on top and sprinkle with remaining cheese. Bake for 30 to 40 minutes, or until golden brown. Cut into 12–16 pieces.

POTATO *MOUSSAKA* WITH YOGURT

Patata Moussaka me Yiaourti

5 medium potatoes, peeled and cut in ¼-
    inch-thick slices
⅓ cup corn or vegetable oil
½ cup chopped onions
2 tablespoons butter or vegetable oil
1½ pounds ground beef
¼ cup dry white or red wine
½ cup tomato sauce
1 tablespoon minced parsley
½ teaspoon paprika
Salt and pepper to taste
1 cup grated *kasseri* cheese
2 tablespoons flour
2 egg yolks
1 cup plain yogurt

Preheat oven to 350°F.

In a skillet, brown the potatoes lightly in the oil; set aside. Sauté the onions in the butter. Add the meat and brown. Add the wine, tomato sauce, parsley, paprika, and salt and pepper. Simmer for 10 minutes. Grease a 9- x 12- x 2-inch baking dish. Arrange half the potato slices on the bottom of the dish. Spread the meat sauce evenly over the potatoes. Sprinkle with a little of the cheese. Arrange remaining potato slices on top. Prepare a sauce by beating flour, egg yolks, and yogurt together. Pour over the top of the casserole. Sprinkle with the remaining cheese and bake for 30 minutes. Serves 8–10.

VEAL ROLL IN *PHYLLO*

Mosharaki se Filo

6 tablespoons butter or margarine
1 small onion, chopped
1½ pounds ground veal
½ cup chopped tomatoes
1 stick cinnamon, or 1 teaspoon ground
    cinnamon
Salt and pepper to taste
1 tablespoon minced fresh basil, or ½
    teaspoon dried basil
2 eggs, separated
4 tablespoons flour
2½ cups milk
1 egg, beaten
½ cup grated *kefalotiri* cheese
½ teaspoon ground nutmeg
1 sheet cooking parchment (20 x 20
    inches)
10–12 sheets *phyllo* pastry
⅓ cup melted butter for brushing *phyllo*
1 tablespoon minced parsley

Preheat oven to 350°F.

Heat 2 tablespoons of the butter in a frying pan and sauté the onion until wilted. Add meat and cook until raw color disappears. Add tomatoes and cinnamon. Cover and simmer for 20 minutes. Remove lid and season with salt, pepper, and basil. Remove the cinnamon stick and allow the meat to cool. When cooked, mix the egg whites into the meat.

Prepare a Béchamel Sauce by melting 4 tablespoons of the butter in a saucepan over low heat. Add the flour and stir to blend. Gradually add first the milk and then the beaten egg. Cook, stirring constantly, until the sauce thickens.

Combine the Béchamel Sauce with the egg yolks, cheese, and nutmeg. Spread out the cooking parchment on a counter. Lay a sheet of *phyllo* in the center. Brush with melted butter. Continue layering buttered sheets of *phyllo* to make a base on which to roll the meat loaf. Spread half the sauce in the center of the *phyllo*, allowing wide margins for turning. Spread meat mixture over the sauce. Cover with remaining sauce and sprinkle with parsley. Turn edges of the *phyllo* up over the meat and roll into a loaf. Fold the paper over the loaf, secure it, and place seam side down in a baking pan. Brush outer surface with butter. Bake for 1 hour. Remove paper after 35 minutes to allow *phyllo* to get crisp. Use electric knife to slice the roll. Serves 8.

PASTITSIO WITH EGGPLANT
Pastitsio me Melitzana

1 large onion, peeled and chopped
4½ tablespoons butter
1 pound ground lamb or beef
1 (1-pound) can whole tomatoes, drained
    and chopped
1½ teaspoons salt
¼ teaspoon pepper
¼ teaspoon ground nutmeg
¼ teaspoon ground cinnamon
2 eggs, beaten
½ cup grated *kefalotiri* or Parmesan
    cheese
1½ cups elbow macaroni, cooked
    according to package directions
1 medium-size eggplant, cut into ¼-inch-
    thick slices
¼ cup olive oil
1 teaspoon cornstarch
1½ cups milk, heated
3 eggs, beaten
Salt and pepper to taste

Preheat oven to 350°F.

Sauté onion in 2 tablespoons of the butter until wilted. Add the meat and cook until it loses its raw look. Add tomatoes and cook until mixture is almost dry. Season with salt, pepper, nutmeg, and cinnamon. Add eggs and ⅓ cup of the grated cheese. Combine meat mixture with macaroni. Pour into well greased 13- x 9- x 2-inch pan (pan should be about half full). Sauté eggplant slices in olive oil and drain on paper towels. Place eggplant slices over macaroni and meat mixture. Make a custard by melting 2 tablespoons of the butter and blending in the cornstarch. Gradually add the hot milk and cook over low heat, stirring, until slightly thickened. Pour in eggs, beating constantly. Season lightly with salt and pepper. Pour custard evenly over pan ingredients. Sprinkle top with remaining melted butter and cheese. Bake for 45 minutes, or until custard is set and golden brown. Serves 6–8 as main meal, more as a buffet item.

PASTITSIO TURNOVERS
Pastitsio Trigona

1 pound large-size elbow macaroni
½ pound butter, melted
2 onions, finely minced
1½ pounds ground beef
1 teaspoon salt
½ teaspoon pepper
1 large bay leaf
1 cup tomato sauce
¾ pound mild *feta* cheese, crumbled
3 eggs, lightly beaten
1 pound *phyllo* pastry
¾ pound melted butter for brushing
    phyllo

Preheat oven to 350°F.

Boil the macaroni according to package directions. In the meantime, melt the butter in a large frying pan, add the onion and the ground meat and cook over fairly high heat until meat juices are absorbed. Add salt, pepper, and bay leaf. When well browned, add the tomato sauce and simmer until liquid is absorbed. When macaroni is cooked, rinse in cold water and drain very well. When cool, add the meat mixture. In a separate bowl, mix the crumbled *feta* with the beaten eggs. Slowly add to the macaroni mixture and mix carefully. Cool in refrigerator for 1 hour. Butter a cookie sheet. Cut the *phyllo* sheets in half, arrange in a single pile and cover with plastic wrap.

Work with one *phyllo* strip at a time and leave the rest covered. Butter each strip well and place a well rounded tablespoon (about the size of a small ice cream scoop) at the bottom of the strip and form into triangles (see How to Work with *Phyllo*, page 211). Place each triangle on the buttered cookie sheet and butter the tops of the turnovers. Bake for 45 minutes, or until golden brown. YIELD: 4 dozen.

Note: This versatile recipe can be served as a luncheon dish or a first course. It may also be prepared in a 9- x 13- x 1¾-inch baking pan (layer ½ the buttered *phyllo*, all of the meat mixture and the remaining *phyllo*; brush with butter, and bake until golden brown. To serve, cut into squares.) You can also cut the recipe in half or prepare it in advance and freeze it before baking. To serve, bake, without prior thawing, for 1½ hours, or until golden brown.

PASTITSIO WITH PHYLLO

Pastitsio me Phyllo

2 pounds lean ground beef
2 onions, finely minced
1 cup plus 4 tablespoons butter
2 teaspoons salt
¼ teaspoon pepper
½ cup wine (optional)
2 tablespoons tomato paste
1 cup water
1¼ pounds macaroni
½ cup melted butter
10 sheets *phyllo* pastry
3 cups grated *kefalotiri* cheese
12 eggs
1 quart milk

This is a "gourmet" variation of *pastitsio*, the well-known macaroni and chopped meat dish.

Preheat oven to 350°F.

Sauté ground beef and onion in 4 tablespoons butter. Season with salt and pepper. Add wine, tomato paste, and water, and simmer until liquid is evaporated, about 40 minutes. Cook macaroni in boiling, salted water until almost done (do not overcook). Pour into colander; rinse with cold water and drain well. Mix with ½ cup melted butter.

Arrange 5 *phyllo* sheets, brushed one at a time with melted butter, in a 14- x 11-inch baking pan. Place half the macaroni in pan. Sprinkle with grated cheese and cover with beef mixture, spreading evenly over entire surface. Sprinkle grated cheese over meat and cover with remaining macaroni. Beat eggs until light and fluffy, and mix with milk. Carefully pour mixture over ingredients in pan. Top with 5 *phyllo* sheets, each brushed with the remaining melted butter. Bake for 30 to 40 minutes, or until golden brown on top and firm when tested with a knife. Let stand for 15 minutes before cutting into squares. (See How to Work with *Phyllo* page 211 for cutting method.) YIELD: 20–30 squares.

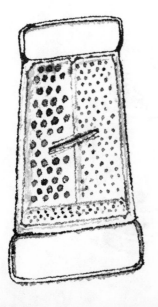

CASSEROLES

Our word "casserole" derives from the Greek "*katsarola*," meaning pot. And whether baked in the oven or cooked on top of the stove, casseroles are the ideal "prepare ahead of time" dishes for the busy cook. The "one-dish meal" recipes presented in this section (such as the countryside favorite, "Lamb and Peas Casserole" and the more sophisticated "Veal *Kapama*") have the added advantage that they improve on reheating and give the cook a wide range to exercise his or her inventiveness.

ISLANDER BAKED LAMB

Nisiotiko Psito Arni

2 pounds lamb from breast or shoulder
1 pound *feta* cheese
2 pounds tomatoes, peeled and sliced
1½ teaspoons salt
Pepper to taste
2 tablespoons olive oil

Preheat oven to 350°F.

Trim all fat from the meat and cut the meat into chunks. Put in an oiled casserole. Crumble the cheese on top of the meat. Cover with the tomato slices. Sprinkle with salt, pepper, and oil. Bake, uncovered, for 2 hours, or until meat is tender, basting occasionally with pan drippings. Serves 4–6.

LAMB WITH WINE SAUCE

✢ ARCADIA

Arni Krassato

2 pounds boneless lamb, preferably leg,
    cut in 1½-inch cubes
1 tablespoon olive oil
1 tablespoon butter
Salt and pepper to taste
½ teaspoon dried rosemary
Pinch of dried sage
1 small clove garlic, crushed
1½ tablespoons flour
¼ cup dry white wine
½ cup red wine vinegar
4 lemon wedges
Minced parsley

Brown the lamb on all sides in the oil and butter mixture. Stir in seasonings and cook for several minutes over low heat. Stir in flour and gradually add wine and wine vinegar. Stir well. Cook over low heat until lamb is tender, about 45 minutes. Garnish with lemon and parsley. Serves 4.

LAMB AND PEAS CASSEROLE

Arni me Araka Giouvetsi

3 pounds rump or leg of lamb, in 1 piece
Salt and pepper to taste
1½ pounds tomatoes, peeled, seeded, and
    chopped, or 1 pound canned
    tomatoes, drained and chopped
½ cup melted butter
4½ pounds peas (see note)
Water as needed
1 tablespoon minced dill

Preheat oven to 325°F.

Pat the meat dry, season with salt and pepper, and put in a casserole. Add one third of the tomatoes and all of the butter and bake for 1 hour. Meanwhile shell, wash, and drain the peas. Add the remaining tomatoes and 1 to 2 cups water to the meat. When this begins to simmer, add the peas and the dill. Sprinkle with additional salt and pepper. Cook slowly for 1 hour, or until the peas are tender. Serves 6.

Note: 4 packages of frozen peas may be substituted for the fresh peas. Add to casserole after meat has cooked for 1½ hours and continue cooking for 30 minutes.

LAMB OR BEEF CASSEROLE WITH *ORZO*

Kritharaki me Kreas

2½ pounds lamb or beef chuck
½ cup butter or oil
1 small onion, minced
1 (8-ounce) can tomato sauce, or 4–5
    medium, ripe tomatoes, peeled,
    seeded, and chopped
¼ teaspoon each salt and pepper
8½ cups water
½ pound *orzo*
1 cup grated *kefalotiri* cheese

Preheat oven to 350°F.

Cut the meat into small, bite-size pieces. Melt butter in a large casserole. Add chopped onion, meat, tomatoes, salt, pepper, and 2 cups water and mix well. Cover and bake for 1 hour. Add 6½ cups boiling water and the *orzo* to the meat mixture. Stir well and continue baking for ½ hour. Serve at once topped with grated cheese. Serves 5–6.

LAMB SHANKS WITH LENTILS

Arnisia Kotsia me Fakes

6 medium lamb shanks, about 8 ounces
    each
2 tablespoons cooking oil
3½ cups water
2 cloves garlic, minced
2 teaspoons salt
⅛ teaspoon dried oregano
Dash of pepper
1½ cups lentils
1 small onion, studded with 3 whole
    cloves
½ cup chopped celery
1 bay leaf
6 thin lemon slices

Preheat oven to 350°F.

In a large skillet, brown the lamb shanks in hot oil. Add ½ cup water, the garlic, ½ teaspoon salt, oregano, and pepper and cook, covered, over low heat for 1 hour. Meanwhile, rinse the lentils and drain. In a medium saucepan, combine the lentils with 3 cups water. Add the onion, celery, bay leaf, and 1½ teaspoons salt. Simmer, covered, for 50 to 60 minutes, or until vegetables are tender. If mixture is too thick, add a little more water. Pour lentil mixture into a 10-inch baking dish. Top with the meat and lemon slices. Bake for 30 to 35 minutes. Discard onion and bay leaf before serving. Serves 6.

Note: This dish may be prepared ahead and baked just before serving.

LAMB CUBES IN MINTED YOGURT SAUCE

Komatiasto Arni me Yiaourti

2 pounds lamb, cut into 1½-inch cubes
1 teaspoon salt
¼ teaspoon pepper
1 cup hot water
1 bay leaf
1 small onion, thinly sliced
1 clove garlic, split in half
2 tablespoons flour
2 teaspoons sugar
1 cup plain yogurt
1 tablespoon finely minced mint

In a skillet, combine the lamb with the salt, pepper, water, bay leaf, onion, and garlic. Cover tightly and simmer for 1¼ hours, or until lamb cubes are tender. Remove meat from pan onto a hot plate. Blend flour, sugar, and yogurt, and stir into the pan drippings. Cook, stirring constantly, until sauce thickens and just begins to simmer. Return the meat to the sauce. Reheat, stirring gently until piping hot but not boiling. Sprinkle with mint and serve immediately over rice. Serves 4–6.

LAMB CHUNKS IN *PHYLLO*

Arni Exohiko

1 (6–8-pound) leg of lamb
2–3 cloves garlic, slivered
Dash of salt and pepper
¼ cup melted butter
Dried oregano to taste
Juice of 1 lemon
2 cups hot water
2 carrots, diced
½ cup celery, diced
4–5 very small onions, peeled
2 cups Béchamel Sauce (see Index)
2 cups cooked vegetables (such as
    chopped artichoke hearts, peas, or
    beans)
1 pound *phyllo* pastry
½ pound melted butter for brushing
    phyllo
2 cups fresh bread crumbs
½ pound *feta* cheese, crumbled

The word *Exohiko* means countryside and is indicative of the origins of this recipe. Easily prepared ahead of time, *Exohiko* is an ideal dish for picnics and cookouts.

Preheat oven to 450°F.

With a sharp knife make incisions all over the lamb and insert the garlic slivers. Season with salt, pepper, and oregano. Brush with the melted butter. Squeeze the lemon juice over the lamb and put it in a roasting pan fat side up. Roast for ½ hour. Lower the oven temperature to 350°F. and add hot water, carrots, celery, and onions. Roast for 1½ hours, adding more water if necessary. Remove from oven when lamb is almost, but not quite, done (150° on a meat thermometer). Cut meat into 1-inch cubes. Make a thick Béchamel Sauce using the pan juices for stock. Add any vegetable you desire to the sauce.

Oven temperature should remain at 350°F.

Unwrap *phyllo* and quickly cover with plastic wrap. Butter one sheet of *phyllo*, sprinkle with bread crumbs. Place a second sheet of *phyllo* on top of the first; butter and sprinkle with bread crumbs. Place several pieces of meat, 1 heaping tablespoon of cream sauce with vegetables and crumbled *feta* on the lower half of the *phyllo*. Fold up the sides of the *phyllo*, envelope-style. Continue this procedure until all *phyllo* and/or filling ingredients are used up. (Recipe may be prepared to this point and frozen. To serve, bake without thawing for 1 hour.) Place on baking sheet seam side down and bake for 30 to 45 minutes, or until golden brown. YIELD: 15 *phyllo* envelopes.

LAMB AND LENTIL CASSEROLE

CHIOS

Arni me Fake

¼ cup finely minced onion
1 clove garlic, minced
¼ cup olive oil or butter
1½ cups dried lentils
3 cups chicken bouillon
3 cups canned tomatoes
1 tablespoon minced parsley
2 cups cubed leftover lamb

Preheat oven to 350°F.

Sauté onion and garlic in oil until golden. Add all remaining ingredients except lamb. Bring to a boil. Reduce heat, cover, and simmer for 2 hours. Add lamb and pour into a casserole. Bake for 20 minutes. Serves 6.

SPRING-LAMB STEW WITH DILL

Arnaki Yiahni me Anitho

2½ pounds boneless lamb, trimmed of fat
    and cut into 1-inch cubes
2 tablespoons oil
12 small white onions, peeled
2 cups water
¾ cup tomato juice
2 teaspoons salt
¼ teaspoon pepper
6 medium carrots, scraped and halved
6 potatoes, peeled and quartered
1 (10-ounce) package frozen peas
¼ cup flour
Fresh dill sprigs

Heat the oil in a heavy Dutch oven, add one third of the meat, and brown well on all sides. Remove and continue adding meat until all of it is browned. Add onions and brown on all sides. Remove and set aside. Pour all fat from pan. Return the lamb to pan and add 2 cups water, the tomato juice, salt, and pepper, bring to a boil. Cover, reduce heat, and simmer, for 30 minutes. Add reserved onions, carrots, potatoes, and peas to lamb mixture. Sprinkle with flour and stir. Cover and simmer for 10 to 15 minutes, or until vegetables are tender. Remove from heat, and let stand for 5 minutes. Skim off any fat. Ladle stew into a heated serving dish. Garnish with fresh dill sprigs. Serves 6.

LAMB WITH WALNUT SAUCE

Arni me Karidia

2 tablespoons oil or butter
2 pounds boned lamb, cut into 2-inch
    cubes
1 (12½-ounce) can condensed chicken
    broth
⅓ cup chopped onion
1 clove garlic, minced
1½ teaspoons salt
¼ teaspoon pepper
2 tablespoons flour
2 tablespoons cold water
½ cup coarsely chopped walnuts

Heat butter in a large, heavy skillet with a tight-fitting cover. Add lamb and sauté, turning until browned on all sides. Add broth, onion, garlic, salt, and pepper. Bring to a boil, cover, reduce heat, and simmer until lamb is tender. Remove lamb to a warm platter and keep warm.

Combine flour with cold water to make a smooth paste. Measure cooking liquid from the lamb and, if necessary, add enough water to make 2 cups. Skim fat and discard. In the skillet, combine liquid with flour mixture and walnuts. Bring to a boil, stirring frequently. Reduce heat and simmer, uncovered, for 5 minutes, or until thickened. Pour over lamb. Serves 4.

LAMB STEW IN FOIL

Arni Yiahni sto Harti

2½ pounds boneless lamb stew meat, cut
    in 2-inch cubes
6 small potatoes
3 small zucchini, cut up
6 ripe tomatoes, quartered
3 green peppers, halved
6 small onions
2 eggplants, cubed
6 whole mushrooms
6 tablespoons minced parsley
Salt and pepper to taste
2 tablespoons dried oregano
2 tablespoons dried mint
2 tablespoons dried thyme
2 tablespoons garlic salt
6 small pieces bay leaf

Preheat oven to 350°F.

Divide the meat into six equal portions and put each portion on a large sheet of heavy-duty foil. Surround meat with equal portions of all the vegetables. Season each mound with salt, pepper, oregano, mint, and thyme. Sprinkle with garlic salt and add a piece of bay leaf to each portion. Fold edges of foil so that juices cannot escape. Place on cookie sheets and bake for 3 hours. Do not turn packages or cover them. Serves 6.

Note: Veal or beef stew meat may be substituted.

LAMB WITH SQUASH IN *AVGOLEMONO* SAUCE

        ❧ PATMOS

Arni me Kolokithakia Avgolemono

3 pounds breast of lamb, cut into 1½-
    inch cubes
¾ cup butter
1½ cups water
Salt and pepper to taste
6 scallions (white part only), chopped
3 pounds small squash
2 eggs
2 tablespoons water
Juice of 2 lemons
Water as needed

Put meat into a pot with the butter and ½ cup water; bring to a boil. Add salt, pepper, and scallions. As soon as the water has been absorbed and the meat begins to sizzle, add another cup of water and cook for 30 to 45 minutes. Meanwhile, clean and scrape the squash; and cut each into 2 or 3 pieces. Add to the meat. Again let it simmer until all but about 1 cup of the liquid has been absorbed. Beat the eggs in a bowl with 2 tablespoons water. Add the lemon juice and beat well. Drain the remaining lamb cooking liquid and add enough water to make 1 cup. Combine this with the lemon/egg mixture and pour the sauce over the meat. Shake the pot gently over very low heat until the sauce is evenly distributed and begins to thicken. Serve hot. Serves 6.

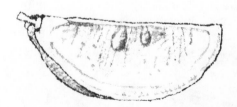

HOLIDAY MEAT PIE

Kreatopeta

2½ pounds lean lamb shoulder or leg, cut
    into 1½-inch cubes
4½ cups warm water
2 medium onions, finely minced
1½ cups chopped celery
1½ cups minced parsley
1 clove garlic, finely minced
1 teaspoon minced fresh mint, or ½
    teaspoon dried mint
2 (8-ounce) cans tomato sauce
½ cup plus 4 tablespoons olive oil
2 teaspoons salt
½ teaspoon pepper
3½ cups sifted flour
1 egg, lightly beaten
2–3 tablespoons warm water
4 eggs
1 cup grated *kasseri* cheese
1 teaspoon ground cinnamon
1 cup rice, uncooked

This is a traditional Carnival time and Ascension Day recipe.

Place the meat in a large pan, add the water and bring to a boil. Add the onions, celery, parsley, garlic, mint, tomato sauce, ½ cup olive oil, 1 teaspoon salt, and ½ teaspoon pepper. Cover and cook over low heat for 1 hour. While meat cooks, prepare the pie crust. Put the sifted flour, 1 teaspoon salt, and 3 tablespoons olive oil into a bowl and mix well with a fork. Add the egg. Gradually add warm water and stir until dough is well blended. Knead for 10 minutes, or until dough is firm. Chill thoroughly (at least 1 hour).

Preheat oven to 400°F.

Remove the pan with the lamb from heat. Beat 4 eggs lightly and add the cheese and cinnamon. Mix well, and add to the meat mixture, along with the rice. Divide the chilled dough into two balls. Roll each ball out on a lightly floured surface to ⅛-inch thickness, making one piece big enough to line a 15- x 11-inch baking pan with a lip to turn over on the top. The other piece should be large enough to fit the top of the pan. Grease the pan with 1 tablespoon butter and 1 tablespoon olive oil; line with the larger piece of dough. Pour in the meat mixture, spreading evenly. Cover with the second crust, turning the lip of the lower crust over, and crimp the edges. Brush lightly with olive oil and sprinkle with additional cinnamon. Prick with a fork. Bake for 45 minutes, or until crust is golden brown. Allow to set for a few minutes before cutting into squares to serve. Serves 6–8.

KEBABS WITH PILAF

Pilafi tas Kebab

2 pounds leg of lamb or veal, cut into 2-
    inch cubes
1¼ cups butter
3 medium onions, chopped
½ cup white wine
1½ pounds ripe tomatoes, peeled, seeded,
    and chopped, or 1 tablespoon
    tomato paste, diluted in 1 cup water
Salt and pepper to taste
1 cup water
6 cups rice pilaf (see note)

Brown the meat in a large skillet, using ¾ cup of the butter. Add the chopped onions and brown lightly. Add the wine, tomatoes, salt, and pepper and cook for 5 minutes. Add the water. Cook, uncovered, for 1½ hours, or until the meat is tender and about 1 cup of sauce remains in the skillet. Melt the remaining butter and add it to the cooked rice. Place the meat and the sauce in the bottom of a tube pan or solid mold. Add the rice and pack lightly. Turn out onto a platter so the meat is on top; the sauce will run down the sides of the rice. Serves 6–10.

Note: For an excellent pilaf recipe, see *The Art of Greek Cookery*, page 142.

VEAL IN *AVGOLEMONO* SAUCE

Moshari me Avgolemono

3 pounds veal leg, boned and cut into 2-inch cubes
Water as needed
½ pound onions, chopped
1 tablespoon chopped celery
1 tablespoon minced parsley
2 bay leaves
Salt to taste
A few peppercorns
4 tablespoons butter
4 tablespoons flour
3 egg yolks
Juice of 2 lemons

Put the meat into a large pot and add enough water to cover. Add the onions, celery, parsley, bay leaves, salt, and peppercorns and simmer for 1 hour, or until tender. Remove meat from pot. Measure stock and add enough water to make 3 cups. Return meat to pot. In a separate saucepan, melt the butter, add the flour and blend well. Add the meat stock and stir until thick. Remove from heat. Beat the egg yolks. Add the lemon juice and beat it in well. Slowly add a little of the sauce from the saucepan to the egg-lemon mixture, stirring constantly. When well blended, stir the egg-lemon mixture into the sauce. Pour the sauce over the meat and shake the pot gently to distribute the sauce evenly. Serve hot. Serves 6.

BAKED EGGPLANT AND VEAL

Mosharaki me Melitzanes

2 eggplants, cut lengthwise into ½-inch-thick slices
Salt to taste
2 pounds veal, cut into 1-inch cubes
3 tablespoons butter
Pepper to taste
2 cloves garlic, minced
1 teaspoon dried oregano
1 (8-ounce) can whole tomatoes, drained
½ cup wine
½ cup flour
Oil for frying
4 large tomatoes, sliced

Preheat oven to 375°F.

Sprinkle 1 teaspoon salt over eggplant slices. Put in a colander and weight down with a plate for 1 hour. Brown veal in butter. Add salt, pepper, garlic, and oregano and sauté for a few minutes. Add the whole tomatoes and wine and cook until partially done. Dry eggplant slices, dust with flour and fry in hot oil until brown. In a baking dish, place 2 slices of eggplant one on top of the other so that they crisscross. Put some of the meat in the center of the cross and fold the edges of the eggplant over the meat. Place a slice of tomato on top and secure with a toothpick. Continue until all the meat and eggplant are used up. Bake for 1 hour. Serves 6–8.

Variations: Chunks of *kasseri* cheese (about ¼ pound) may be mixed into the filling, or grated cheese may be sprinkled over the tomatoes.

VEAL WITH MACARONI

Moshari me Makaronaki Kofto

3 pounds lean veal roast
Salt and pepper to taste
¾ cup butter
2 teaspoons grated onion
2 pounds ripe tomatoes, peeled, seeded,
  and chopped
Water as needed
1 pound cut macaroni
Grated *kasseri* or *kefalotiri* cheese

Preheat oven to 350°F.

Cut the meat into six thick slices, and sprinkle lightly with salt and pepper. Melt the butter in a heavy pot, add the meat, and brown evenly on all sides. Add the onion and tomatoes. Cover and cook for 1½ hours, or until meat is tender. Watch the meat during the cooking and add water if necessary. Meanwhile, cook the macaroni according to package directions (the pasta should be *al dente*, or firm to the bite). Remove the meat from the pot; put it on a platter and keep warm. Measure the sauce and add enough water to make six cups. Return to the pot and add the cooked macaroni. Put the slices of meat on top of the macaroni. Bake for 15 minutes. Serve with grated cheese. Serves 6.

VEAL WITH OLIVES

Moshari me Elies

2½ pounds veal, cut into 2-inch cubes
Salt and pepper to taste
½ cup flour
¼ cup oil (or half oil, half butter)
1 medium onion, peeled and chopped
½ cup white wine
1 (2-pound, 3-ounce) can tomatoes,
  mashed
2 tablespoons minced parsley
1 cup pitted black olives, drained
1 cup pitted green olives, drained

Season the meat with salt and pepper and flour it lightly. Heat the oil in a large skillet, add the meat, and brown. Add the onion, wine, mashed tomatoes, and parsley. Cover and cook for 45 minutes, or until almost done. Check for tenderness. Add the olives and continue cooking until all liquid is absorbed. May be served over rice. Serves 5–6.

VEAL WITH SPINACH

Moshari me Spanaki

3 pounds veal, cut into 2-inch cubes
Salt and pepper to taste
¾ cup butter or margarine
2 medium onions, chopped, or 1 bunch
    scallions, chopped
1 tablespoon minced fresh dill
3½ cups water
3 pounds fresh spinach (see note)
2 eggs
Juice of 2 lemons

Sprinkle the meat with salt and pepper. Melt the butter in a large pot, add the meat, and brown lightly. Add the onions and dill and cook until they soften, but do not brown. Add the water, cover, and simmer for 1 hour. While the meat is cooking, wash the spinach well. Add the spinach and salt and pepper to the saucepan, and add a little more water if necessary. Cook the meat and spinach for 5 to 8 minutes. Remove from heat. Prepare the *Avgolemono* Sauce by beating the eggs well. Add the lemon juice and beat well. Slowly add some of the hot liquid from the pot, beating constantly. Pour into the pot and shake gently to distribute and thicken the sauce. Serve hot. Serves 6.

Note: 3 packages of frozen leaf spinach may be substituted. Simply thaw and drain. Also 1 tablespoon tomato paste diluted with 2 cups water may be substituted for the *Avgolemono* Sauce. As soon as the meat is browned add the tomato sauce. Cook for 1 hour, add the spinach, and cook 5 minutes.

PORK WITH GREEN OLIVES

Hirino me Prasines Elies

2 pounds pork tenderloin
2 tablespoons butter or margarine
1 clove garlic, crushed
2 tablespoons slivered almonds
1½ teaspoons salt
¼ teaspoon pepper
1 cup sliced onions
½ pound sliced mushrooms (optional)
1 cup dry white wine
1 teaspoon minced mint (optional)
2 tablespoons minced parsley
12 pitted *tsakistes* olives (see note)

Cut pork into 1-inch-thick slices; cut slices in half. Brown in the butter with the garlic and almonds. Season with salt and pepper. Add the onions and mushrooms and sauté until tender. Add the wine, mint, and parsley. Cover and simmer for 30 minutes. Add the olives and heat. Serves 6.

Note: *Tsakistes* are green olives, cracked and marinated in herbs and brine. They may be purchased in Greek specialty shops.

Variation: Omit slivered almonds and *tsakistes* olives. Slice 12 green olives stuffed with almonds and add with 2 tablespoons lemon juice to the cooked tenderloin. Heat to blend flavors.

SAUSAGE SPARTAN STYLE

⤏ SPARTA

Loukaniko

1 pound sweet sausages
6 small onions, sliced
6 green peppers
3 cloves garlic, minced
2–3 whole cloves
2 teaspoons dried oregano
1 (8-ounce) can tomato sauce

This great luncheon dish goes well with a leafy green salad. It is also suitable as an appetizer or for a party buffet.

Cut sausages into 1-inch-thick slices. In an ungreased frying pan, sauté until brown. Remove and set aside. Drain drippings from sausages, leaving 3 tablespoons of dripping in pan. Sauté the onions in the drippings. Add the peppers, garlic, cloves, and oregano. Cook until onions and peppers are wilted. Add the tomato sauce and browned sausage and simmer for 5 minutes. Serve hot with crusty bread. Serves 4–6.

SAUSAGE STEW

⤏ AMORGOS

Loukanika Stefado

¼ cup olive oil
2 pounds sweet sausage, sliced
1 pound small white onions, peeled
2–4 cloves garlic, finely minced
2 bay leaves
½ teaspoon ground cumin
1 cup tomato sauce
⅛ cup red wine
½ cup water
Salt and pepper to taste

In a large skillet, heat the oil, add the sausages and cook until brown. Remove sausage; brown onions and garlic in the same skillet. Add sausages and the remaining ingredients. Simmer for 30–40 minutes. Serve with rice pilaf. Serves 4.

BEEF ONION STEW

⤏ RHODES

Stefado

3 tablespoons butter
3 pounds top round of beef, cut into 2-
    inch pieces
1 cup red wine
2 cups tomato sauce
4 tablespoons tomato paste
1 cup hot water
3 tablespoons olive oil
3 pounds small white onions, peeled
4 cloves garlic, crushed
1 teaspoon ground cinnamon
1 bay leaf
Salt and pepper to taste
Dash of minced parsley
Dash of dried oregano

Melt the butter in a heavy casserole or Dutch oven, add the meat, and brown on all sides. Add ¼ cup of the wine and simmer for a few minutes. Add the tomato sauce and the tomato paste diluted in the hot water. Cover and continue to simmer. In a skillet, heat the olive oil, add the onions, and brown. Add the onions to the meat along with the garlic, spices, bay leaf, and salt and pepper. Cover and simmer over very low heat for 1 to 1½ hours, or until the meat is very tender. As the meat cooks, gradually add the remaining wine. Sprinkle with parsley. Serves 6–8.

BEEF OR VEAL *KAPAMA*

Vothino oi Mosharaki Kapama

2 pounds veal or beef, cut into 1-inch
    cubes
¼ pound butter
2 tablespoons olive oil
2 medium onions, chopped
2 cloves garlic, crushed
1 pound fresh or canned tomatoes,
    peeled, seeded, and chopped
2 teaspoons salt
¼ teaspoon pepper
⅛ teaspoon ground cinnamon
1 quart water

Sauté the meat in the butter and oil until well browned. Add the onions, garlic, and tomatoes. Cook until the tomatoes begin to simmer. Add the spices and water and cook for 15 minutes. Reduce the heat, cover, and cook until the meat is tender. The sauce should not be watery; if it is, cook, uncovered, until the proper consistency is reached. Serves 4.

BEEF WITH ARTICHOKES AND PIGNOLIA NUTS

Kreas me Anginares ke Koukounaria

2 tablespoons oil
2 cloves garlic, crushed
1½ pounds fillet of beef, flank steak, or
    London broil
1 cup beef broth
8 artichoke hearts, canned or frozen
½ cup pignolias (pine nuts)
¼ teaspoon salt
¼ teaspoon pepper
¼ teaspoon ground cumin

Heat the oil in a casserole. Add the garlic and beef and sauté over high heat until the beef is well browned on all sides. Add the broth, artichokes, pignolias, and seasonings and bring to a boil. Lower the heat, cover, and simmer for 10 to 15 minutes, or until the beef reaches the desired degree of doneness. Slice the beef and arrange on a serving plate. Garnish with the artichoke hearts and pour the sauce on top. Serves 4.

POT ROAST WITH VEGETABLES

Komatiasto me Hortarika

1 (4-pound) rolled beef roast
2 tablespoons vegetable oil
Salt and pepper to taste
1 large onion, chopped
1 cup water
1 (8-ounce) can tomato sauce
⅓ cup red wine
1 tablespoon red wine vinegar
1 bay leaf
1 clove garlic, crushed
½ teaspoon ground cumin
1 large eggplant, peeled and cut in
    chunks
2 green peppers, cored, seeded, and cut
    in chunks
1 (1-pound) jar whole onions, drained

Brown the meat in the oil in a large heavy pot. Season with salt and pepper. Remove meat and add onion to fat in pan and cook, stirring, until golden. Add the water and tomato sauce, wine, wine vinegar, bay leaf, garlic, and cumin and bring to a boil. Return meat to pot and simmer, covered, for 2 hours, or until meat is very tender. Skim fat from top and add eggplant, green pepper, and onions. Season with more salt and pepper, if necessary. Cover and simmer ½ hour more, or until eggplant is tender. Put meat and vegetables on a platter and pour cooking liquids on top. Serves 6.

MEAT WRAPPED IN FOIL

Klephteko

4 large thick chops, about 2 pounds
1 tablespoon olive oil
1 teaspoon salt
¼ teaspoon pepper
Juice of 1 lemon
2 tablespoons butter
1 large onion, chopped
4 scallions, cut in 1-inch pieces
1 cup canned tomatoes with juice
3 tablespoons dry red wine
½ teaspoon dried dill
4 large slices *feta* cheese

This method of cooking meat was developed during the Turkish occupation by guerrillas hiding in the mountains. There, ingenious fighters would wrap meat in skins before cooking it so that the cooking aroma would not escape and reveal their hideouts. Today aluminum foil is a handy substitute for skins. Lamb chops, beefsteak, ground beef, veal cutlets, pork tenderloin, and chicken can all be prepared this way.

Preheat oven to 350°F.

Sprinkle the meat with the olive oil, salt, a pinch of pepper, and lemon juice and let stand 1 hour. Melt the butter in a skillet and sauté the onions and scallions until brown. Add the tomatoes, wine, remaining pepper, dill, and additional salt, if desired. Cover and cook until the sauce is thick. Remove from heat and cool. Cut four pieces of foil large enough to completely wrap each piece of meat. Place the meat in the center of the foil; spoon some of the sauce over it and add a slice of cheese. Fold the foil around the meat and seal. Place on a baking sheet and bake for 1½ hours for lamb, 2 hours for pork and thick beef, or 50 minutes for chicken or thin veal cutlet. Serves 4.

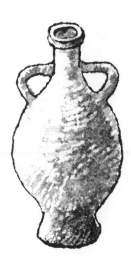

CHICKEN-ARTICHOKE CASSEROLE

Ornitha me Anginares Plaki

1 (3-pound) chicken, cut into serving
    pieces
1 onion, chopped
6 tablespoons butter
1½ teaspoons salt
½ teaspoon pepper
½ pound fresh mushrooms, cleaned and
    sliced, or 1 (8-ounce) can sliced
    mushrooms
2 tablespoons flour
1 cup chicken broth or bouillon
¼ cup dry white wine
1 (12–15-ounce) can artichoke hearts,
    drained

Preheat oven to 375°F.

In a large skillet, brown the chicken and onion in 4 tablespoons of the butter. Season with salt and pepper. Remove chicken and onions and put in a 2-quart casserole. Add the remaining 2 tablespoons of butter to the skillet and sauté the mushrooms for 5 minutes. (If using canned mushrooms, sauté for only 1 minute). Sprinkle the flour over the mushrooms and stir in broth and wine; simmer 5 minutes, stirring constantly, until thickened and smooth. Arrange the artichokes among the chicken pieces. Pour the mushroom sauce over the chicken and artichokes. Cover and bake for 40 minutes. Serves 6.

Note: This casserole can be prepared the day before serving and stored in refrigerator. Bake as above.

ISLANDER CHICKEN

Ornitha Nisiotikia

2 (3-pound) chickens, cut into serving
    pieces
Salt and pepper to taste
½ cup olive oil
1 clove garlic, minced
1 cup chopped scallions (include some of
    the green tops)
1 cup white wine, or 1 cup water
    flavored with lemon juice
2 small eggplants, diced
6 zucchini, diced
6 ripe tomatoes peeled, seeded, and
    diced
Black olives, chopped chives, and
    anchovy fillets for garnish

Sprinkle the chicken with salt and pepper. In a large deep skillet, sauté the chicken in the olive oil. Add the garlic, scallions, and wine and simmer for 20 minutes. Add the eggplant, zucchini, and tomatoes and simmer for 25 minutes, or until chicken and vegetables are cooked. Arrange chicken and vegetables on a serving platter and garnish with sliced black olives, anchovy fillets, and chives. Serves 6.

CHICKEN WITH *ORZO*

CORFU

Kritharaki me Kota

½ cup butter
2 medium onions, finely minced
1 (3-pound) frying chicken, cleaned and
    cut in serving pieces
2 cups water
1 cup *orzo*
Salt and pepper to taste
½ cup grated *kefalotiri* cheese
2 cups plain yogurt

In a large skillet, melt the butter, add the onions, and cook until wilted. Add the chicken and brown on all sides. Add the water and bring to a boil. Add the *orzo* and salt and pepper. Lower the heat and simmer, covered, for 30 to 40 minutes. Garnish with grated cheese and serve with plain yogurt on the side. Serves 3–4.

CHICKEN WITH SPINACH *AVGOLEMONO*

LESBOS

Kota me Spanaki Avgolemono

4 tablespoons butter
1 (3-pound) frying chicken, cleaned and
    cut into serving pieces
1 onion, chopped
1 cup water
Salt and pepper to taste
3 pounds fresh spinach
3 eggs
2 tablespoons flour
Juice of 2 lemons

Melt the butter in a large pot. Add the chicken and onion, and brown lightly. Add water and salt and pepper. Bring to a boil, cover, and simmer for 30 minutes. Wash spinach thoroughly and tear each leaf into 2 or 3 pieces. Scald in boiling water; remove and drain. Add spinach to chicken and cook for 15 to 20 minutes. Remove from heat. Prepare *Avgolemono* Sauce by beating the eggs until frothy. Add the flour and lemon juice, beating well. Slowly add some of the hot liquid from the pot, beating constantly. Pour the sauce into the pot, shaking the pot gently to distribute the sauce. Do not allow sauce to boil. Serve immediately. Serves 4.

EGGPLANT AND CHICKEN STEW

Ornitha ke Melitzanes Plaki

3 small eggplants, peeled and cut
    crosswise into 6 thick slices each
3 medium onions, thinly sliced
2 tablespoons butter
5 tomatoes, peeled, seeded, and chopped
1 large green pepper, cored, seeded, and
    sliced into rings
1 (2½–3-pound) frying chicken, cut into
    serving pieces
Salt and pepper to taste
⅓ cup lemon juice
1 cup olive or vegetable oil

Preheat oven to 350°F.

Salt the sliced eggplant, spread out on paper towels, weight down, and let drain for 30 minutes. Meanwhile, in a large heavy casserole greased with 1 tablespoon butter, arrange a layer of onion slices. Cover the onions with a layer of chopped tomatoes. Spread a few pepper rings over the tomatoes. Place chicken over pepper rings. Sprinkle with salt and pepper. Continue layering onions, tomatoes, and pepper until ingredients are all used, seasoning with salt and pepper to taste. Pour lemon juice over casserole and dot with 1 tablespoon butter. Cover tightly. Bake for 45 minutes. While casserole is baking, rinse and dry eggplant slices. In a large skillet, fry eggplant in oil until soft and golden brown on both sides. Arrange eggplant slices in the casserole. Cover loosely and bake for 20 minutes. Let stand for 20 to 30 minutes before serving. Serve with rice. Serves 4.

BAKED EGGPLANT AND CHICKEN

Ornitha ke Melitzanes Psites

1 large eggplant
¼ cup vegetable or olive oil
2 tablespoons butter
2 tablespoons flour
1 cup milk
Salt and pepper to taste
1 teaspoon ground cumin
1 tablespoon dry white wine
½ cup grated *kasseri* cheese
3 cups finely minced cooked chicken
1 cup cooked peas
Buttered soft bread crumbs

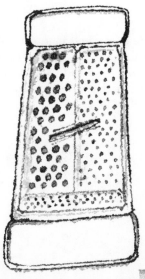

Preheat oven to 350°F.

Remove the eggplant stem. Cut the eggplant crosswise in six thin slices from its narrower end. Slice the remaining eggplant thinly lengthwise. Fry all slices in the oil on both sides until tender. Drain on paper towels. Line six small baking dishes, custard cups, or ovenproof glass cups with the longer eggplant slices. Reserve the round slices for later. Chop any remaining slices and set aside. Melt the butter in a saucepan. Add the flour and blend well. Gradually stir in the milk. Season with salt, pepper, cumin, and wine. Cook for 5 minutes over low heat, stirring constantly, until sauce thickens. Add the cheese, chicken, and any chopped eggplant to the sauce and cook for 5 minutes. Add the peas. Carefully spoon the mixture into the lined dishes. Sprinkle with bread crumbs and top with reserved round slices of eggplant. Bake for 20 minutes. Serves 6.

CHICKEN LIVERS WITH EGGPLANT
Sikotakia me Melitzanes

1 eggplant (about 1 pound), cut into ½-inch-thick slices
5 tablespoons flour
1 teaspoon salt
2 tablespoons vegetable oil
4 tablespoons butter or margarine
1½ pounds chicken livers, washed and cut in half
1 medium onion, chopped
½ teaspoon dried basil, crumbled
1 (15½-ounce) can condensed chicken broth
2 tomatoes, peeled, seeded, and cut in eighths
2 tablespoons minced parsley

Dip the eggplant slices in 3 tablespoons of the flour mixed with the salt. In a large skillet sauté the eggplant in oil and 2 tablespoons of butter for 3 minutes on each side, or until soft. Arrange, overlapping, as a border around the edge of a heated serving dish. Keep warm in oven. In the same skillet, sauté the chicken livers and onion in the remaining butter for 6 minutes, or until browned. Stir in the remaining 2 tablespoons of flour and basil. Gradually stir in the broth. Heat, stirring constantly, for 1 minute, or until the mixture thickens and bubbles. Add tomatoes, cover, reduce heat and simmer for 5 minutes. Spoon into the center of the serving dish with the eggplant border. Sprinkle with parsley and serve with hot cooked rice, if desired. Serves 4–6.

BARBECUE

Though the term is of New World origin, the méthod of cooking is typically Greek. Easy to prepare and delicious to eat, spit-roasted meats spiced with oregano and lemon juice are one of the quintessential flavors of Greece. No day trip anywhere in Greece would be complete without a meal of kebabs at a roadside *psistaria*, or outdoor barbecue restaurant.

BARBECUED LEG OF LAMB
Bouti Arni tis Skaras

MARINADE:
1 cup oil
2 cups red wine
4 cloves garlic, crushed
1 tablespoon salt
1 teaspoon pepper
2 tablespoons dried oregano
Juice of 2 lemons

1 (7-pound) leg of lamb, boned and rolled

Combine all the marinade ingredients in a bowl. Marinate the lamb at room temperature for 4 hours, turning two or three times. Skewer the lamb and place on rotisserie. Barbecue for 2½ hours, basting with the marinade. Serves 6.

BARBECUED LEG OF LAMB STEAKS
Arni Brizoles tis Skaras

MARINADE:

1 cup oil
4 cloves garlic, crushed
1 tablespoon salt
½ tablespoon pepper
2 tablespoons dried oregano
Juice of 2 lemons

1 (8-pound) leg of lamb, cut into 1-inch-
    thick slices (your butcher can do
    this for you)

Combine all the marinade ingredients in a bowl. Arrange the lamb slices on the grill and baste with the marinade. Barbecue for 15 minutes on each side, basting frequently. Serves 10.

BARBECUED BABY LAMB
Arni tou Galactos sti Souvla

MARINADE:

2 cups oil
1 cup lemon juice
3 tablespoons salt
1 tablespoon pepper
½ cup dried oregano
4 cloves garlic, crushed

1 (12–16-pound) baby lamb

Combine all the marinade ingredients in a bowl. The lamb may be marinated for several hours prior to cooking. Tie the legs of the lamb together. Push the hot white coals away from the center of the grill; place a sheet of aluminum foil in the free area to catch the falling fat. This will prevent the coals from igniting when the fat splatters on them. Barbecue the lamb for 3 to 4 hours, basting frequently with the marinade. Serves 12–16.

MARINATED LAMB SHOULDER CHOPS   ↭ KOS
Paidakia Marinata

MARINADE:

2 cups red wine
⅛ cup lemon juice
Squeezed lemon halves
1 medium onion, chopped
2 cloves garlic, split
¼ cup minced celery leaves
½ teaspoon dried oregano

6 large lamb shoulder chops

Combine all the marinade ingredients in a bowl. After the juice has been squeezed from the lemon halves add the squeezed halves to the marinade for additional flavor. Marinate the chops for 1 hour or longer (overnight if possible). Remove meat from marinade and pat dry. Put chops on an oil-rubbed grill 2 inches from fire. Cook for 30 to 45 minutes until nicely browned, turning occasionally and brushing with the marinade. Serves 6.

GRILLED LAMB KIDNEYS

Nephra tis Skaras

12 lamb kidneys

MARINADE:
½ cup olive oil
1 small onion, chopped
½ teaspoon dried oregano
½ teaspoon salt
Juice of 2 lemons
1 clove garlic
1 teaspoon brown sugar

Wash and remove membranes from kidneys; soak in salt water for 20 minutes. Cut each kidney into four pieces. Combine all the marinade ingredients. Marinate the kidneys in a jar for 1 hour, occasionally shaking the jar. Arrange the kidneys on skewers and broil 3 inches from heat, turning frequently until lightly brown. Serve with pilaf. Serves 4–6.

Note: Lamb liver may also be prepared in this way, or may be alternated with the kidneys on skewers.

LAMB, LIVER, AND KIDNEY KEBABS

Arni, Sikoti kai Nefra tis Skaras

MARINADE:
½ cup oil
1 cup red wine
2 cloves garlic, crushed
1 tablespoon salt
1 teaspoon pepper
1 tablespoon dried oregano
Juice of 1 lemon

1 pound lamb, cubed
1 pound liver (preferably calf), cubed
1 pound lamb kidneys, cut in half
8 tomatoes, quartered
12 mushroom caps
4 onions, peeled and quartered

Combine all the marinade ingredients in a bowl. Marinate the meats for 1 hour. Skewer, alternating lamb, liver, kidneys, tomatoes, and onion, leaving the mushroom cap to finish each skewer. Broil, turning frequently, until meat is lightly browned. Serves 6 as main dish, 12 as an appetizer.

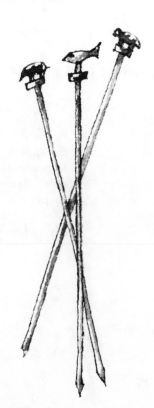

BARBECUED PIG

Gourounaki tis Souvlas

1 (4–5-week-old) suckling pig
½ cup butter, melted
½ cup olive oil
Salt and pepper to taste
Dried oregano to taste
Minced parsley to taste

GARNISH:

Parsley
Watercress
Raisins
1 red apple

Rinse the piglet with cold water inside and out and pat dry. Rub outside with salt and pepper. Pull front legs forward and tie together; tie back legs together. Open mouth with a block of wood. Insert spit through body from tail to center of head. Combine the butter, olive oil, salt, pepper, oregano, and parsley. Rub the pig with the butter mixture and broil slowly over a charcoal fire for 4 hours, or until meat is cooked. (Pig may also be placed on a rack in an open pan and roasted in a 400°F. oven for 20 to 25 minutes, then lower the temperature to 300°F. and cook for 30 minutes per pound.) Baste every 20 minutes with the butter mixture. When cooked, place the piglet on a platter and encircle with parsley and watercress. Insert raisins for eyes and put a bright red apple in the mouth. Serves 6–8.

PORK KEBABS

Hirino tis Skaras

⚓ LEFKAS

½ teaspoon salt
¼ teaspoon crushed dried sage
1 pound lean tender pork, boned and cut
    into ½-inch cubes
¼ cup olive oil
4 lemon wedges

Rub salt and sage into the meat, then brush meat with the oil. Skewer the meat and cook over charcoal, turning frequently, until meat is brown. Serve at once with lemon wedges. Serves 4.

BEEF KEBABS

Vothino tis Skaras

MARINADE:

½ cup oil
1½ cups red wine
3 cloves garlic, crushed
1½ tablespoons salt
1 teaspoon pepper
2 tablespoons dried oregano
½ cup lemon juice

3 pounds round steak (or lamb), cubed
8 tomatoes, quartered
6 onions, quartered
6 green peppers
24 mushroom caps

Combine all the marinade ingredients in a bowl. Marinate the meat at room temperature for at least 8 hours. Skewer, alternating meat, tomato, onion, green pepper, and mushroom caps. Broil for 20 to 25 minutes, turning frequently. Serves 6–8.

GROUND MEAT KEBABS

Keftedes tis Skaras

1½ pounds ground lean beef or lamb
1½ tablespoons minced parsley
½ cup finely minced onion
1 teaspoon dried, crushed mint
1 egg, beaten
1½ teaspoons salt
½ cup pignòlias (pine nuts), chopped

Combine all ingredients, working into a paste with the fingers. Shape into small, plump sausages around bamboo skewers. Grill over hot charcoal. YIELD: 2 dozen.

BARBECUED CHICKEN

Kota tis Skaras

MARINADE:
½ cup oil
½ cup dry white wine
2 tablespoons dried oregano
1 tablespoon salt
1 teaspoon pepper
1 tablespoon paprika
½ tablespoon garlic powder

3 (2-pound) chickens

Combine all the marinade ingredients in a bowl. Remove the wings and backs from the chickens and quarter the remaining chicken. Marinate the chicken pieces for 2 hours at room temperature. Remove the chicken from the marinade and put on a hot grill. Barbecue for 20 minutes, or until golden brown, turning and basting often with the marinade. Serves 6.

CHICKEN *SOUVLAKIA*

Ornithenia Souvlakia

MARINADE:
⅔ cup salad oil
¼ cup lemon juice or wine vinegar
1 small clove garlic, crushed
¼ cup red wine
1 teaspoon dried oregano

3 chicken breasts, boned and cut into
    bite-size squares
¼ pound chicken livers (optional)
2 green peppers, cut into 12 squares
1 tomato, cut into 6 wedges
6 mushroom caps

Combine all the marinade ingredients in a bowl. Add the chicken and livers and marinate for 3 hours. Using 2 long (8- to 9-inch) skewers, arrange alternating pieces of chicken, green pepper, mushroom, chicken liver, and vegetables. Brush with some of the marinade; put under the broiler, about 4 inches from the flame, or on a barbecue and cook for 20 to 25 minutes, brushing with marinade and turning frequently. Serves 6.

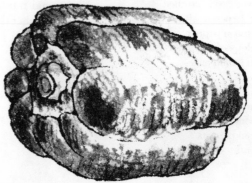

BARBECUED CHICKEN WINGS

Fterouges tis Kotas tis Skaras

MARINADE:

½ cup oil
2 tablespoons oregano
1 tablespoon salt
1 teaspoon pepper
1 tablespon paprika
½ cup lemon juice

24 chicken wings

Combine all the marinade ingredients in a bowl. Marinate the chicken wings for 1 hour. Barbecue to a golden brown, basting frequently with the marinade. Serves 6.

Seafood

Though Greece's mountainous, arid terrain makes it less than ideal for large-scale agriculture, its thousands of miles of coastlines and literally hundreds of islands make it a fisherman's paradise. Think of a Greek island and the emerald-blue Aegean, and your next thought inevitably will be of a luxuriant array of fish and shellfish. Here we present the pick of the catch, from Lobster Tails with *Feta* Cheese and Octopus Pilaf to such island specialities as Shrimp Scorpios and Baked Fish *Spetsa*.

FISH

BAKED FISH

Psari Psito

✢ SPETSA

3 pounds thick fish slices (about ¾ inch thick), such as bass, cod, red snapper, or swordfish
Salt and pepper to taste
Lemon juice
2 cups fresh or canned tomatoes, chopped
½ cup white wine
1 cup olive oil
2 cloves garlic, minced
2 tablespoons minced parsley
Dry bread crumbs

Preheat oven to 400°F.

Place fish in a lightly greased baking dish, sprinkle with salt, pepper, and lemon juice, and set aside. In a saucepan, combine the tomatoes, wine, oil, garlic, and parsley and cook for 20 minutes. Pour sauce over fish and sprinkle with bread crumbs. Bake uncovered for 45 minutes, or until golden. Serves 5–6.

BAKED FISH WITH ONIONS

Psari me Kromidia

✢ THASSOS

5 pounds onions, chopped
1 teaspoon salt
1½ cups tomato sauce
Salt and pepper to taste
¾ cup olive oil
1 (5–7-pound) whole fish, such as striped bass, sea bass, sea trout, or any other baking fish, cleaned and dressed (leave head on)
½ cup bread crumbs

Preheat oven to 400°F.

Cook the onions in a heavy covered saucepan over very low heat with 1 teaspoon salt for 5 to 10 minutes, stirring occasionally. Remove from heat. Add tomato sauce, salt and pepper, and ½ cup olive oil. Pour onion mixture into a large roasting pan. Place the fish on the onions. Sprinkle fish with additional salt and pepper and the bread crumbs. Drizzle remaining ¼ cup oil over fish and onions. Bake for 1 hour or slightly longer if onions are too watery. Add a little more bread crumbs to thicken, if necessary. Serves 6–8.

Variation: Omit bread crumbs and add 1 cup red wine, 2 tablespoons vinegar, and 2 cloves chopped garlic to the tomato sauce and bake.

BAKED FISH WITH MIXED VEGETABLES

✦ KOS

Psari Tourlou

1 eggplant, diced (2 cups)
1 cup water
1 tablespoon salt
1 cup vegetable or olive oil
2 onions, chopped
4 scallions, cut into thin slices
2 cloves garlic, minced
1 green pepper, sliced thin
4 potatoes, sliced (2 cups)
1 (1-pound) can tomatoes, chopped
1 package frozen okra, thawed (cut large
    ones into 1-inch pieces)
2 tablespoons minced parsley
1 bay leaf
3 pounds fish fillets or steaks (blue fish,
    black fish, striped bass, sea bass, red
    snapper, or porgy)
Salt and pepper to taste
2 tablespoons butter
1 lemon, sliced

Preheat oven to 350°F.

Soak the eggplant in 1 cup salted water for ½ hour, then drain. Heat the oil in a heavy pot. Add the onions, scallions, garlic, green pepper, potatoes, eggplant, tomatoes, okra, parsley, and bay leaf. Cook over low heat for 20 minutes, stirring occasionally. Arrange vegetables in a baking pan and bake for 20 minutes. Season fish with salt and pepper, place on top of vegetables, dot with butter and add lemon slices. Bake for 45 minutes, or until fish flakes easily. Serves 4–6.

BAKED CODFISH CAKES

✦ CORFU

Bakaliaros Keftedes

1 pound salt codfish
4 medium potatoes, cooked and mashed
¼ cup milk
1 tablespoon minced onion
Cayenne pepper
1 egg
1 recipe Garlic Sauce (*Skordalia*) (see
    below)

Soak codfish in cold water overnight. Drain. Put in a pan and cover with boiling water. Cover pan and let stand for 20 minutes. Drain.

Preheat oven to 350°F.

Cover fish with boiling water for 20 minutes and drain again. Flake the fish with a fork. Mix flaked fish with mashed potatoes, milk, onion, pepper, and unbeaten egg. Shape into cakes and bake for 35 minutes. Serve with Garlic Sauce. Serves 4–6.

GARLIC SAUCE

Skordalia

4 medium potatoes
4½ cups water
6 cloves garlic
1 teaspoon salt
½ cup olive oil
4 tablespoons vinegar

Boil the potatoes in 4 cups water. Peel them and cut in quarters. Place ½ cup water in blender. Add the garlic, salt, and potatoes and blend for 2 minutes. Add the oil and vinegar, a little at a time, and continue blending until smooth, about 3 minutes. Serve chilled as a sauce over fish, game, or vegetables. YIELD: 2 cups.

BAKED FISH WITH EGGPLANT AND TOMATO SAUCE

Kefalos me Melitzana Saltsa

2 pounds fish fillets or steaks (sea bass,
    porgies, halibut, or any other baking
    fish)
2 tablespoons lemon juice
Salt and pepper to taste
1 large green pepper
1 pound eggplant
⅓ cup salad oil
1 large onion, chopped
2 (8-ounce) cans tomato sauce
½ cup dry white wine
1 clove garlic, minced
1 bay leaf

Preheat oven to 350°F.

Sprinkle the fish with the lemon juice, salt, and pepper. Cut the green pepper into ½-inch strips. Peel the eggplant and cut into ½-inch cubes. In a large skillet, heat the oil and add the green pepper and onion; cook until tender. Add the eggplant, tomato sauce, wine, garlic, and bay leaf and simmer for 15 minutes. Put the fish in a baking pan, cover with the sauce, and bake for 35 minutes. Serves 4–6.

FISH PATTIES

Psarokeftedes

2 cups cooked fish (cod or flounder)
1 tablespoon minced mint leaves
1 large onion, minced
2 eggs
1 cup bread crumbs
⅓ cup grated *kefalotiri* cheese
¾ cup water
Salt and pepper to taste
1 cup flour
Vegetable oil for frying
Juice of 2 lemons
1 recipe Rosemary Sauce (*Savoro*) (see
    below)

Mash the fish with a fork. Add the mint leaves, onion, eggs, bread crumbs, *kefalotiri* cheese, water, and salt and pepper. Mix thoroughly. Form into small patties. Roll each patty in flour and fry in hot oil until golden brown. Sprinkle with lemon juice. Serve hot with Rosemary Sauce. Serves 5–6.

ROSEMARY SAUCE

Savoro

Oil
3 tablespoons flour
⅓ cup vinegar
½ tablespoon tomato paste
2 cups water
1 clove garlic, finely minced
½ teaspoon dry rosemary
1 bay leaf
Salt and pepper to taste

After frying fish, add enough oil to the remaining frying pan oil to make ½ cup and heat. Add the flour and then the vinegar and continue to stir. Dilute the tomato paste with the water and add to the pan with the garlic, rosemary, bay leaf, and salt and pepper. Cook over medium heat, stirring, until the sauce thickens. YIELD: 1½ cups.

Note: To heighten the flavor of this dish, return the fried fish to the pan when the sauce thickens and let it simmer for 3 minutes. Refrigerate for several hours and serve at room temperature. *Savoro* Sauce is also an excellent accompaniment for sautéed liver.

BARBECUED BASS

Psari tis Skaras

1 cup oil
½ cup lemon juice
1 tablespoon salt
1 teaspoon pepper
2 tablespoons dried oregano
2 tablespoons flour
Bread crumbs
1 (3½–4-pound) whole sea bass

Combine the oil, lemon juice, salt, pepper, oregano, flour, and enough bread crumbs to make a very thick paste. Coat the sea bass with the paste. Spread the hot white coals away from the center of the grill. Place the coated fish in the center of the grill and cook for ½ hour on each side. Serves 4–6.

BRAISED SWORDFISH WITH MUSSELS

❧ LIMNOS

Xifias me Midia

2-2½ pounds swordfish (in 1 piece)
1 clove whole garlic plus 1 clove crushed
    garlic
2 tablespoons flour
¼ cup olive oil
½ cup butter
¼ pound mushrooms
½ pound lean salt pork, cut in small
    pieces
1 teaspoon dried thyme
2 bay leaves
½ cup cognac
2 quarts mussels, cleaned and bearded
⅛ cup white wine
Minced parsley

Rub the fish with the whole garlic clove and flour lightly. Sear fish in the oil and ¼ cup butter in a heavy Dutch oven. Set aside. In a skillet sauté the mushrooms and pork in 3 tablespoons butter. Add to the fish. Season with the thyme and bay leaves. Heat the cognac; pour over the fish and ignite. Simmer for 35 minutes. While fish is simmering, steam the mussels in the remaining butter with the crushed garlic and white wine. Add mussels and liquid from the mussel mixture to the fish. Stir to blend the two sauces. Arrange the fish and mussels in a dish and garnish with the parsley. Serves 4–6.

PORGIES WITH *AVGOLEMONO* SAUCE

❧ KITHIRA

Tsipoura Avgolemono

1 head celery
3 cups water
2 onions, finely minced
½ cup vegetable or olive oil
3–4 whole porgies, cleaned
2 eggs
Juice of 2 lemons
1 tablespoon flour
Salt and pepper to taste
Fresh parsley or dill for garnish

Clean celery and cut into 3-inch pieces. Poach in 2 cups boiling water for 5 minutes, or until limp. Drain. In a large skillet, sauté onions in the oil until wilted. Place the celery on top of the onions, and the fish on top of the celery, sprinkle with salt and pepper. Add 1 cup water, cover, and simmer for 20 minutes, or until fish flakes. Remove fish and vegetables, place on a heated platter and keep warm. Strain remaining broth, measure, and add water to make 1 cup. Heat the broth. Beat eggs, lemon juice, and flour in a blender. Gradually blend in the heated broth. Pour into a saucepan and heat over very low flame until slightly thick. Pour over fish. Garnish with parsley or dill. Serves 8.

Note: Striped bass may be substituted for porgies.

BROILED FILLETS WITH *KASSERI* AND TOMATOES

Fetes Psari me Kasseri kai Domates

2 pounds skinless flounder or other fish
    fillets
2 tablespoons grated onion
Salt and pepper to taste
3 tomatoes, chopped
¼ cup melted butter
1 cup grated *kasseri* cheese

Preheat broiler.

Place fillets in a single layer in a well-greased shallow baking dish. Sprinkle fish with onion, 1½ teaspoons salt, ¼ teaspoon pepper, and tomatoes. Sprinkle tomatoes lightly with salt and pepper. Drizzle butter over all. Broil 4 inches from the flame for 5 minutes, or until fish flakes easily. Sprinkle with cheese and broil 2 more minutes. Serves 4.

DODECANESIAN FISH

Psari Dodekanisa

2 cloves garlic, minced
¼ cup vegetable or olive oil
3 medium onions, chopped
¼ pound fresh mushrooms, sliced
1 cup canned plum tomatoes, chopped
3 tablespoons minced parsley
½ cup water
½ teaspoon dried oregano
Salt to taste
½ cup red wine
2 pounds striped bass or sea bass fillets,
    or a 1-inch-thick halibut steak

Preheat oven to 350°F.

In a large skillet, sauté the garlic in hot oil until golden. Add the onions and mushrooms and cook until soft, stirring often. Add the tomatoes, parsley, water, oregano, ½ teaspoon salt, and wine to the vegetables and simmer for 5 minutes, stirring occasionally. Sprinkle the fish with additional salt. Place fish on vegetable mixture and simmer, uncovered, for 40 to 50 minutes, or until fish flakes easily. Serves 6.

POACHED FISH WITH *AVGOLEMONO* SAUCE

Psari Avgolemono

1 cup water
½ cup dry white wine
1 onion, quartered
2 carrots, sliced
¼ cup chopped parsley
1 sprig thyme, or ⅛ teaspoon dried
    thyme
2 bay leaves
1 teaspoon salt
3–4 peppercorns
1 (3½-pound) whole, cleaned fish, such as
    striped bass or sea trout

Avgolemono SAUCE:

2 eggs
Juice of 1 lemon
1 cup hot fish stock

Combine all but the fish and the sauce ingredients in a deep pot or fish poacher. Note that liquid should cover fish (adjust wine and water accordingly). Bring to a boil and cook for 5 minutes. Immerse fish into water and immediately lower flame to a gentle simmer. Cover and poach for 25 to 30 minutes, or until fish flakes easily. Remove fish from poaching liquid and keep warm. Beat the eggs for the sauce in a saucepan. Gradually add the lemon juice. Slowly add 1 cup hot poaching liquid, stirring constantly. When all liquid is added, put saucepan on a low flame and heat gently, stirring constantly, until sauce thickens. Be careful not to bring to a boil. Spoon a light coating of sauce over the fish and serve remaining sauce on the side. Serves 4–6.

Note: This recipe may also be made with fish fillets. Cook as directed for 15 to 20 minutes, or until fish flakes easily.

ROLLED STUFFED FILLETS WITH *AVGOLEMONO* SAUCE ⚓ ITHAKI

Fetes Psari Gemistes Avgolemono

¾ cup butter or margarine
1 clove garlic, crushed
1 small onion, minced
¼ cup minced green pepper
12 fresh or frozen shrimp, shelled,
    deveined, and cooked briefly in
    boiling water (until shrimp turn
    pink) with 1 cut up carrot, 2 onions,
    1 bay leaf, and a few peppercorns
    (save 1 cup of the cooking liquid)
¼ cup flavored bread crumbs
1 tablespoon minced parsley
½ teaspoon salt
⅛ teaspoon pepper
4 fillets of sole or flounder (about 1½
    pounds)

Avgolemono SAUCE:

3 eggs
1 cup shrimp broth
Juice of 2 medium lemons

Preheat oven to 350°F.

Melt 2 tablespoons of the butter in a large skillet. Stir in garlic, onion, and green pepper and sauté until onion is golden. Dice 8 shrimp and add to the skillet mixture. Add bread crumbs, parsley, salt, and pepper and blend. Remove from heat. On boned side of each fillet spread 2 tablespoons of the shrimp mixture. Roll fillets carefully and tuck in any extra mixture into end of rolled fillets. Melt 2 tablespoons of butter in a 10- x 6- x 2-inch baking dish. Arrange the fillets flapside down in the dish. Brush with more melted butter. Bake for 25–30 minutes. Prepare the *Avgolemono* Sauce by beating the 3 eggs until creamy. Very slowly add the warm broth reserved from the cooked shrimp. Add the lemon juice and beat until thick. When fish is baked, place on a platter and pour sauce over all. Garnish each fillet with the remaining shrimp. Serves 4.

SEAFOOD *BOUREKIA* ⚓ KOS

Bourekia me Garides kai Glossa

1 pound flounder fillets
1 pound shrimp, peeled, deveined,
    boiled briefly until they turn pink,
    and coarsely chopped
4 tablespoons butter
1 large onion, chopped
2 stalks celery, chopped
4 scallions, including green, chopped
1 hard-cooked egg, chopped
½ cup bread crumbs
½ cup chicken stock
1 pound *phyllo* pastry
½ pound melted butter for brushing
    phyllo

Preheat oven to 350°F.

Steam flounder fillets for 10 minutes, or until fish flakes easily. Flake fish, add cooked shrimp, and set aside. Melt the 4 tablespoons butter in a skillet. Add onion, celery, and scallions and sauté until onion is wilted. Add flounder, shrimp, egg, bread crumbs, and ½ cup chicken broth or enough to moisten mix. Work with 1 *phyllo* sheet at a time and keep remainder covered with plastic wrap. Brush a *phyllo* sheet with melted butter and fold in half width-wise. Place 2 tablespoons of mixture at one of the narrow ends. Fold ends over mixture and roll. (Read How to Work with *Phyllo*, see Index.) Place in baking pan. Repeat procedure until all of the mixture is used up. Brush all the rolled pastry with butter. Bake for 25 to 30 minutes, or until golden. Serve warm with tossed Greek salad. Serves 8.

Note: For an excellent appetizer, the *phyllo* in this recipe may be cut into quarters, instead of folded in half. Use 1 teaspoon filling and roll. Recipe may also be baked in a 9- x 12-inch baking pan. Butter 8 sheets of *phyllo* one at a time and place in pan. Spread filling over *phyllo*. Top with 12 sheets of buttered *phyllo*. Score top of *phyllo*. Bake in a 350°F. oven.

SKEWERED SWORDFISH
Xifias Souvlakia

2 pounds swordfish, boned, skinned, and
    cubed
Salt and pepper to taste
Juice of 1½ lemons, strained
¼ cup olive oil
2 teaspoons chopped fresh thyme, or 1
    teaspoon dried thyme
3 firm ripe tomatoes, quartered, or 8
    cherry tomatoes
8 bay leaves
2 green peppers, seeded and cubed

Season the cubed swordfish lightly with salt and pepper. Combine the lemon juice, oil, and thyme. Add the seasoned swordfish and marinate for several hours, or overnight. When ready to serve, thread on metal skewers, alternating with the tomatoes, bay leaves, and peppers. Broil 4 to 5 inches from the heat or grill over coals for 15 minutes, turning frequently and brushing occasionally with the remaining marinade. Serve hot with rice and salad. Serves 6.

STEWED FISH WITH ONIONS
Bourtheto

⚘ CORFU

3½ pounds red snapper, cod, turbot, or
    haddock
1½ cups water
½ cup olive oil
1 teaspoon salt
1 teaspoon pepper
1 teaspoon paprika, or to taste
⅛ teaspoon cayenne pepper
½ pound onions, sliced

Cut the fish into large serving pieces. Put the water, oil, seasonings, and onions in a saucepan and simmer for 15 minutes. Add the fish and cook over low heat for 18 minutes. Serves 6.

TUNA FISH WITH CHICK-PEAS
Tonos me Revithia

1 (20-ounce) can chick-peas
1 (7-ounce) can tuna fish
4 scallions, white parts only, minced
1 tablespoon finely minced fresh parsley
1 tablespoon minced celery

DRESSING:

½ cup olive oil
4 tablespoons lemon juice
½ tablespoon dried oregano
½ tablespoon dried marjoram
½ teaspoon salt
½ teaspoon pepper
1 clove garlic, crushed
¼ teaspoon powdered mustard

This is an excellent appetizer or luncheon main course.

Drain the chick-peas and the tuna. Mix together with the chopped vegetables. Combine the dressing ingredients and shake well. Pour the dressing over chick-peas and tuna mixture and stir well. Serves 4–6.

SHELLFISH

BAKED LOBSTER TAILS WITH *FETA*

↴ SKORPIOS

Astakos Psitos me Feta

3 tablespoons olive oil
2 large onions, finely minced
1 clove garlic, minced
1½ pounds fresh plum tomatoes, peeled, seeded, and finely chopped, or 3 cups solid-packed canned plum tomatoes
½ teaspoon dried oregano
Dash of powdered mustard
Dash of sugar
¼ cup finely minced parsley
1 tablespoon finely minced dill
Pepper to taste
12 frozen baby lobster tails
1 cup flour
¼ pound butter
4 large tomatoes, peeled and cut into ¼-inch-thick slices
¾ pound *feta* cheese, sliced thinly

This recipe comes to us from Leon Lionides, owner of New York's famed Coach House Restaurant.

Preheat oven to 375°F.

Heat the oil in a saucepan. Add the onions and gently sauté until wilted. Add garlic and stir in plum tomatoes, oregano, mustard, sugar, parsley, dill, and pepper. Simmer for 30 minutes, or until sauce is moderately thick. Thaw the lobsters and shell them, taking care to remove the meat of each in one piece. Roll lobster tails in flour; sauté briskly in the butter, stirring the pieces for 2 minutes, or just until they are firm. Remove them to a shallow baking dish. Pour the sauce over the lobster and arrange the tomato slices on top. Cover with the *feta* cheese and bake for 15 minutes, or until the cheese melts. Serve with rice pilaf and a crispy salad. Serves 6.

(Lenten)
MUSSELS WITH WINE SAUCE

Midia Krassata

½ cup chopped onion
1 clove garlic, minced
3 tablespoons vegetable or olive oil
3 quarts mussels, cleaned and bearded (see page 35 for Preparation of Fresh Mussels)
1 cup dry white wine
4 sprigs parsley
1 sprig fresh thyme, or ½ teaspoon dried thyme
1 bay leaf
½ teaspoon pepper
¼ cup vinegar
2 tablespoons prepared mustard
½ teaspoon salt
1 cup olive oil
¾ cup diced, blanched celery
1 tablespoon each minced parsley and tarragon

This is an excellent first course dish.

In a heavy kettle sauté the onion and garlic in the oil until wilted. Add the well-scrubbed mussels, wine, parsley sprigs, thyme, and bay leaf. Sprinkle with ¼ teaspoon pepper. Cover, bring to a boil, lower heat, and simmer for 6 to 7 minutes, shaking pan, until the mussels open. Transfer the mussels to a large bowl. Strain the cooking liquid through cheesecloth, boil, and reduce to 1 cup. In another bowl, combine the vinegar, mustard, salt, and ¼ teaspoon pepper. Pour in 1 cup olive oil in a stream. Add celery, parsley, and tarragon and stir the mixture into the sauce. Pour over the mussels and reheat. Serves 4–6.

(Lenten)

MUSSELS *YIAHNI*
Midia Yiahni

2 large onions, chopped
¼ cup vegetable or olive oil
1 cup tomato sauce
½ cup raw rice
1 cup water
2 quarts mussels, cleaned and bearded
    (see page 35 for Preparation of
    Fresh Mussels)

Brown the onions in oil. Add tomato sauce and raw rice, stirring constantly. Cook for 5 minutes. Add 1 cup water and cook for 10 minutes. Add cleaned raw mussels, still in their shells, and cook for 15 minutes, or until rice is tender, and mussel shells open. Add more liquid, if necessary. Serves 4.

OCTOPUS PILAF
Oktapodi Pilafi

2 pounds fresh octopus, skinned
2 medium onions, minced
¼ pound plus 2 tablespoons butter
1 clove garlic, minced
1 bay leaf
1 teaspoon dried oregano
2 tablespoons tomato paste
1 (16-ounce) can whole tomatoes with
    liquid
1 cup white wine
3½ cups water
2 cups raw rice

Pound the octopus to tenderize it, and cut into cubes. Sauté the onions in ¼ pound butter until golden brown. Add the garlic, bay leaf, oregano, and octopus. Sauté for a few more minutes. Add the tomato paste, whole tomatoes, and wine. Stir well, cover, and simmer over low heat for 1 hour, or until octopus is tender. When octopus has cooked for about 35 minutes, put 3½ cups water, ½ cup octopus cooking liquid, and 2 tablespoons butter in a saucepan. Bring to a boil, add rice, stir, lower heat, and simmer for 20 minutes. To serve, shape the rice into individual mounds with a cup and cover with octopus and remaining sauce. Serves 4.

SCALLOPS WITH RICE
Ktenia me Rize

⤙ IKAROS

1 large onion, chopped
¼ cup butter
2 pounds bay scallops
2 tablespoons olive oil
1 cup raw rice
Water
1½ teaspoons salt
Minced parsley

Preheat oven to 400°F.

In a skillet sauté the onion in butter until golden. Wash the scallops and add to the onion and simmer for 7 minutes, turning occasionally. Meanwhile, heat the oil in a 2-quart heavy pot, add rice, and stir to coat. Drain the liquid from the scallop mixture and measure, adding enough water to make 2½ cups. Add the salt to the liquid and pour over the rice. Cover and bake for 20 minutes. Stir in scallop mixture and bake for 10 minutes. Sprinkle with parsley. Serves 4.

ARTICHOKES STUFFED WITH SHRIMP

Aginares Gemistes me Garides

6 medium artichokes
3½ quarts water
2 tablespoons salad or olive oil
2 cloves garlic, slivered
1 teaspoon salt
1 teaspoon sugar

SHRIMP STUFFING:

1 pound fresh or frozen shrimp, cleaned,
    deveined, and chopped
½ cup minced scallions
½ cup salad or olive oil
1 cup flavored bread crumbs
¼ cup minced parsley
1 teaspoon salt
½ teaspoon garlic salt
⅛ teaspoon pepper

Trim the artichokes by cutting off the stalk and snipping off tops of all leaves. Place in large (5-quart) saucepan containing 3½ quarts boiling water, seasoned with oil, garlic, salt, and sugar. Boil, covered, for 30 minutes, or until tender. Drain well. Spread leaves apart and scoop out choke with a small spoon.

Preheat oven to 350°F.

Prepare stuffing by sautéing the shrimp and scallions in ½ cup oil for 2 to 3 minutes, or until shrimp turns pink. Remove from the heat and add the bread crumbs, parsley, salt, garlic salt, and pepper. Toss lightly to mix well. Fill centers of the artichokes with shrimp stuffing, using approximately ½ cup stuffing for each artichoke. Place stuffed artichokes in a well-greased baking dish, cover lightly with foil and bake for 15 minutes, or until just heated through. Serves 6.

(Lenten)

MARINATED SHRIMP

Garides se Lathoxitho

MARINADE:

2 large red onions, thinly sliced
1 (2½-ounce) bottle capers, drained and
    rinsed
3 bay leaves
1½ cups vinegar
1½ cups water
1½ cups olive oil
1 teaspoon salt
½ teaspoon pepper
½ teaspoon dried oregano

3 pounds medium-size shrimp, cooked
    and shelled
2 (8-ounce) cans button mushrooms
2 (8-ounce) cans artichoke hearts, cut in
    thirds

An excellent party dish any time of the year.

Combine all the marinade ingredients. Refrigerate overnight. On the second day add the cooked shrimp, mushrooms, and artichoke hearts. Refrigerate overnight and serve on the third day. Serves 16–20.

BRANDIED SHRIMP

Garides tis Flogas

2 tablespoons butter
1 medium onion, chopped
1 tablespoon minced parsley
1 tablespoon finely minced scallions
⅛ teaspoon dried thyme
1 small bay leaf
2 pounds shrimp, cleaned and deveined
2 fresh tomatoes, seeded and chopped
1 cup dry white wine
¼ cup brandy

Melt the butter, add the onion, and sauté until golden. Add the parsley and scallions and cook until the scallions become translucent. Simmer for 2 minutes and add the thyme, bay leaf, and shrimp. Stir and simmer for 5 minutes, or just until the shrimp turn pink. Do not overcook. Add the tomatoes and wine and cook for 2 minutes. Remove bay leaf. Heat the brandy and add to the shrimp mixture. Serve on rice. Serves 6–8.

(Lenten)

SHRIMP AND OKRA

Garides me Bamies

⅔ cup chopped green onions (include
    tops)
3 cloves garlic, finely minced
⅓ cup vegetable or olive oil
2 cups sliced fresh okra, or 1 package
    frozen baby okra, thawed
1 pound shrimp, cleaned
1 cup hot water
1 cup tomato juice
2 whole bay leaves
1 cup canned tomatoes
½ teaspoon salt
½ teaspoon pepper

Sauté the onion and garlic in the oil. Add the okra and cook, stirring constantly, for 10 minutes, or until okra appears dry. Add the shrimp and cook for 5 minutes. Add the water, tomato juice, bay leaves, tomatoes, salt, and pepper. Cover and simmer for 20 minutes. Remove bay leaves. Serve over cooked rice. Serves 4.

(Lenten)

SHRIMP AND SCALLOPS ON SKEWERS

Garides kai Ktenia Souvlaki

MARINADE:
½ cup olive oil
¼ cup lemon juice
2 tablespoons brandy
¼ teaspoon each salt, pepper, dried
    oregano, dried thyme, and garlic
    powder

2 pounds fresh scallops
2 pounds raw shrimp, cleaned

Combine all the marinade ingredients. Add the shrimp and scallops to the marinade, mix well, and let stand for 2 to 3 hours at room temperature. Place on skewers, alternating 1 scallop and 1 shrimp. Broil over charcoal or under the broiler for 10 minutes, turning once. Serves 6–8 as a main course, or 12 as an appetizer.

SHRIMP CASSEROLE WITH BÉCHAMEL SAUCE

Garides tou Fournou me Krema

3 dozen shrimp
1 large onion, minced
2 tablespoons butter
3 tablespoons brandy
1 cup white wine
2 medium tomatoes, sliced
1 cup chicken broth
1 tablespoon minced parsley
¼ teaspoon dried mint
¼ teaspoon dried dill
1 bay leaf
¼ pound butter
½ cup plus 2 tablespoons flour
½ cup milk
½ cup crumbled *feta* cheese

Preheat oven to 450°F.

Shell shrimp and poach shells in water to extract flavor; reserve liquid for Béchamel Sauce. In a large skillet, sauté the onions in butter over medium heat. Add shrimp and cook just until they turn pink. Flame the brandy and pour it over the shrimp. Add the wine, tomatoes, broth, and herbs and simmer for 5 minutes. Make the Béchamel Sauce by melting the butter in a saucepan (do not let it brown). Stir in the flour and cook over low heat for 1 minute. Gradually add ½ cup milk and ½ cup fish broth to make a thick, creamy sauce. Butter a 1-quart casserole and make layers of sauce and shrimp; sprinkle each layer with *feta* cheese. Finish with a layer of sauce. Sprinkle generously with *feta* cheese. Bake for 20 to 30 minutes. Serves 6–8.

(Lenten)

SHRIMP WITH SPAGHETTI CASSEROLE

Garides me Macaronia sto Fourno

2 pounds spaghetti
2 pounds shrimp
½ cups olive or vegetable oil
¾ cup chopped onion
½ cup Retsina or white wine
1 pound ripe tomatoes, peeled and
    strained, or 2 tablespoons tomato
    paste, diluted with 2 cups water
½ cup minced parsley
1 green pepper, cored, seeded, and
    chopped
1 teaspoon salt
½ teaspoon pepper
3 fresh tomatoes for garnish, sliced thin

Preheat oven to 300°F.

Cook the spaghetti according to package directions (pasta should be "al dente" or firm to the bite) and drain well. Shell, wash, and devein the shrimp. In a large pot, heat the oil and sauté the onions until light golden in color. Add the wine, tomatoes, parsley, green pepper, salt, and pepper. Cook the sauce until it begins to thicken. Add the shrimp and cook for 3 minutes. Remove the sauce from the heat. Stir the shrimp and sauce mixture into the spaghetti, mixing well. Butter a 9- x 12-inch pan and pour this mixture evenly into it. Arrange the fresh tomato slices over all. Bake for 15 minutes. Serves 8–10.

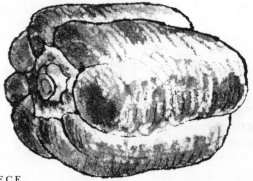

SHRIMP SCORPIO

Garides me Saltsa

3 tablespoons olive oil
2 cups minced onion
1 clove garlic, minced
¼ cup finely minced parsley
1 tablespoon finely minced dill (optional)
⅛ teaspoon powdered mustard
¼ teaspoon sugar
2 cups fresh or canned peeled tomatoes
½ cup tomato sauce
1 pound shrimp, peeled and deveined
1 cup crumbled *feta* cheese

Preheat oven to 425°F.

Heat the oil in a saucepan and add the onion. Cook, stirring, until the onion starts to brown. Add the garlic, parsley, and dill. Stir in the mustard and sugar. (Do not add salt at any time.) Add the tomatoes and tomato sauce and simmer for 30 minutes. Add the shrimp to the sauce and cook for 3 minutes. Pour the mixture into a 1½-quart casserole and sprinkle with the crumbled cheese. Bake for 10 to 15 minutes, or until cheese melts. Serve immediately. Serves 4.

SHRIMP WITH *FETA* AND DILL

Garides me Feta kai Anithos

½ cup chopped onion
4 tablespoons butter
2 cups cooked rice
1 pound shrimp, peeled and deveined
1½ cups loosely packed, crumbled *feta* cheese
1½ tablespoons finely minced fresh dill, or ½ teaspoon dried dill
1 (1-pound 14-ounce) can whole tomatoes, drained and chopped

Preheat oven to 350°F.

Sauté onion in the butter. Mix with the cooked rice and spread in a 1½-quart casserole. Arrange the shrimp and *feta* on top of the rice. Sprinkle with dill. Add the tomatoes and bake for 35 minutes, or until the shrimp are opaque. Serves 3.

(Lenten)

SNAILS STEW

Saligaria Stifado

2 pounds fresh snails (see note), or 2 (12-ounce) cans snails
3 onions, thinly sliced
1 cup olive oil, or half olive and half vegetable oil
2 cloves garlic, finely minced
½ cup red wine
2 pounds well-ripened tomatoes, chopped, or 1 (35-ounce) can tomatoes, chopped
1 bay leaf
1 teaspoon salt
½ teaspoon pepper

Follow directions for Preparation of Fresh Snails, if used (see page 20). In a heavy skillet, sauté the onions in the oil until golden brown. Add the garlic, wine, and tomatoes and let simmer for 15 minutes. Add the bay leaf, salt, and pepper. Add prepared snails, cover, and simmer for 45 minutes. Uncover and continue simmering until all liquid is absorbed. (If canned snails are used, reduce cooking time by 15 minutes.) Serve with rice or french fries. Serves 4–6.

Note: Snails may be purchased at many fishmarkets, supermarkets, and Greek specialty stores.

SQUID IN RED WINE

Kalamarakia me Krassi

3 pounds squid
3 cups chopped onion
½ cup vegetable or olive oil
1 teaspoon salt
½ teaspoon pepper
1 teaspoon mashed garlic
1 cup red wine

Remove the ink sac, sand sac, the innards, and the chitinous "pen" bone of the squid; use only the body and the tentacles. Blanch the squid for a few minutes in boiling water, drain well, and cut into pieces. In a saucepan, cook the onions in the oil until tender but not brown. Add the squid and heat through. Add the salt, pepper, and garlic and stir. Add the red wine and stir. Cook for 20 minutes, or until the squid is tender. Serve over rice. Serves 6.

Note: Frozen, cleaned squid are an acceptable substitute. Thaw and proceed with the recipe.

Cereals and
Dairy Products

The traditional accompaniment to many a Greek meal is rice pilaf or the distinctive Greek pasta, shaped like tiny almonds, called *orzo*. Here we present variations on the traditional recipes, such as Tipsy Rice (flavored with *ouzo*) and *Orzo* and Rice Pilaf. Though eggs play an important role in many Greek dishes, we concentrate in this section on the Greek way with omelets, a popular choice for the traditional light supper or that new-fangled invention (in Greece at any rate), the one-hour lunch. And finally we present a glossary of Greek Cheeses, an important part of the Greek diet which, fortunately for cheese-lovers everywhere, is becoming more widely available outside the country (this is especially true of the ever-popular *Feta*).

EGGS

EGGS WITH SPINACH

Avga me Spanaki

2 (10-ounce) packages frozen spinach, thawed, or 2 (10-ounce) packages fresh spinach
3 tablespoons butter or margarine
1 onion, finely minced
Salt and pepper to taste
Dash of nutmeg
4 eggs

In a skillet, briefly cook the spinach in the butter until wilted. Add the onion, salt, pepper, and nutmeg. When the onion is soft and golden make four depressions in the spinach mixture with the back of a large spoon. Break 1 egg into each depression. Season with additional salt and pepper, and cook until the eggs are set, covering the pan if necessary. Serves 4.

TOMATO OMELET

Avga me Ntomates

3 to 4 tablespoons olive oil, butter, or margarine
4 scallions, with green parts, sliced
5 ripe tomatoes, peeled and sliced
Salt and pepper to taste
1 teaspoon sugar
8 eggs, lightly beaten
Fresh parsley for garnish

Heat the oil in an omelet pan. Add the scallions and cook until soft. Layer the tomatoes over the scallions and sprinkle with salt, pepper, and sugar. Cover and simmer for 20 minutes, or until the tomatoes are tender. Pour the eggs over the tomatoes and cook for 4 minutes, then flip the omelet over and cook the bottom until the eggs are a golden chestnut color. Transfer to a warm platter, garnish with parsley, and serve hot. Serves 4–5.

OMELET WITH VEGETABLES

Omeleta me Hortarika

4 eggs
2 tablespoons *feta* cheese, crumbled
1 tablespoon minced parsley
4 tablespoons butter
1 (10-ounce) package frozen, thawed,
    well-drained artichoke hearts, with
    1 tablespoon finely chopped dill, or
1 (10-ounce) package frozen, thawed,
    well-drained asparagus, cut into
    1-inch pieces, or
2 medium potatoes, thinly sliced and
    fried, or
2 medium zucchini, cut into ½-inch-thick
    slices and fried in oil until lightly
    browned
Salt and pepper to taste

Though various vegetables may be used for this omelet, artichokes, asparagus, potatoes, and zucchini are among the traditional favorites.

Beat the eggs. Add the *feta* cheese and parsley. In a large frying pan, melt the butter. Add prepared vegetables and the beaten egg mixture. Sprinkle with salt and pepper. Cook for several minutes first on one side, then flip the omelet and cook on the other side. Serves 4–6.

POACHED EGGS WITH YOGURT

Tsilbiri

2 pints plain yogurt
8 poached eggs
¼ pound butter, melted and browned
Salt and pepper to taste

Bring yogurt to room temperature. Spoon ½ pint of the yogurt into each of 4 ramekins or soup bowls. Carefully place 2 poached eggs on top of yogurt. Spoon browned butter over all. Sprinkle with salt and pepper. Serve with garlic bread and a cooked vegetable. Serves 4.

RICE

(Lenten)

EGGPLANT AND RICE

Melitzana kai Rize

3 tablespoons vegetable oil
1 large onion, chopped
1 medium eggplant, peeled and cubed
1 large tomato, peeled, seeded, and
    chopped
¼ pound fresh mushrooms, sliced
1 teaspoon salt
1 bay leaf
½ teaspoon dried thyme
1 cup cooked rice

Heat the oil in a 10-inch skillet. Add the onions and sauté until wilted. Add the eggplant, tomato, mushrooms, salt, bay leaf, and thyme and sauté for 10 minutes, stirring occasionally. Stir in the rice and cook until heated through. Serve immediately. Serves 6.

BAKED EGGPLANT AND RICE CASSEROLE
Melitzana kai Rize sto Fourno

2 large eggplants
1 teaspoon salt
¼ cup vegetable or olive oil
3 cups finely minced onion
2 cloves garlic, minced
1 green pepper, seeded and cut into 1-
    inch cubes
1 teaspoon dried oregano
1 bay leaf
3 tomatoes, peeled, seeded, and chopped
1 cup raw rice
3¼ cups chicken broth
Salt and pepper to taste
½ cup grated *kefalotiri* cheese
2 tablespoons butter

Preheat oven to 400°F.

Slice unpeeled eggplants and cut into 1-inch cubes. Sprinkle with salt. Place in a colander, cover with a weighted plate, and let stand for 30 minutes. Heat oil in a heavy skillet. Carefully dry off eggplant pieces and add to the skillet. Cook over high heat, stirring occasionally, until lightly browned. Add the onion, garlic, green pepper, oregano, and bay leaf while stirring. Stir in the tomatoes and reduce the heat. Simmer for 5 minutes, or until most of the liquid has evaporated. Bring the chicken broth to a boil. Pour the vegetable mixture into a casserole and stir in the rice and boiling chicken broth. Season with salt and pepper. Sprinkle with cheese and dot with the butter. Bake, uncovered, for 30 minutes, or until the liquid is absorbed by the rice. Serves 8–10.

BAKED RICE
Rize sto Fourno

½ cup butter
1 large onion, chopped
¼ cup chopped green pepper
1 cup sliced mushrooms
1 cup rice
2 cups chicken broth
2 teaspoons salt or to taste
1 teaspoon pepper
Dash of dried thyme

Preheat oven to 350°F.

Melt ¼ cup butter in a 1-quart Dutch oven. Add the onion and sauté until wilted. Add the green pepper and mushrooms and sauté until tender. Remove mixture and set aside. In same pot melt the remaining butter. Add rice and brown slightly. Meanwhile, heat broth to the boiling point and add the salt. Stir the broth into the rice mixture. Add the reserved vegetables and season with pepper and thyme. Cover and bake for 30 to 40 minutes. Serves 4–5.

(Lenten)

RICE NISTISIMO
Nistisimo Rize

1 clove garlic, finely minced
4–5 sprigs of parsley, minced
½ cup oil
1 pound well-ripened tomatoes, peeled,
    seeded, and chopped, or 1 (1-
    pound) can tomatoes
1 cup water
1 cup rice
Salt and pepper to taste
Kalamata olives and parsley for garnish

In a heavy pot, sauté the garlic and parsley in the oil. Add the tomatoes and water and bring to a boil. Lower heat and simmer for 10 minutes. Add rice and stir. Cover and cook for 20 minutes, or until rice is done and water is absorbed. Season with salt and pepper and serve immediately. Garnish with *kalamata* olives and extra parsley, if desired. Serves 4.

LENTILS AND RICE PILAF

Fakorizo

1 cup lentils, picked over
5 cups chicken broth
1 cup rice or *orzo*
Salt to taste
1 medium onion, chopped
½ cup vegetable or olive oil
1 cup canned plum tomatoes, drained
    and chopped
Pepper to taste

Wash the lentils. Boil them in the chicken broth in a deep pot for 5 minutes. Add rice and salt and simmer until all liquid is absorbed, about 30 minutes. In the meantime, prepare the sauce by sautéing the onion in the oil for 3 minutes. Add the tomatoes and simmer for 10 minutes. As soon as the lentil-rice mixture is cooked, remove from the heat and add the sauce. Sprinkle with pepper. Serves 6.

Note: This may be served as a Lenten dish if plain water is substituted for the chicken broth.

(Lenten)

LIMA BEAN PILAF

Fasolia Pilafi

1 cup lima beans
5 tablespoons vegetable or olive oil
4 cups water
1 bay leaf
1 whole carrot
½ cup raw rice
½ teaspoon dried oregano
⅛ teaspoon sugar
Juice of ½ fresh lemon
Salt and pepper to taste

Rinse the lima beans in cold water. Put the beans in a large pot with 2 tablespoons of the oil, the water, bay leaf, and carrot. Bring to a boil and simmer for ½ hour. Remove bay leaf and carrot and discard. Add the rice, oregano, sugar, lemon, and salt and pepper. Bring to a boil, stirring with a fork a few times to prevent the rice from sticking. Lower the heat to a simmer and cook for 20 minutes, or until rice and beans are done. Heat 3 tablespoons oil to a sizzle and pour over the rice. Cover tightly. Remove from heat and let stand for 5 minutes before serving. (This dish may also be served cold.) Serves 4.

PILAF WITH ARTICHOKES

Pilafi me Anginares

4 tablespoons butter or margarine
1 medium onion, finely minced
1 tablespoon dried dill, or ½ cup fresh
    minced dill
2 (10-ounce) packages frozen artichokes,
    thawed
2 cups converted rice
5 cups chicken broth
1 (8-ounce) can tomato sauce
¼ pound butter
Salt and pepper to taste

Melt the 4 tablespoons butter in a deep pot. Add the onion, dill, and artichokes and brown. Add the rice and allow to brown for 2 minutes. In a saucepan bring the chicken broth and tomato sauce to a boil and add to the rice and artichokes. Cover and simmer over low heat for 20 minutes, or until all water is absorbed. Brown the ¼ pound butter, pour over the rice mixture and season with salt and pepper. Stir to blend. Remove from the heat and let stand for 5 minutes before serving. Serves 8–10.

RICE PILAF WITH NOODLES

Pilafi me Hilopetes

4 tablespoons butter
1 cup thin noodles
1 cup raw rice
2½ cups chicken broth
½ teaspoon salt

Melt 2 tablespoons butter in a heavy pot. Add the noodles and sauté over medium heat for 3 minutes, or until they turn golden brown. Remove noodles and set aside. Melt the remaining butter in the same pot. Add the rice and sauté until it turns a pale yellow color. In a saucepan bring the broth to a boil and add it to the rice along with the salt and the sautéed noodles. Stir, cover, and simmer over medium heat without stirring for 20 to 25 minutes, or until rice has absorbed all the liquid. Remove from the heat, uncover, and place a linen towel over the pot. Replace the cover and let stand for 5 minutes before serving. (If desired additional butter may be browned and poured over the rice just before serving.) Serves 4.

PILAF WITH CREAM SAUCE *AVGOLEMONO*

Pilafi me Aspri Saltsa Avgolemono

10 cups chicken broth or water
4 cups converted rice
1 cup butter
¼ cup flour
1 cup milk
3 egg yolks
Juice of 1 lemon
½ pound *kefalotiri* or Parmesan cheese, grated

Put 9 cups of the broth into a large pot and bring to a boil. Add the rice and stir with a fork. Cover and cook until the rice is fluffy and soft, about 20 minutes. Heat the remaining cup of broth. As the rice cooks, melt ¼ cup butter in a saucepan. Add the flour and blend well. Slowly add the remaining cup of hot broth and the milk. Cook over low heat until the sauce thickens, stirring constantly to prevent lumping or burning. Remove from the heat. Beat the egg yolks with the lemon juice and slowly add to the sauce, stirring constantly. Return the sauce to the heat, continuing to stir until thickened. Remove from the heat. Add the remaining butter and half the cheese. Pack the rice into a 10-cup mold and turn out on a platter. Pour the sauce over the rice. Sprinkle the remaining cheese over it. Serve hot. Serves 15–20.

Note: This recipe may be successfully halved. Use 2 egg yolks.

(Lenten)

RICE WITH CHESTNUTS

Rize me Kastana

1 cup converted rice
4 tablespoons vegetable or olive oil
½ cup chestnuts, shelled and broken into
    small pieces (see page 175 for
    Preparation of Chestnuts)
½ cup chopped seedless raisins
½ teaspoon fennel seeds
Salt and pepper to taste
2½ cups hot water
Lemon juice to taste (optional), or 1 cup
    plain yogurt (optional)

In a wide, heavy-bottomed pot, sauté the rice in the oil until it turns golden. Add the chestnuts, raisins, fennel seeds, and salt and pepper. Add 2½ cups water and bring to a boil. Stir a few times to prevent rice from sticking, cover pot, and simmer over low heat for 20 minutes, or until rice is tender. Remove from heat and let stand for 5 minutes before serving. Serve hot with lemon juice, or cold, smothered in yogurt. Serves 4–6.

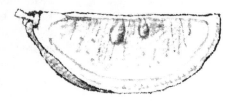

(Lenten)

SPINACH WITH RICE

Spanakorizo

2 pounds fresh spinach, or 2 (10-ounce)
    packages frozen spinach, thawed
¾ cup oil
1 large onion, finely minced
4–5 sprigs dill, or 1 teaspoon dried dill
2 tablespoons tomato paste
2½ cups water
Salt and pepper to taste
1 cup converted rice
Lemon wedges

A popular saying when preparing this dish is *To spanaki me to rize ti orea pou mirizi*, which means "How wonderful spinach with rice smells."

Wash the spinach well and drain in a colander; if frozen, thaw. Heat the oil in a heavy pot and sauté the onion until wilted. Add the dill and spinach and sauté for 5 minutes. Add the tomato paste diluted in the water and season with salt and pepper. Bring to a boil, add the rice, stir, cover, and cook for 20 minutes, or until rice is done and water is absorbed. Serve with lemon wedges and additional pepper. Serve 4–6.

TIPSY RICE

Methesmeno Rize

↝ CORFU

1 cup water or meat stock
1½ cups port wine
1 teaspoon salt
1 cup converted rice
1 tablespoon dried oregano
2 tablespoons butter

Combine the water, wine, and salt in a saucepan. Bring to a boil and add the rice. Cover and boil gently for 18 minutes. Add the oregano and butter and mix well. Serves 4.

PASTA

(Lenten)

CABBAGE, CELERY, AND NOODLES CASSEROLE
Lahano me Fide

½–¾ cup vegetable oil
2 large onions, finely minced
1 small head of cabbage, sliced thin
(about ¼-inch thick slices)
8–10 ribs celery, cut in 1-inch pieces
1 (8-ounce) can tomato sauce
1 tablespoon tomato paste
Salt and pepper to taste
¼ pound extra-fine noodles or *orzo*
½ cup *kefalotiri* cheese (optional)

Heat the oil in a 5-quart Dutch oven and sauté the onions, cabbage, and celery until lightly browned or limp. Add the tomato sauce and tomato paste (if mixture seems too thick add a little water) and simmer over medium heat until the vegetables are almost cooked, adding more water if necessary. Add salt and pepper. Add noodles and simmer until noodles are cooked. (This casserole may be sprinkled with grated *kefalotiri* cheese. If cheese is used, however, this ceases to be a Lenten dish.) Serves 6–8.

ORZO AND RICE PILAF
Kritharaki me Rize

 KITHIRA

2 tablespoons butter or margarine
⅔ cups rice
½ cup *orzo*
3 cups chicken broth
Grated *kefalotiri* cheese or Eggplant-
Tomato Sauce (optional, see below)

In a medium saucepan melt the butter and lightly brown the *orzo* and the rice. Bring the broth to a boil and add to the rice-*orzo* combination. Cover tightly and simmer for 20 minutes, or until all the liquid is absorbed. Serve with grated cheese and/or tomato sauce, if desired. Serves 4–5.

Variation: Preheat oven to 350°F. Proceed as above but bake for 30 minutes, or until all liquid is absorbed.

EGGPLANT-TOMATO SAUCE
Saltsa me Melitzana

¼ cup butter or margarine
1 clove garlic, crushed
½ cup chopped onion
2 cups finely chopped eggplant
1 (8-ounce) can tomato sauce
½ teaspoon dried oregano
¼ teaspoon salt
1 teaspoon sugar
½ cup water (or more if sauce seems too
thick)

Melt the butter in a medium saucepan, and sauté the garlic, onion, and eggplant for 5 minutes, or until tender. Add the tomato sauce, oregano, salt, sugar, and water. Simmer, uncovered, for 20 minutes, stirring frequently. YIELD: 2 cups.

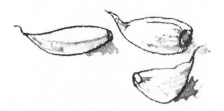

(Lenten)

ZUCCHINI WITH *ORZO*

Kolokithakia me Kritharaki

4–5 medium zucchini, scrubbed,
    trimmed, and diced
¼ cup vegetable or olive oil
1½ cups boiling water
⅛ cup *orzo*
Salt and pepper to taste
½ teaspoon oregano

In a large heavy pot sauté the zucchini in the oil until brown. Put the *orzo* in boiling water and simmer until tender, about 15 minutes. Stir a few times to prevent sticking. Drain. Add the *orzo* to the zucchini, and season with salt, pepper, and oregano. Cover and cook over low heat for 10 minutes. Shake the pot a few times to prevent mixture from becoming lumpy. Do not stir in order to avoid mashing zucchini. Serve hot or cold. Serves 4–6.

SPAGHETTI WITH BROWNED BUTTER SAUCE

Makaronia me Kavourdismeno Voutero

1 pound spaghetti (#8 or #9), or 1
    pound macaroni
½ cup butter
½ cup grated *kefalotiri* cheese

Cook spaghetti according to package directions and drain well. Meanwhile, melt the butter in a small frying pan. Add 2 or 3 tablespoons of grated cheese to the butter and allow both the butter and the cheese to brown lightly, stirring all the while. Put the drained spaghetti into a serving bowl. Sprinkle with the remaining grated cheese and keep tossing so that the cheese penetrates throughout. When the butter and cheese mixture is lightly browned, pour over the spaghetti. Serves 4–5.

MACARONI WITH SPINACH

Makaronia kai Spanaki Gouvetsi

1 pound ground beef
½ cup chopped onion
1 clove garlic
2 tablespoons butter
1 teaspoon salt
Pepper to taste
Dash of ground allspice
1 (8-ounce) can tomato sauce
2 tablespoons tomato paste
1 cup water
½ pound macaroni
4 tablespoons melted butter
2 (10-ounce) packages frozen chopped
    spinach, thawed and drained
¾ cup *feta* cheese, crumbled
¼ cup milk
2 eggs
1 cup grated *kefalotiri* cheese
1 tablespoon grated onion
¼ cup bread crumbs

Preheat oven to 350°F.

Brown the meat, onion, and garlic in 2 tablespoons butter. Add 1 teaspoon salt, a dash of pepper and allspice, tomato sauce, tomato paste, and water. Simmer until thickened, about 30 minutes. Cook macaroni according to package directions, drain well, and toss with 4 tablespoons of melted butter. Grease an 8- x 12-inch casserole. Put half the macaroni in the casserole and spread the spinach on top. Sprinkle crumbled *feta* over the spinach, add remaining macaroni, and top with the meat sauce. Combine ¼ cup milk, the 2 eggs, grated cheese and grated onion, mix well and pour over meat sauce. Sprinkle bread crumbs on top and bake for 30 minutes. Let stand at room temperature for 10 minutes before cutting. Serves 6–8.

BAKED MACARONI WITH *FETA*

Makaronia me Feta

1 pound ziti macaroni
1 pound *feta* cheese
6 eggs
1 quart milk
2 tablespoons minced onion
6 tablespoons grated *kefalotiri* cheese

Preheat oven to 350°F.

Cook ziti according to package directions and drain well. Mash the *feta* cheese. Separate the eggs and beat the egg whites until frothy. Beat the egg yolks until creamy. Fold the yolks into the whites, and add the *feta* cheese, milk, and the onions. Spread the macaroni in a buttered 10- x 14-inch pan. Pour the egg mixture over the macaroni and sprinkle the cheese over the mixture. Bake for 1 hour. Serves 4–6.

MACARONI WITH *FETA*

Makaronia me Feta

½ cup bread crumbs
½ cup grated *kefalotiri* cheese
½ pound macaroni, cooked and drained
¼ cup butter, melted
½ pound *feta* cheese, crumbled
2 cups milk
4 eggs, well beaten

Preheat oven to 350°F.

Grease a 10-inch square pan with butter. Sprinkle the pan with half the bread crumbs and half the grated cheese. Combine the macaroni with the melted butter and crumbled *feta*. Pour into the pan and sprinkle with the remaining bread crumbs. Combine the milk with the eggs and pour over the macaroni mixture. Sprinkle with remaining grated cheese. Bake for 30 minutes, or until brown. Serves 4–5.

HOW TO MAKE *FETA* CHEESE

Traditional *feta* is made of sheep's milk, though goat's (and, rarely, cow's milk) is also used. The second most important ingredient is cheese yeast, obtainable in food specialty shops, health food stores and some gourmet shops. It is essential that you follow the instructions that appear on the package of cheese yeast.

Boil the milk until it reaches 150°F., and allow it to cool to 90°F. For every 20 quarts of milk, add ¼ tablet of yeast (diluted in water according to package instructions). Stir thoroughly over low heat until the milk thickens, about 45 minutes. Cut into 1-inch cubes and stir again with a ladle. Allow to settle off heat for about 20 minutes and transfer to cheese strainers.

Leave cheese in strainers for at least 12 hours, or until thoroughly drained, at which point you begin the salting process. Sprinkle the cheese with salt every 24 hours for 4 days, turning cheese over after each salting. Total amount of salt used should equal about 2 percent of the weight of the cheese.

Take the cheese out of the strainers and place in large pots and cover with light brine. Let cheese stand in a cool place (about 60°F.) for about 16 days before using.

THE CHEESES OF GREECE

Many Greeks consider a meal incomplete without a slab of cheese and a piece of crusty homemade bread. The following is a list of some of the more popular Greek cheeses, all of which are now available in this country.

ANTHOTYRO: A soft (though firmer than cream cheese), white, goat's milk cheese, with a mild, sweet taste.

FETA: The most widely known of Greek cheeses, *feta* is made of a combination of sheep's and goat's milk. Pure white, crumbly, and salty, it is excellent in salads and in a wide variety of baked dishes. To keep it moist, *feta* should be stored in brine or tightly wrapped in plastic wrap.

GRAVIERA (or Kefalograviera): A mild, Gruyére-type cheese made of sheep's or cow's milk. A good all-purpose cheese with a particularly delicious flavor.

HALOUMI: A semi-soft cheese, similar to mozzarella but quite salty. Good as a snack with crackers.

KASSERI: A mild, creamy cheese made of sheep's or goat's whole milk. Suitable for baking, *kasseri* is also a good after-dinner accompaniment for fruit.

KEFALOTIRI: A light yellow, very hard cheese made of sheep's or goat's milk, salty *kefalotiri* is widely used in Greek cuisine. It is especially suited for grating.

MANOURI: This soft, unsalted sheep's and goat's milk cheese closely resembles soft *mizithra* (see below) and its Italian counterpart, ricotta, and can be used interchangeably with both.

MIZITHRA: Comes in two types: the first is soft, unsalted, and resembles ricotta *manouri*. The second type is lightly salted and semi-hard. Mildly flavored, this type is a delicious accompaniment for fruits.

TOULOUMOTYRI: A semi-hard, flaky white cheese, prepared and aged in animal hides. Similar to *feta*, but less salty, *touloumotyri* is excellent with fruit, especially grapes.

Vegetables

In a land where the private vegetable and herb garden is a common sight, it is no surprise that vegetable dishes hold pride of place on the Greek menu. Though eggplant and artichokes are probably the vegetables most associated with Greece, cabbage, squash, cauliflower, fresh peas, string beans, and tomatoes are also standard fare (it is almost redundant to say "fresh" peas, since processed foods have made few inroads in Greece . . . as yet). In the legume family, lentils, chick-peas, fava beans, and white beans are commonly, and inventively, used throughout Greece.

Perhaps one of the reasons for the importance of vegetables in the Greek diet is the strict observance of Lent among the majority of Greeks. During the 40-day period of abstinence from meat and animal protein, religious Greeks must rely (without too much hardship, mind you) on such tempting fare as Cauliflower *Stifado*, *Dolmades* with Eggplant, and Artichokes with Lima Beans, to name only a few.

ARTICHOKES BÉCHAMEL
Anginares Béchamel

8–10 whole, fresh artichokes
2 or more lemons, as needed
1 recipe Béchamel Sauce (see following)
½ pound *feta* cheese
1 cup chopped cooked ham or chicken
1 cup grated *kefalotiri* or Parmesan
  cheese
⅓ cup melted butter
2–3 tablespoons toasted bread crumbs

Preheat oven to 350°F.

Prepare artichokes by breaking off the outer three layers of leaves. Slice 1 inch off the tips of the remaining leaves and snap off the stem. Rinse in cold water and rub cut surfaces with a lemon half. To prevent darkening, drop prepared artichokes in a bowl of cold water acidulated with the juice of 1 lemon until ready to use. When all the artichokes are prepared, put in a large kettle, add salted water to cover, and boil for 45 minutes, or until you can pull off a leaf easily. Remove artichokes from the kettle with tongs and drain upside down in a colander. When cool, spread leaves apart and remove thistly choke.

Prepare a Béchamel Sauce according to directions given below.

Break up the *feta* cheese and mix it with the meat in a mixing bowl. Add ½ cup of Béchamel Sauce and mix well. Sprinkle the mixture with half of the *kefalotiri* cheese and mix well. Line up the artichokes in rows in a buttered baking pan. Drizzle some of the melted butter over them. Fill with the meat and cheese mixture. Cover the tops with the remaining Béchamel, then sprinkle with the rest of the *kefalotiri*. Top with the bread crumbs, drizzle on the melted butter, and bake for 20 minutes, or until the cheese and sauce take on a golden color. Serves 4–5 or 8–10, depending upon the size of the artichokes.

BÉCHAMEL SAUCE

8 tablespoons butter
10 tablespoons flour
4 cups hot milk
2 egg yolks, lightly beaten
Salt and pepper to taste

Melt the butter in a saucepan and slowly add the flour. Blend well, over a low flame. Add the hot milk, stirring it in rapidly with a clean wooden spoon until the sauce thickens. Remove the sauce from the heat and add egg yolks and salt, and pepper. Stir to blend.

ARTICHOKES WITH *KEFALOTIRI* SAUCE
Anginares me Kefalotiri

Coarse salt
Juice of 1 lemon
8–10 small artichokes, prepared for
    cooking (see page 11 for
    Preparation of Fresh Artichokes), or
    2 (10-ounce) packages frozen
    artichoke hearts
½ cup melted butter
Salt and pepper to taste
1 recipe Béchamel Sauce°
2 cups grated *kefalotiri* cheese
3–4 tablespoons toasted bread crumbs

Preheat oven to 350°F.

Add coarse salt to taste and the lemon juice to a large kettle of water. Bring to a boil. Add artichoke hearts and boil for 35 to 45 minutes, if fresh, or according to package directions, if frozen. Remove artichokes with a slotted spoon and cut into cubes. Pour half the melted butter over the artichokes and season with salt and pepper. Prepare the Béchamel Sauce. Butter a small 9- x 7-inch pan. Spread a thin layer of the sauce in it and sprinkle with about one-third of the cheese. Spread the artichokes evenly on top and sprinkle additional cheese over them. Pour the remaining Béchamel Sauce over all, and top with the remaining cheese and the bread crumbs. Drizzle the remaining butter over the bread crumbs. Bake for 20 minutes, or until golden brown. Serves 6.

(Lenten)

BRAISED ARTICHOKES
Anginares Laderes I

2 (10-ounce) packages frozen artichoke
    hearts
4 scallions, chopped
1 tablespoon minced fresh dill, or ½
    tablespoon dried dill
¼ cup vegetable or olive oil
¼ teaspoon salt
⅛ teaspoon pepper
1 cup water
1 tablespoon lemon juice

Thaw the artichokes and drain any excess liquid. Sauté the scallions and dill in the oil. Add the artichokes and sauté for 3 minutes. Add salt, pepper, water, and lemon juice and simmer for 20 to 25 minutes, or until liquid is absorbed. Serves 6–8.

Note: This recipe may be served with an *Avgolemono* Sauce (see Index), made with 1 cup of artichoke cooking liquid. The use of *Avgolemono* makes this a non-Lenten dish.

(Lenten)

ARTICHOKES WITH LIMA BEANS

Anginares Laderes II

½ pound onions, chopped
½ pound small white onions, peeled, or medium onions, peeled and cut in half
2–3 carrots, trimmed, scraped, and cut into thin rounds
1 cup cooked lima beans
1 can artichokes in brine (8–10 artichokes)
½ cup vegetable or olive oil
1 cup water
Salt and pepper to taste
Juice of 2 lemons
1½ tablespoons flour, diluted in ½ cup water
⅓ cup minced dill or parsley
Dash of dried oregano

Spread all of the onions on the bottom of a large pot. Add the carrots and lima beans. Put the artichokes on top. Add the oil, water, salt and pepper, lemon juice, and flour-water paste. Sprinkle with dill and oregano. Cover the pot with a piece of aluminum foil and pierce a hole in the center. Place the cover on the pot and cook over moderate heat for 45 minutes. This dish is best served cold. Serves 4.

(Lenten)

BLACK-EYED BEANS WITH FENNEL

Mavromatika Fasolia

1 cup black-eyed beans
4 cups cold water
7 tablespoons vegetable or olive oil
1 small onion, finely minced
1 small green pepper, chopped finely
1 small potato, diced
1 large bunch fresh fennel
1 tablespoon honey
1 tablespoon wine vinegar
Salt and pepper to taste

Wash the beans in cold water and drain. Put them in a large pot with 4 cups cold water and 3 tablespoons oil. Slowly bring to a boil and simmer until beans begin to get soft, about 30 minutes. In a skillet, heat 2 tablespoons oil and sauté the onion, green pepper, and potato. Add to the beans and continue simmering until beans begin to crack. Wash the fennel in cold water and chop it. Add to the beans along with the honey, wine vinegar, and salt and pepper. Simmer until fennel is soft but not mushy, about 12 minutes. Remove from heat and add remaining oil. Serve hot or cold with olives and *feta* cheese. Serves 4–6.

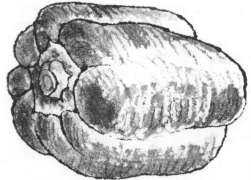

(Lenten)

BLACK-EYED BEANS WITH GARLIC SAUCE

Mavromatika Fassolia me Skordalia

1 cup black-eyed beans
4 cups cold water
2 bay leaves
1 stalk celery
1 carrot, scraped
1 tablespoon honey
4 tablespoons vegetable or olive oil
Salt and pepper to taste
1 recipe Garlic Sauce *(Skordalia)*°
Chopped parsley for garnish

Wash the beans in cold water and drain. Put them in a pot with 4 cups cold water, the bay leaves, celery, carrot, honey, and 3 tablespoons of the oil. Slowly bring to a boil. Boil about 10 minutes, then simmer until beans begin to crack, about 20 minutes. Remove bay leaves, celery, and carrot from the beans. Add remaining oil and salt and pepper to the beans. Simmer a few minutes more; there should be almost no liquid. Serve hot or cold, garnished with plenty of Garlic Sauce and chopped parsley. Serves 4–6.

(Lenten)

FAVA BEAN STEW

Koukia Yiahní

½ cup vegetable or olive oil
2 medium onions, chopped
3 stalks celery with leaves, chopped
2 cloves garlic, minced
1 (8-ounce) can tomato sauce
½ cup water
½ cup wine
1 (20-ounce) can fava beans
Salt and pepper to taste

In a large pot, heat the oil and sauté the onions and celery until wilted. Add the garlic and sauté for 2 minutes. Add the tomato sauce, water, and wine and simmer for 5 to 10 minutes. Wash and drain fava beans and add to mixture with salt and pepper. Simmer for 5 minutes. Serves 4.

(Lenten)

BRAISED CAULIFLOWER

⚓ PATMOS

Kounoupithi Kapama

1 large head cauliflower (approximately
   4 pounds)
Juice of 2 lemons
1 cup olive oil
1 medium onion, chopped
1 tablespoon tomato paste
1 cup water
Salt and pepper to taste

Wash the cauliflower and break into flowerets. Place on a platter and sprinkle with lemon juice. Heat the oil in a frying pan and fry the cauliflower, a few pieces at a time. Carefully transfer these to a large pot. Gently sauté the onions in the same frying pan. Add the tomato paste, 1 cup water, and salt and pepper. Stir and bring to a boil. Cook for 3 minutes. Pour the sauce over the cauliflower and bring to a boil over medium heat. Cook for 30 minutes, or until all the liquid except the oil has been absorbed. Serves 6–8.

(Lenten)

CAULIFLOWER *STIFADO*
Kounoupithi Stifado

3 small heads cauliflower
1¼ cups oil
12 small white onions, peeled
3 cloves garlic, peeled and cut in half
    lengthwise
1 tablespoon tomato paste, diluted with 2
    cups water
½ cup vinegar
½ tablespoon dried rosemary
1 bay leaf
6 peppercorns

Wash the cauliflower and break it into flowerets. Heat the oil in a pot and lightly brown the whole onions. Add the garlic and cook until golden. Add the diluted tomato paste, vinegar, rosemary, and bay leaf and cook for 30 minutes. Bring a large pot of salted water to a boil. Add the cauliflower and cook for 5 minutes. Drain and add the cauliflower to the sauce. (Add a little water if necessary.) Add the peppercorns. Cover and simmer for 30 to 45 minutes, or until all the liquid, except the oil, has been absorbed. Serves 6–8.

CELERY WITH *AVGOLEMONO* SAUCE
Selino Avgolemono

1 large onion, chopped
¼ cup butter
1 head celery (2 pounds)
2 cups chicken stock
Salt and pepper to taste
2 egg yolks
Juice of 1 lemon

In a large saucepan sauté the onion in butter until golden brown. Wash the celery, remove strings, and cut into 2-inch lengths. Add to the onion with the chicken stock and salt and pepper. Simmer for 30 minutes. Beat the egg yolks and add the lemon juice. Slowly add some of the hot stock to the yolks while beating. Stir into the remaining stock, cover, remove from heat, and let stand for 5 minutes. Serves 6.

Note: Chicory, escarole, or leeks may be substituted for the celery. The cooking time, however, should be reduced to 15 to 20 minutes. Any combination of the above is also delicious.

CREAMY EGGPLANT CUSTARD

Melitzana Galatopeta

1 large eggplant (about 1¼–1½ pounds)
4 eggs
1 cup light cream (or half-and-half)
2 tablespoons butter
½ teaspoon salt
⅛ teaspoon pepper
¼ teaspoon minced fresh dill
¼ cup finely minced parsley

Preheat oven to 325°F.

Peel the eggplant and cut it into 1-inch cubes. Bring 1½ inches salted water to a boil in a 4-quart saucepan. Add the eggplant, cover, and cook for 8 minutes, or until tender, stirring occasionally. Drain well. Turn eggplant into a large bowl and whip until smooth. Add the eggs, cream, butter, salt, pepper, dill, and parsley and beat until light and fluffy. Pour the mixture into a greased, shallow, 1½-quart baking dish. Bake, uncovered, for about 35 minutes, or until set. Serve immediately. Serves 6.

EGGPLANT PIE

Melitzanopitta

1 large or 2 medium eggplants (2 pounds total)
½ cup oil
1 medium onion, chopped
1 green pepper, chopped
3 tablespoons butter
1 (1-pound) can plum tomatoes
Salt and pepper to taste
1 recipe Béchamel Sauce°
1 pound *feta* cheese, crumbled
4 eggs, beaten
½ pound *phyllo* pastry
½ cup melted butter for brushing *phyllo*
Oil for frying

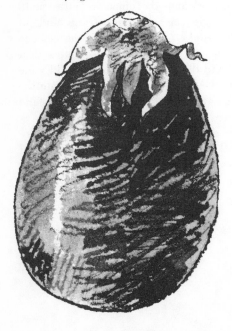

Preheat oven to 350°F.

Cut eggplant into slices. Sprinkle with salt and place in a colander to drain. Heat oil in a large skillet and fry eggplant slices a few at a time; drain on paper towels. (If you prefer, lightly oil each slice and brown under a preheated broiler, taking care not to burn the eggplants.) In a large saucepan, brown the onion and green pepper in the 3 tablespoons butter. Add the tomatoes and salt and pepper. Simmer for 20 to 25 minutes. Prepare Béchamel Sauce. Add one half of the *feta* cheese and the beaten eggs to the Béchamel Sauce. Brush a sheet of *phyllo* with melted butter and place in a 9- x 12-inch baking pan (keep remaining *phyllo* covered with plastic wrap). Repeat with 7 additional sheets. (Read How to Work with *Phyllo*, see Index.) Spread half of the eggplant slices over the *phyllo*. Sprinkle with the remaining *feta* cheese and spread with half of the Béchamel Sauce. Top with half of the onion-tomato sauce. Add the remaining eggplant slices and top with Béchamel Sauce and onion-tomato sauce. Cover with the remaining *phyllo* sheets, individually brushed with butter as before. Score the top lightly with a sharp pointed knife into serving-size pieces. Bake for 30 to 35 minutes. YIELD: 32 appetizer-sized pieces or 20 entree-sized pieces.

Note: Zucchini (or a mixture of zucchini and eggplant) may be substituted for eggplant.

(Lenten)

DOLMADES WITH EGGPLANT

Dolmadakia me Melitzana

1 medium eggplant
⅔ cup vegetable or olive oil
1 medium onion, chopped
2 tablespoons lemon juice
1½ teaspoons dried oregano
1 teaspoon dried dill, or ¼ cup minced
    fresh dill
2 cloves garlic, minced
1 teaspoon salt
1 teaspoon pepper
1½ cups water
3 cups cooked rice
1 (8-ounce) jar grape leaves
½ teaspoon basil
1 (1-pound) can peeled tomatoes

Here is a popular islander dish that is frequently served during the Lenten period.

Peel the eggplant and chop it finely. Heat ⅓ cup oil in a skillet. Add the onion, eggplant, lemon juice, oregano, dill, and garlic. Season with salt and pepper and add the water. Simmer, covered, until the eggplant is tender and the water is almost completely absorbed. Turn off the heat and stir in the cooked rice. Rinse the grape leaves with cold water. Place a spoonful of filling in the center of each leaf; fold in the sides and then roll (see page 38 for fuller directions). Line a deep pot with small or broken grape leaves and place the rolled *Dolmades* on the leaves in one layer. Mix basil and tomatoes together and pour half over the *Dolmades*. Make another layer of rolled grape leaves. Pour the remaining tomatoes and ⅓ cup oil over the top. Cover with a weighted plate and cook over low heat for 1 hour. Serves 6.

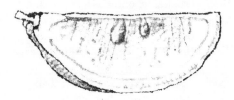

LEEK PIE

Prasopitta

10 medium-size leeks
½ cup butter or margarine
1 tablespoon minced fresh dill
Salt and pepper to taste
2 cups crushed tomatoes
¼ cup white wine
4 eggs
1 pound *mizithra* or ricotta cheese
20 sheets *phyllo* pastry
½ cup melted butter for brushing *phyllo*

Preheat oven to 375°F.

Prepare the leeks by cutting off roots and coarse tops; wash well to remove grit and peel off any yellowed or bruised outer layers. Cut into 1-inch-thick slices. In a large frying pan, melt the butter, add the leeks, dill, and salt and pepper and sauté lightly. Add the tomatoes and wine and simmer until all the liquid has been absorbed. Let cool. Beat the eggs and add the *mizithra* cheese and mix well. Add to the cooled leeks. Line a 9- x 13- x 2-inch pan with 8 individually buttered sheets of *phyllo*. (Read How to Work with *Phyllo*, see Index.) Add the leek mixture and cover with 12 buttered sheets of *phyllo*. With a sharp knife score the top layers of *phyllo* into squares and bake for 30 to 40 minutes. When pie cools, cut all the way through the squares and serve warm. YIELD: 24 pieces.

MOLDED SPINACH PIE

Spanakopita se Forma

1 bunch scallions, chopped
2 tablespoons butter
2 pounds fresh spinach, picked over,
    washed, and drained
6 eggs, lightly beaten
½ pound *feta* cheese, crumbled
8 ounces cottage cheese
2 tablespoons farina
½ cup minced parsley
½ cup fresh snipped dill, or 1 tablespoon
    dried dill
Salt and pepper to taste
1 pound *phyllo* pastry
1 cup melted butter for brushing *phyllo*

Preheat oven to 375°F.

Sauté the scallions in 2 tablespoons butter until tender. Chop the spinach and place in a large saucepan. Cover and cook until wilted, about 15 minutes. Drain, pressing out as much moisture as possible. Mix together the scallions, eggs, *feta*, cottage cheese, farina, parsley, dill, and spinach. Season lightly with salt and pepper. Butter a 2-quart decorated ring mold. Unfold the *phyllo* and place under a damp towel or plastic wrap to keep it from drying out. Remove one sheet of pastry at a time, brush with melted butter, and begin lining the mold with the *phyllo* (1½ inches of pastry should hang over the outer edge of the mold). Continue fitting *phyllo* sheets into the mold, turning it as you go in order to make even layers. (The sheets will overlap in the center hole of the mold.) Use about 20 sheets of *phyllo*. Fill the mold with the spinach mixture. Draw up the overhanging outer edges of the *phyllo* pastry over filling. Arrange the remaining sheets of *phyllo*, buttered one at a time, to completely cover the filling; cut out and discard the pastry over the center hole of the mold.

Put the mold on a cookie sheet to catch the butter dripping. Place in the oven and lower the temperature to 350°F. Bake for 1¼ hours, or until golden brown and puffed. Let stand in the mold for 5 to 15 minutes before unmolding onto a warm platter. YIELD: 12–16 pieces.

Note: If when unmolded the crust is not crisp and golden brown, return to oven to brown the top. This dish may be frozen, unbaked. To serve, bake without prior thawing, for about 1¾ hours, or until golden brown and puffed.

SPINACH AND EGGPLANT SOUFFLÉ

Melitzana kai Spanaki Sfougato

2 medium eggplants
1 cup boiling water
10 egg whites
Butter or margarine
½ pound fresh spinach
½ cup butter
1 cup unsifted all-purpose flour
2 cups milk
8 egg yolks
1 cup grated *kefalotiri* cheese
½ cup grated *kasseri* cheese
1 tablespoon minced parsley
2 teaspoons powdered mustard
1¼ teaspoons salt
Dash of pepper
1 recipe Eggplant-Tomato Sauce°

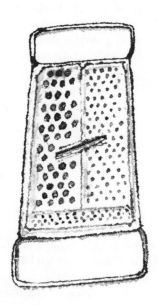

Preheat oven to 350°F.

Wash eggplants and halve lengthwise. Make several gashes in the flesh on cut sides but do not cut skins. Place, cut side down, in a single layer in a large roasting pan. Add 1 cup boiling water. Bake, uncovered, for 30 minutes, or until tender, but not mushy. Meanwhile, in the large bowl of an electric mixer, let egg whites warm to room temperature, about 1 hour. Cool the eggplants on a wire rack. With a large spoon, scoop pulp from the eggplants, leaving a ¼-inch-thick shell. Reserve pulp for sauce. Cut shells in half lengthwise. Butter a 2-quart soufflé dish (8 inches in diameter). Line the bottom and sides of the dish with eggplant shells. Make a collar around the dish by folding a 26-inch length of wax paper or foil lengthwise in thirds. Lightly butter one side. Wrap around the soufflé dish to form a 2-inch collar above the rim. Tie securely with string. Wash and dry spinach, remove stems and discard. Chop spinach coarsely (there should be about 1 cup). In a medium saucepan, melt ½ cup butter and stir in flour until smooth. Gradually stir in the milk. Cook, stirring, over medium heat until the mixture thickens. In large bowl, beat the egg yolks with a wire whisk. Gradually beat the Béchamel Sauce into the egg yolks. Beat in the spinach, both cheeses, parsley, mustard, and salt and pepper until well combined. Set aside. Beat egg whites at high speed just until stiff peaks form when beater is slowly raised. Gently fold spinach mixture into egg whites just until well combined. Turn into eggplant-lined soufflé dish. Bake for 65 to 70 minutes, or until puffed and golden. Serve at once, right from dish, with Eggplant-Tomato Sauce. Or let cool several minutes and invert onto a serving dish. Serves 6–8.

Note: Eggplant shell, Eggplant-Tomato Sauce, and spinach mixture may be prepared 1 day in advance. Combine spinach mixture with egg whites just before baking.

SQUASH PIE

Kolokithopita

3 pounds small zucchini
¾ pound *feta* cheese
½ cup butter
Salt and pepper to taste
5 eggs
2 tablespoons minced parsley
2 tablespoons minced dill
½ cup toasted bread crumbs
½ cup milk
¾ pound *phyllo* pastry
½ cup melted butter for brushing *phyllo*

Preheat oven to 300°F.

Clean and scrape the squash. Grate it coarsely and put in a colander to drain for 1 hour. Cut or crumble the cheese into pieces about the size of peas. Brown ½ cup of the butter in a large pot. Add the squash and toss a few times (they should not brown). Add salt and pepper and remove from heat. Beat the eggs in a bowl. Add the cheese, parsley, dill, bread crumbs, and milk. Season with salt and pepper and mix well. Pour into the pot with the squash and mix again. Butter a 9- x 12- x 2-inch baking pan. Brush half the *phyllo* with melted butter one sheet at a time (keep remainder covered in plastic wrap to keep from drying out) and overlap in the baking pan so that bottom and sides are completely covered and 2 inches of pastry extend beyond the rim of the pan all around. (Read How to Work with *Phyllo*, see Index.) Pour the squash mixture into the pan and spread evenly. Fold the overhanging *phyllo* up over the squash and brush well with melted butter. Lay the remaining *phyllo* sheets on top, again brushing with butter one sheet at a time. Butter the top very well. Score top layers of *phyllo*, and bake for 1 hour. Cool and cut into serving pieces. Serves 6–8.

(Lenten)

SWISS CHARD AND RICE CASSEROLE

Sescoula me Rizi

2 pounds Swiss chard
½ cup vegetable oil
2 large onions, chopped
Salt and pepper to taste
1 (8-ounce) can tomato sauce
1 cup water
1 cup raw rice
1 teaspoon crushed mint

After washing Swiss chard throughly, cut into 2-inch pieces and allow to drain in a colander. Meanwhile, heat the oil in a large saucepan, and add the onion and salt and pepper and sauté until onion is wilted. Add tomato sauce, cover, and simmer for 5 minutes. Add water, chard, rice, and mint. Cover and simmer over medium heat for 20 minutes, sitrring frequently. Taste for salt and pepper. This casserole may be served as a Lenten main dish or as a side dish. Serves 4–6.

TOMATOES STUFFED WITH EGGPLANT

Ntomates Gemistes me Melitzana

12–15 tomatoes
Salt and pepper to taste
2 medium eggplant, cubed
1 cup flour
½ cup vegetable oil
½ cup raw rice
½ cup bread crumbs
½ cup *feta* cheese, cut into chunks
4 tablespoons minced parley
4 teaspoons minced onion
3 hard-cooked eggs, sliced

Preheat oven to 350°F.

Wash the tomatoes. Cut off and reserve the tops. Scoop out pulp and reserve. Salt and pepper the tomatoes and invert to drain. Immerse the eggplant cubes in cold water as you cut them; drain well on paper towels. Roll eggplant in flour and fry in oil until golden. Remove and drain on paper towels. Combine eggplant with rice, bread crumbs, cheese, and parsley. Sauté the onion in the same oil in which you fried the eggplant; add to the eggplant mixture. Season with salt and pepper, add half the tomato pulp and mix well. Stuff tomatoes with this mixture and top with a slice of egg and the tomato tops. Place tomatoes in a shallow baking pan. Drizzle oil from the frying pan and the remaining tomato pulp over tomatoes. Bake for 40 minutes. Serve as a main course (allow 2 per serving) or as a vegetable (allow 1 per serving).

ZUCCHINI WITH *FETA* AND MINT

❧ CRETE

Kolokithia me Feta

2 pounds zucchini
2 tablespoons salt
½ cup flour as needed
½ cup grated *kefalotiri* or Parmesan cheese
2 tablespoons minced fresh mint, or 1 teaspoon dried mint
½ pound *feta* cheese, crumbled
⅛ cup salad or olive oil

Wash squash well and cut lengthwise into ½-inch-thick slices. Layer squash and salt in a colander and let stand for 2 hours.

Preheat oven to 400°F.

Rinse squash well, squeezing out excess water. Coat each slice with flour and place a layer of squash in a 9- x 9-inch greased baking pan. Sprinkle with one third of the grated cheese, mint, and *feta*; continue layering until all ingredients are used up. End with a layer of squash. Pour oil evenly over top and bake for 45 minutes, or until squash is tender. Cool for 30 minutes. Cut into squares. Serve hot or at room temperature. Serves 4.

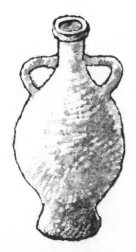

Salads and Salad Dressings

Very few dishes are as evocative of Greece as a simple assortment of lettuce, tomatoes, olives, *feta* cheese, a sprinkling of oregano, some good virgin olive oil and a splash of lemon juice—in other words, the classic Greek salad. From this very solid foundation springs a large number of regional and seasonal variations, employing anything from artichokes and cauliflower to tiny new peas, eggplants, and sweet peppers. Other more exotic salads presented in this chapter include Eggplant and Yogurt Salad and a superb Cold Lentil Salad.

ARTICHOKE-TOMATO SALAD WITH FRESH-HERB DRESSING

Ntomatosalata me Anginares

3 large artichokes, prepared for cooking
    (see Index) or 1 (10-ounce) package
    frozen artichoke hearts
1 quart water
1 lemon, cut into eighths
1 teaspoon salt

FRESH-HERB DRESSING:
½ cup tarragon vinegar
1 cup olive or salad oil
¼ cup minced parsley
2 tablespoons finely snipped chives
1 tablespoon minced fresh tarragon, or 2
    teaspoons dried tarragon
1 tablespoon minced fresh basil
1 teaspoon sugar
1 teaspoon salt
⅛ teaspoon pepper

4 tomatoes
8 pitted ripe olives
Chicory

If using fresh artichokes, cut prepared hearts into quarters. Bring water, lemon, and salt to a boil. Drop artichokes into boiling water, cover, and cook until tender, approximately 30 to 40 minutes. Drain well. (Otherwise cook frozen artichoke hearts according to package directions.) Put artichokes, cut side up, in a single layer in a shallow dish. In a pint jar with a tight-fitting lid, combine vinegar, oil, parsley, chives, tarragon, basil, sugar, salt, and pepper and shake well. Spoon about two thirds of the dressing over the warm artichokes. Cover and refrigerate, basting occasionally with the dressing, until very well chilled—at least 4 hours. Cover and refrigerate remaining dressing. At serving time, cut tomatoes into eighths and place in a bowl. Add olives and reserved dressing and toss to mix. Arrange artichokes around edge of large serving platter. Pile tomato mixture in center. Garnish with chicory. Serves 6–8.

Note: 1½ cups bottled oil-and-vinegar dressing may be substituted for Fresh-Herb Dressing. If you make dressing, ½ tablespoon dried tarragon leaves and ½ tablespoon dried basil leaves may be used instead of fresh herbs.

ARTICHOKE SALAD

Salata me Anginares

1 (1-pound) can artichoke hearts,
    drained
⅓ cup olive oil
⅓ cup freshly squeezed lemon juice
1 head romaine or other lettuce
2 tablespoons crushed dried mint
2–4 green onions
1 cup pitted black Greek olives
2 ripe tomatoes, peeled and cut in
    wedges
Salt to taste

Marinate artichoke hearts for 2 to 3 hours in olive oil and lemon juice. Tear lettuce into bite-size pieces and combine with the mint, onions, olives, and tomatoes in a large salad bowl. Add the artichoke hearts with marinade and season with salt. Toss lightly. Serves 6.

CAULIFLOWER-MUSHROOM SALAD WITH YOGURT

Salata me Yiaourti

2 cups tiny raw cauliflowerets
2 cups thinly sliced raw mushrooms
2 cups sliced pitted black olives
1 cup diced green pepper
1 cup plain yogurt
½ cup olive oil
¼ cup vinegar
¼ cup minced parsley or dill
1 clove garlic, crushed
¼ cup lemon juice
1 teaspoon salt
½ teaspoon pepper
1 small head of romaine

Combine the cauliflowerets, mushrooms, olives, and green pepper in a bowl and toss lightly to mix. Combine the yogurt, olive oil, vinegar, parsley, garlic, lemon juice, salt, and pepper: Mix well and pour over raw vegetables. Serve salad on lettuce leaves. Serves 6.

COLD LENTIL SALAD

Salata Faki

1 cup lentils, rinsed
1 onion, studded with 2 cloves
1 bay leaf
1 teaspoon salt
4 cups water
½ cup olive oil
⅓ cup vinegar
1 tablespoon dried oregano
1 cup minced celery
2 tablespoons minced scallions or onions
Crisp lettuce
2 tomatoes, quartered

Put the lentils, onion, bay leaf, salt and water in a large, heavy saucepan. Bring to a boil and simmer for 30 to 40 minutes, or until tender. Drain. Discard onion and bay leaf. Combine oil, vinegar, and oregano and pour over the lentils. Let cool to room temperature and refrigerate for at least 2 hours. When ready to serve add the celery and scallions and toss. Serve in a bowl lined with lettuce. Garnish with tomatoes. Serves 4.

COUNTRY-STYLE SALAD

Horiatiki Salata

4 cups salad greens (escarole, romaine,
  chicory, or other greens)
4–8 radishes, cut into "roses"
1 red onion, peeled and cut into rings
  (use according to taste)
1 small green pepper, cored, seeded, and
  cut into thin rings or strips
1–2 tomatoes cut into wedges
½ cup crumbled *feta* cheese
Coarse salt
1 clove garlic
8 *kalamata* or other black olives
4–8 flat anchovy fillets (optional)
2 tablespoons lemon juice or vinegar
Salt and pepper to taste
½ cup olive oil

Wash the salad greens and pat dry and tear into bite-size pieces. Prepare the radishes, onion, green pepper, tomatoes, and cheese. Pour a little coarse salt into a salad bowl, crush the garlic clove with a mortar over the salt and rub it around the surface of the bowl. Add the salad greens, prepared vegetables, cheese, olives, and anchovy fillets. Sprinkle with lemon juice, salt, and pepper and toss lightly. Add the oil and toss again. Add more lemon juice or vinegar and oil to taste. Serve immediately. Serves 4–6.

CRACKED WHEAT SALAD
Pligouri Salata

1 cup *pligouri* (fine cracked wheat) or
    bulghur wheat
4 scallions
1 bunch curly parsley
1 pint cherry tomatoes
½ cup olive oil
¼ cup vinegar
1 clove garlic (or to taste), minced
Salt and pepper to taste

Soak cracked wheat in cold water for ½ hour. Meanwhile chop scallions and parsley and cut the cherry tomatoes in half. Drain the wheat and mix with the greens and tomatoes. Combine the oil, vinegar, garlic, and salt and pepper and pour over the salad. Toss, then let stand a few minutes before serving. Serves 6–8.

EGGPLANT AND TOMATO SALAD
Melitzana kai Ntomata Salata

❧ CORFU

1 medium eggplant
2 large tomatoes
½ onion, finely minced
¼ cup minced parsley
½ cup olive oil
1 teaspoon salt
½ teaspoon pepper

Preheat oven to 350°F.
Put the eggplant in an ungreased pan and bake for 1 to 1½ hours, or until tender. When cool, skin the eggplant and put the pulp into a medium-size mixing bowl. Mash the pulp or chop it finely. Skin and chop the tomatoes and add them to the eggplant pulp. Add the onion and parsley and mix well. Stir in the olive oil, salt, and pepper. Serve at room temperature. Serves 4–5.

EGGPLANT AND YOGURT SALAD
Melitzanes me Yiaourti

2 cups plain yogurt
1 medium-to-large eggplant
3 tablespoons minced fresh dill
½ cup chopped scallions
1 clove garlic, finely minced
3 tablespoons olive oil
Juice of ½ lemon
Salt to taste

Line a mixing bowl with cheesecloth and empty the yogurt into it. Bring the edges of the cheesecloth up to make a bag; tie with string and suspend over the bowl to let the yogurt drip. Let stand in a cool place for 2 to 3 hours. The yogurt will become thick like sour cream. Place the eggplant on a square of aluminum foil and bake in preheated 375°F. oven for 1 hour, or until very soft. Remove the eggplant and put it in a colander to drain and cool. Remove outer skin. Place the soft interior of the eggplant in the bowl of an electric mixer. Beat on high speed. Add the yogurt and continue beating to blend well. Add the remaining ingredients and chill thoroughly. Garnish, if desired, with tomato wedges and imported Greek olives. Serves 4–6.

SPINACH AND *FETA* SALAD
Spanaki kai Feta Salata

2 pounds fresh spinach
½ cup olive oil
2 tablespoons white wine vinegar
2 tablespoons lemon juice
¼ teaspoon ground cinnamon
¼ teaspoon powdered mustard
Salt and pepper to taste
2 cucumbers
4 hard-cooked eggs
¼ pound *feta* cheese, crumbled
2 green onions, chopped

Remove stems from spinach. Wash and drain leaves, then cut in 1-inch-wide strips. Put in a salad bowl. Blend together the oil, vinegar, lemon juice, and spices. Pour half the dressing over the spinach and mix well. Thinly slice the cucumbers (with or without peel) and arrange on top of the spinach. Slice the eggs and arrange on top of the cucumbers. Sprinkle with cheese and onions. Pour remaining dressing over salad. Serves 8.

SPINACH-YOGURT SALAD
Salata Spanaki me Yiaourti

1½ pounds fresh spinach
1 onion, chopped
Juice of 1 large lemon
½ teaspoon salt
Pepper to taste
1 cup plain yogurt, drained
¼ cup slightly roasted walnuts (optional)
1 tablespoon chopped fresh mint, or 1
    teaspoon crushed dried mint

Remove stems from spinach and wash in cold water. In a large pot, combine the spinach and the onion, and cook, covered, over medium heat for 10 minutes, using only the water that clings to the spinach after washing. Drain the spinach well in colander or strainer. Transfer to a bowl and chop coarsely. Add the lemon juice, salt, and pepper. Stir in the yogurt. Transfer to a serving dish and sprinkle with walnuts and mint. Serve cold. Serves 4.

SPRING GREENS SALAD
Maroulosalata

1 head romaine lettuce
1 bunch scallions, finely minced
½ bunch dill, finely minced

DRESSING:
½ cup olive oil
¼ cup vinegar
1 teaspoon salt
½ teaspoon pepper
2 tablespoons lemon juice
¼ cup grated *kefalotiri* cheese (optional)

Wash and dry lettuce and tear into bite-size pieces. Combine with scallions and dill in a large bowl. Just before serving, mix all the ingredients for the dressing and pour over the salad. Toss. Serves 6–8.

SUMMER SALAD

Kalokerini Salata

3 tomatoes, cut in wedges
1 cucumber, sliced
1 onion, sliced
2 green peppers, cut in rings
6 tablespoons olive oil
2 tablespoons wine vinegar
Salt and pepper to taste
½ pound *feta* cheese
12 black olives
½ teaspoon crumbled dried oregano or
minced parsley

Put the tomatoes, cucumber, onion and peppers in a large salad bowl. Combine the olive oil, vinegar, and salt and pepper and pour over the salad. Sprinkle *feta* cheese and olives over the salad. Add the oregano and toss. Serves 4–6.

FETA DRESSING

Saltsa me Feta

2 cups mayonnaise (preferably
Homemade, see below)
2 cloves garlic, minced
½ cup red wine vinegar
1 teaspoon dried oregano
3 tablespoons olive oil
2 cups crushed *feta* cheese

Combine all the ingredients except the *feta* in a bowl and blend well. Crumble the *feta* and add to the mixture. Refrigerate in a covered jar. YIELD: 1 quart.

Note: All ingredients except the *feta* may be placed in a blender and creamed until smooth. Add *feta* and refrigerate.

HOMEMADE MAYONNAISE

Spitikia Mayoneza

1 teaspoon powdered mustard
¼ teaspoon sugar
Dash of white pepper
1 teaspoon salt
2 teaspoons white vinegar
2 egg yolks
1⅔ cups olive oil
Juice of 1 lemon

Combine the mustard, sugar, pepper, and salt and stir. Add the vinegar and egg yolks and beat well. Add the oil one drop at a time, beating constantly. When the mayonnaise starts to thicken, thin with lemon juice and continue beating, alternately adding lemon juice and oil. YIELD: 2 cups.

Breads

Bread is the staff of life in Greece, as elsewhere. But there it takes on an almost religious significance, especially during the Christmas and Easter seasons. No holiday would be complete without a festive bread, rich in eggs, sweet butter, and sesame seeds. But in a country where bread is still routinely baked in the home, unique, marvelously-flavored breads are common the year round. In this latter category, we include Olive Muffins, Yeast Tea Rolls, and the marvelous Sweet Bread Rings sold by street vendors as a mid-day snack.

Note: Unless otherwise indicated, the following recipes have been tested with all-purpose flour.

ADVENT BREAD

Eftazymo

1 pound chick-peas
1 teaspoon salt
1 teaspoon wood ashes
2½ cups very hot water
4 pounds plus 3 cups flour
1 teaspoon ground anise seeds
⅓ cup sugar
1 beaten egg, for brushing
Sesame seeds

The traditional bread of the pre-Christmas season, *Eftazymo* (or "bread kneaded seven times") entails a good deal of work as the name implies. But its aroma while baking plus its marvelous flavor makes it more than worth the effort. This bread is unusual in that a foam made from fermented chick-peas is used instead of yeast as a leavening agent.

The night before: Grind the chick-peas and put them in a heavy crock pot. Add salt, wood ashes, and water. Cover and let stand overnight in a warm place free of drafts.

The next morning: Check and see if foam has formed on the top. If not, add 2 more cups very hot water and cover again. Place in a warm place or in a hot sunny spot. After 2 to 3 hours the foam should form. If not, discard and start again another day with a different batch of chick-peas. Without the foam the *Eftazymo* cannot be made.

In a bowl put a cup of flour and add enough foam to make a soft dough. Cover and let stand in a warm place until double in bulk. Add another cup of flour and more foam until a soft dough is formed. Let rise again. Repeat a third time. When it rises the third time add the starter to 4 pounds of flour. Add anise seeds, sugar, and enough water to make a soft dough. Divide into four round loaves and let rise again. Preheat oven to 350°F. Brush with egg and sprinkle with sesame seeds. Bake for 30 minutes. YIELD: 4 loaves.

(Lenten)

ENVELOPE BREAD

Peta

1 package dry yeast
3½-4 cups flour
1¼ cup warm water
2 tablespoons oil
1 teaspoon salt
¼ teaspoon sugar

The ubiquitous bread of Greece and the Middle East with a thousand and one uses.

In a mixing bowl, combine the yeast with 1½ cups of the flour. Combine the water, oil, salt, and sugar and add to the yeast mixture. Beat for ½ minute with an electric beater at low speed; then beat for 3 minutes at high speed. Work in the remaining flour by hand. Put in a warm spot, cover, and let rise for 45 minutes. Punch dough down, divide into 12 pieces, and roll each into a ball. Let rest for 10 minutes. Flatten each ball into a circle 5 inches in diameter. Place on a baking sheet; cover and let rest for 20 to 30 minutes.

Preheat oven to 400°F.

Bake bread for 9 or 10 minutes, until puffed and lightly brown on bottom. Immediately wrap in foil and cool. YIELD: 12 *petas*.

(Lenten)

FLAT BREAD

Plati Psome

2 packages dry yeast
2 cups warm water
1 tablespoon sugar
2 teaspoons salt
6–7 cups flour
Cornmeal
Sesame seeds

Preheat oven to 400°F.

Sprinkle yeast over water and stir in. Add sugar, salt, and 3 cups flour. Beat until very smooth and shiny. Gradually add remaining flour. Knead until dough is elastic. Place in a greased bowl and turn to grease dough completely. Cover with a damp cloth. Let rise in a warm place until double in bulk. Punch down and turn over in bowl. Cut off egg-size pieces and roll into rounds. Place on a greased cookie sheet that has been sprinkled with cornmeal. Brush tops with water and sprinkle with sesame seeds. Let rise. Bake for 10 to 12 minutes. YIELD: 36 pieces.

Variation: Roll dough into 6-inch-long cylinders. Brush with water and sprinkle with coarse salt. Bake as above.

ISLANDER BREAD

Nisiotiko Psome

1 cup milk
3 tablespoons sugar
1 tablespoon salt
¼ cup melted butter or margarine
1 egg, lightly beaten
2 yeast cakes
½ cup lukewarm water
6 cups sifted flour
2 tablespoons light cream or evaporated milk
4 tablespoons sesame seeds

Scald the milk and cool to lukewarm. In a large bowl, combine the sugar, salt, butter, and egg. Stir in the cooled milk. Dissolve the yeast cakes in the water and add to the milk mixture. Add the sifted flour and mix well. Turn the dough out onto a floured board and knead until very smooth. Grease a large warm bowl. Transfer the dough to the bowl and turn to grease the dough completely. Cover with a cloth and put in a warm place to rise for 1½ to 2 hours, until double in bulk.

Turn the dough out onto a floured board and knead a few minutes. Divide dough into two pieces and fit each into a well-greased 9-inch round cake pan. Brush each loaf with cream and sprinkle with sesame seeds. Cover and put in a warm place to rise for 2 hours. Preheat oven to 350°F. Bake for 40 minutes. YIELD: Two 9-inch round loaves.

ISLANDER CORN BREAD

Bobota

1 cup light cornmeal
1 cup sifted flour
1 teaspoon double-acting baking powder
¼ teaspoon baking soda
½ teaspoon salt
¼ cup sugar
3 tablespoons honey
⅓ cup orange juice
¾ cup warm water
3 tablespoons vegetable oil, warmed
1 teaspoon grated orange rind
½ cup currants
½ cup Basic Sweet Syrup° or powdered sugar

This is a modified and far more palatable version of a Greek wartime staple made only of cornmeal, honey, and water. Though today's *Bobota* has come a long way from its humble origins, it is not popular everywhere in Greece because of its association with war and poverty.

Preheat oven to 375°F.

Sift all dry ingredients together into a large bowl. Combine the honey, orange juice, water, and warm oil and stir into the dry mixture, beating with a large wooden spoon until smooth. Fold in the orange rind and currants. Pour the batter into a well-greased 7- x 7- x 2-inch square pan and bake for 25 minutes. Leave in the pan to cool, then pour warm Basic Sweet Syrup over it or sprinkle with powdered sugar and serve immediately. YIELD: 9 large or 16 small pieces.

OLIVE MUFFINS

Eliopsomakia

2 cups (1¼ pound) chopped pitted black
    olives
4 cups flour
2 onions, grated
1½ cups olive oil, plus additional oil to
    brush muffin tins
1½ cups water
3 tablespoons chopped fresh mint, or 2
    teaspoons crushed dried mint
2 tablespoons sugar
2 heaping tablespoons double-acting
    baking powder

Preheat oven to 350°F.

Combine all the ingredients, adding the baking powder last. Brush muffin cups with oil and dust with flour. (Do not use paper baking cups.) Bake for 40 to 45 minutes. Serve warm. YIELD: 36 muffins.

Variation: Recipe may be baked in loaf pans. Increase baking time by 15 minutes. YIELD: 2 loaves.

ROUND LOAVES

Psome

3 packages dry yeast
1 cup warm water
13½ cups flour
6 tablespoons plus 1 teaspoon sugar
2 tablespoons plus a pinch of salt
4 cups lukewarm water
¼ cup shortening, melted
2 teaspoons cornstarch
2 tablespoons water

Sprinkle yeast over water and stir. Stir ½ cup of the flour, 1 teaspoon sugar, and pinch of salt into the dissolved yeast and set aside to form a sponge. Sift together 13 cups flour, 6 tablespoons sugar, and 2 tablespoons salt. Add the 4 cups water and melted shortening. Mix and knead, adding the starter to make a stiff dough. Continue to knead until smooth and elastic. Place in greased bowl; turn to grease dough completely. Cover with plastic wrap and a damp towel. Let rise in a warm place until double in bulk. Punch down and turn over. Let rise again. Shape into 3 round loaves and place in round pans. Make cuts, sunburst fashion, on top. Let rise until double in bulk.

Preheat oven to 425°F.

Place a pan of water on the bottom of the oven. Bake the bread for 15 minutes. Reduce oven temperature to 350°F. and bake for 1 hour. Meanwhile, dilute the cornstarch in the water and brush baked loaves with the paste. Turn off oven; leave loaves in oven for 15 minutes. Cool on racks. YIELD: 3 loaves.

SALT STICKS
Bastounakia

2 packages dry yeast
2 cups lukewarm water
1 tablespoon sugar
1 tablespoon salt
5 cups flour (approximate)
Cornmeal
Coarse salt
Sesame seeds

In a warmed large bowl, mix yeast, water, sugar, and salt and let stand until bubbly, approximately 5 to 10 minutes. Gradually add flour, kneading well, until dough is stiff. Put the mixture in a greased bowl. Cover first with wax paper and then with a damp towel. Let rise in a warm place (82 degrees) until double in bulk. Punch dough down, turn over, and let rise for another 15 minutes. Pinch off pieces of dough, roll out into sticks, and place on cookie sheets that have been sprinkled with cornmeal. Let the sticks rise again until double in bulk.

Preheat oven to 400°F.

Dampen tops of sticks with water and sprinkle with coarse salt and sesame seeds. Bake for 10 minutes, or until brown. YIELD: 4 dozen.

Note: Coarsely ground pepper or whole caraway seeds may be substituted for the sesame seeds.

SESAME SEED ROLLS
Psomakia

2 yeast cakes
5 tablespoons sugar
2 cups milk
⅓ cup melted butter
1 teaspoon salt
2 eggs, well beaten
2 tablespoons orange juice
2 tablespoons orange rind
6 cups flour

TOPPING:
¼ cup light cream
½ teaspoon sugar
1 cup sesame seeds

In a small bowl crumble the yeast cakes. Sprinkle with 2 teaspoons of the sugar and set aside for 10 minutes. Scald 1 cup milk and let it cool. Combine the cooled milk with the butter, remaining sugar, salt, eggs, orange juice, and orange rind and beat with electric mixer for 5 minutes. Heat the remaining milk until lukewarm and dissolve the yeast in it. Add this to the mixture and blend thoroughly. Add the flour and mix by hand. Put the dough on a floured board and knead until smooth. Put it in a large, well-greased, warm bowl, and turn to grease dough completely. Cover with a cloth and let rise in a warm place for 1½ to 2 hours, or until double in bulk. Turn the dough out on a floured board and knead a few times. Cut off pieces the size of a lemon, roll between palms of the hands into 8-inch-long ropes and tie in a knot. Mix the cream and sugar together for the topping and brush on knotted rolls. Dip in sesame seeds and place on a greased cookie sheet 3 inches apart. Cover with a cloth and put in a warm place to rise for 1½ hours.

Preheat oven to 350°F.

Bake for 25 to 30 minutes. YIELD: 2 dozen rolls.

(Lenten)

TOAST
Paximade

3 cups flour
¾ cup sugar
½ teaspoon salt
¼ teaspoon finely crushed aniseed
½ cup shortening
½ teaspoon double-acting baking powder
½ cup sweet wine
1 yeast cake
¼ cup warm water
1 teaspoon sesame seeds

This bread, made without butter or eggs, is served during Lent, as well as after funerals and during periods of mourning.

Sift the flour, sugar, salt, and aniseed into a bowl. Melt the shortening and blend into the dry mixture. Dissolve the baking powder in the wine and add to the mixture. Dissolve the yeast in the lukewarm water and add to mixture. Mix, then knead the dough until very smooth. Grease a 13- x 4-inch loaf pan and fit the dough into the pan. Mark off loaf into 1-inch diagonal slices, cutting about halfway down. Sprinkle the top with sesame seeds. Put in a warm place to rise for 1½ to 2 hours, or until double in bulk.

Preheat oven to 350°F.

Bake toast for 1 hour. Cool before removing from pan. When loaf is cold, slice all the way through. Place slices on an ungreased cookie sheet and return to a 350°F. oven for 15 minutes, or until golden brown. Store in airtight containers. YIELD: 40 slices.

(Lenten)

WHOLE WHEAT BISCUITS
Paximadia me Sitarenio Alevri

⚓ KARPATHOS

3 envelopes dry yeast
½ teaspoon sugar
1 cup lukewarm water for dissolving yeast
5 pounds whole wheat flour
¼ cup salt
5–6 cups lukewarm water for kneading dough

These very hard biscuits should be dipped in water before eating. For breakfast, they are traditionally dipped in a little olive oil and eaten with cheese.

In a bowl dissolve the yeast and sugar in 1 cup of luke-warm water. Cover and put in a warm place until quite foamy. Put flour in another bowl. Make a well in the flour, and pour the yeast mixture into the well, adding flour from the sides of the bowl. Let rest for 3 minutes. Dissolve the salt in the 5 cups lukewarm water and add it slowly into the flour while kneading. Continue kneading until dough is smooth but firm, about 10 minutes. (More water may be added if dough becomes unworkable.) Divide the dough into seven balls and shape into seven loaves. Mark loaves into 1-inch diagonal slices, cutting halfway down. Cover with a towel and let rise in a warm place until double in bulk.

Preheat oven to 375°F.

Place loaves on cookie sheets and bake for 40 minutes. Remove from oven and slice all the way through. Place slices on cookie sheets and return to oven. Lower oven temperature to 250°F. and bake for 3 hours, or until the biscuits are hard. YIELD: 9 dozen.

Note: Biscuits may be used as croutons in salads: Lightly sprinkle biscuits with cold water and cut into bite-size pieces.

CHRISTMAS FRUIT BREAD

Christopsomo me Frouta

↙ RHODES

3 packages dry yeast
½ cup water
1 teaspoon sugar
2 tablespoons flour
Pinch of salt
4 eggs
1½ cups sugar
1 teaspoon salt
1½ cups milk, scalded and cooled
7–8 cups flour
1 cup sweet butter, melted
1 cup slivered blanched almonds
½ cup white raisins
1 teaspoon grated lemon peel
1 cup mixed candied fruit
Beaten egg

Mix first five ingredients and set aside in a warm place until mixture bubbles and foams. Beat together the eggs, sugar, salt, cooled milk, and last of all the yeast sponge. Beat in about 3 cups of flour. Add the melted butter, almonds, raisins, lemon peel, and candied fruits. Continue to add flour and knead well until the dough is quite stiff but still elastic. Place the dough in a greased bowl. Cover first with wax paper and then with a damp towel. Let dough rise in a warm place until double in bulk. Punch down and turn over in bowl. Let rise for 30 minutes more. Shape dough into 6 ropes and braid 3 at a time. Place braids on a lightly greased cookie sheet and allow to rise for 40 minutes. Brush each braid with lightly beaten egg and bake in a 350°F. oven for 30 minutes, or until golden brown. YIELD: 2 large braids.

EASTER TWISTS

Tsourekia

¾ cup warm water
4–5 packages dry yeast
½ cup flour
1 tablespoon sugar
Pinch of salt
12 eggs
3 cups sugar
2 cups milk, scalded and cooled
1 tablespoon salt
1 tablespoon ground mastic flavoring or
    1 teaspoon ground *mahlepi* (see "A
    Greek Spice Rack" in Appendix)
5 pounds sifted flour or more as needed
1¼ pounds butter, melted
1 or 2 eggs, beaten
Sesame seeds

Mix first five ingredients and let rise in a warm place until mixture bubbles and foams, about 10 to 15 minutes. In a very large bowl beat the 12 eggs. Add the sugar, cooled milk, and salt. Stir in the yeast sponge. Blend mastic (or *mahlepi*) with about half of the sifted flour. Add to the bowl. Stir in the butter and enough flour to make a stiff dough. Knead well on a floured board. Place dough in a greased bowl; cover with a damp towel and let rise until double in bulk. Punch down and turn over in bowl. Cover with a damp towel and let rise again until almost double in bulk. (The second rising should not take as long as the first.) Shape dough into 14-inch-long ropes, braid 3 at a time and place on bread pans or cookie sheets to rise. When they have doubled in bulk brush with beaten eggs and sprinkle with sesame seeds.

Preheat oven to 350°F.

Bake twists for 30 to 40 minutes. YIELD: about 6–8 large twists.

ISLANDER EASTER BREAD

Nisiotiko Lambropsomo

2 packages dry yeast
¼ cup lukewarm milk
⅔ cup plus 1 teaspoon sugar
½ cup butter, softened
1 tablespoon grated orange or lemon
    rind
1 teaspoon salt
¾ cup scalded milk
4 eggs, lightly beaten
6 cups flour
5 hard-cooked eggs, dyed scarlet with
    vegetable food color
1 egg white, lightly beaten

In a small bowl, dissolve yeast in the lukewarm milk with 1 teaspoon sugar and let stand for 10 minutes. In a large bowl, combine the butter cut into bits, ⅔ cup sugar, grated fruit rind, and the salt. Stir in the scalded milk and let the mixture cool until it is lukewarm. Stir in the yeast mixture and the eggs. Gradually beat in 4½ cups flour, or enough to make a soft dough. Turn the dough out onto a lightly floured surface and knead in about 1½ cups more flour. Continue kneading for about 10 minutes, or until the dough is smooth and satiny. Shape the dough into a ball, place it in a buttered bowl, and turn to coat it completely with butter. Let rise, covered, in a warm place until double in bulk, about 1½ hours. Punch down the dough. Pinch off a piece the size of a large egg and set aside. Shape the remaining dough into a round loaf about 8 inches in diameter and place on a buttered baking sheet. Place 1 of the dyed eggs in the center of the loaf and arrange the other eggs around the edge to form the tips of a cross. Roll out the reserved dough into 10 thin strips about 4 inches long and cross 2 strips over each egg, pushing down the ends of the strips to secure them to the loaf.

Preheat oven to 325°F.

Let the dough rise about 30 minutes, or until double in bulk. Brush the surface with the egg white. Bake the bread for 50 to 55 minutes, or until brown. Transfer the bread to a rack. Serve warm. YIELD: 1 loaf.

ORANGE SWIRL BREAD

Psome Portokaliou

7 cups flour
2 teaspoons salt
⅔ cup sugar
2 packages dry yeast
2 eggs, well beaten
1 cup butter, melted
2 cups milk, scalded and cooled
Orange marmalade

Sift together the flour, salt, and sugar. Add the yeast. Mix together the beaten eggs, ½ cup of the melted butter, and the milk. Add to the flour mixture. Knead until smooth and elastic. Place dough in a greased bowl and turn to grease completely. Cover with plastic wrap and a damp towel. Let rise in a warm place until double in bulk. Punch down, turn over, and let rise again. Divide into 3 equal portions and roll out thinly into 3 rectangles. Spread each with one third of the remaining butter and a generous layer of marmalade and roll up tightly, jelly-roll style. Place in 8-inch bread pans and let rise again. Bake in a 350°F. oven for 40 minutes, or until golden brown. YIELD: 3 loaves.

LATTICE TARTS

Gyristaria

2 packages dry yeast
1 tablespoon plus ½ teaspoon sugar
2½ cups warm water
6–6½ cups all-purpose flour
2 teaspoons salt
1 teaspoon ground mastic flavoring (See "A Greek Spice Rack" in the Appendix)
1 teaspoon ground cinnamon
1 egg, beaten
Sesame seeds

In a small bowl or saucepan, combine the yeast, ½ teaspoon sugar, 1½ cups of the warm water, and 2 cups of the flour. Cover and let rest in a warm place until mixture bubbles and foams. Punch down and combine in a large mixing bowl with the remaining water, salt, mastic, remaining sugar and cinnamon and gradually add only enough of the remaining 4 to 4½ cups flour to make a soft dough. Knead for 10 to 15 minutes, until smooth and elastic. Place in a floured bowl, cover, and let rise in a warm place until double in bulk. Punch down the dough and break off 12 pieces about the size of a small orange. Roll each piece into a 6-inch long rope and seal the ends to form circles. Break off pieces of the remaining dough to form 6 pencil-thin strips for each dough ring. Create a lattice effect by criss-crossing the strips over the dough rings. If any dough remains, continue adding and criss-crossing strips to make a tighter lattice. Place on a buttered baking sheet, brush with egg and sprinkle with sesame seeds.

Preheat oven to 375°F.

Cover and allow tarts to rise for 30 minutes. Bake for 25 minutes. Cool on racks. YIELD: 12–15 rings.

YEAST TEA ROLLS

Prozimi Koulourakia

2 packages yeast
⅓ cup warm water
3 tablespoons flour
½ teaspoon sugar
Pinch of salt
2 cups milk, scalded and cooled
1 cup sugar
3 eggs, beaten
1 teaspoon ground mastic flavoring
2 teaspoons salt
7–7½ cups flour
½ cup butter, melted and cooled
1 egg, beaten
Sesame seeds

Mix first five ingredients and set aside in a warm place until mixture bubbles and foams, about 10 to 15 minutes. Combine the milk, sugar, eggs, mastic and salt and add to the yeast mixture. Sift half of the flour into the yeast mixture and beat well with a spoon. Add cooled butter. Start adding remaining flour (as much as necessary) and knead until dough is smooth and elastic. Place in a greased bowl, cover with wax paper and a damp towel, and let rise in a warm place until double in bulk. Punch down, turn over in bowl, and let rise again until almost double in bulk. Pinch off walnut-size pieces of dough and roll into thin ropes. Tie these into knots or twist. Place on a greased cookie sheet and let rise again.

Preheat oven to 350°F.

Brush with beaten egg and sprinkle with sesame seeds. Bake until golden brown, about 12 to 20 minutes, depending on size. YIELD: about 4 dozen rolls.

SWEET BREAD RINGS

Koulourakia

7 cups sifted flour
¼ cup warm water
½ cup warm milk
2 yeast cakes
1 teaspoon salt
½ cup melted butter
3 eggs, lightly beaten
⅛ cup cold milk
¾ cup sugar
1 tablespoon vanilla
2 tablespoons brandy
1 cup light cream

Though called "cookies" in Greek, these rings are actually yeast breads commonly sold by street vendors throughout Greece.

Sift 2 cups of the flour into a large bowl. In a small bowl, combine the warm water and milk. Dissolve the yeast in this liquid and add to the flour. Mix thoroughly to make a loose dough. Let rise in a warm place for about 1½ hours. After the first rising, sift together the remaining flour and salt. Add the melted butter and mix until evenly distributed. In another bowl combine the eggs, cold milk, sugar, vanilla, and brandy and mix well. Add egg mixture to the risen dough, mixing with a heavy spoon until smooth. Add the flour and butter mixture and knead together for 10 minutes, or until very smooth. Cut off pieces of dough about the size of a large walnut and roll between the hands to form 3-inch-long ropes. Seal the ends of the ropes to form circles and place 2 inches apart on a greased cookie sheet. Brush tops with cream and let rise for 1½ hours.

Bake rings in a 350°F. oven for 35 minutes. YIELD: 4 dozen.

Desserts
and
Sweets

That Greeks have a sweet tooth is no secret. Just peer into a typical *zaharoplastion*, or pastry shop, and observe the enormous array of calorie-laden delights to get an idea of what a real sweet tooth means. In this chapter we will take you on a tour of that pastry shop and present the highlights of the Greek baker's art—from a rich Chestnut Cake with Whipped Cream and a delectable Pumpkin Pie to Nougat Torte and *Sourota*, a variation of the ever-popular Baklava; from cookies in an unbelievable array of sizes and shapes to Honey Pie and the non-pareil Greek *Halva*. Calorie-counters beware!

Note: Unless otherwise indicated, of the following recipes those that call for the use of flour have been tested with all-purpose flour.

CAKES AND PIES

APRICOT SAUCE CAKE

SYROS

Tourta me Verikoko

¾ cup chopped dried apricots
1 cup water
2 cups sugar
10 tablespoons sweet butter
1 teaspoon vanilla
1 teaspoon grated lemon peel
2 eggs
½ teaspoon salt
2 teaspoons double-acting baking
     powder
2 cups flour
1 cup milk

In a small pan, combine apricots, water, and ½ cup sugar and bring to a boil. Cover and simmer gently for 20 minutes. Purée the mixture in a blender until smooth, or press through a food mill. There should be 1½ cups of purée. If quantity is not correct, either boil, stirring constantly, to reduce, or add water to bring to the exact measure. Blend in 2 tablespoons of the butter. Set aside for up to several hours to cool.

Preheat oven to 350°F.

Beat together the remaining 8 tablespoons butter and 1½ cups sugar until blended. Add vanilla and lemon peel and beat in the eggs one at a time. In another bowl, sift together the salt, baking powder, and flour. Add flour mixture to butter mixture alternately with the milk, beat well after each addition.

Pour the batter into a greased and floured 9-inch square pan. Spoon apricot sauce evenly over batter. Bake for 50 to 55 minutes, or until cake begins to pull away from the sides of the pan. Serve warm. YIELD: 10–12 pieces.

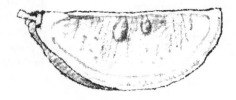

APRICOT ALMOND CAKE

Amigdalopeta me Verikoko

¾ cup sweet butter
2 cups sugar
7 egg yolks
1 whole egg
1 tablespoon flour
1 teaspoon double-acting baking powder
Juice of ½ lemon
12 ounces almonds, shelled and finely
    chopped

FILLING:

1 (8-ounce) jar apricot preserves
Confectioners' sugar

Preheat oven to 350°F.

Cream together the butter and the sugar. Add the egg yolks and the whole egg and blend well. Add the flour, baking powder, lemon juice, and almonds. Butter and flour two 8-inch cake pans. Pour half the batter into each pan. Bake for 20 to 30 minutes, or until lightly brown. Let cakes cool and remove from pans. Spread apricot marmalade over one layer. Place second layer on top and sprinkle with the sugar. YIELD: 8–10 pieces.

CHOCOLATE REFRIGERATOR TORTE

Tourta Sokolatas Psigiou

1 (8-ounce box) social tea biscuits
½ cup milk
1 ounce brandy
½ pound sweet butter
1 cup confectioners' sugar
3 eggs, separated
2 teaspoons vanilla
¼ cup unsweetened cocoa
½ cup almonds, blanched and toasted

Break the biscuits in half and soak in the milk and brandy. Beat the butter with the sugar for about 5 minutes. Add the yolks to the butter-sugar mixture. Mix in the vanilla, cocoa, and nuts. Beat the egg whites until stiff and fold into the mixture. Blend in the moistened biscuits and pour the "batter" into a well-buttered loaf pan lined with wax paper. Put in freezer. Remove from freezer ½ hour before serving. Keep in refrigerator until ready to serve. YIELD: 10–12 pieces.

CINNAMON NUT RING

Tourta Kanelas

1 cup butter, margarine, or vegetable
    shortening
2 cups sugar
4 eggs
1 cup milk
2 teaspoons double-acting baking
    powder
3 cups flour
2 teaspoons ground cinnamon
½ cup chopped almonds
½ cup chopped walnuts

Preheat oven to 350°F.

Blend the butter and sugar well in a mixing bowl. Add the eggs and beat until well blended. Heat the milk until lukewarm. Add the baking powder to the milk and stir well. Add to the batter and blend. Add the flour and beat until batter is creamy and smooth. Add the cinnamon, almonds, and walnuts. Grease a 10-inch tube pan and dust with flour. Pour batter into pan and bake for 50 minutes. Cool 15 minutes before removing cake from pan. YIELD: 12–14 pieces.

Note: This cake is commonly referred to in Greek as the "one, two, three cake." Note that other nuts (pecans, for instance) may be substituted.

CINNAMON SAUCE CAKE

Keïk me Kanela

2 cups flour
1 cup sugar
2 teaspoons double-acting baking
    powder
½ teaspoon salt
2 teaspoons ground cinnamon
2 tablespoons butter
1 cup milk

SAUCE:

1½ cups sugar
1½ cups water
2 tablespoons sweet butter
1 teaspoon ground cinnamon
1 teaspoon rum flavoring
½ cup chopped walnuts

Preheat oven to 350°F.

In a large bowl, combine the flour, sugar, baking powder, salt, cinnamon, butter, and milk. Beat at medium speed until well blended. Spread batter in a 9-inch square pan which has been greased on the bottom only. To make the sauce combine the sugar, water, butter, and cinnamon in a saucepan. Bring to a boil and add rum flavoring. Pour hot sauce over cake and sprinkle with walnuts. Bake for 35 to 40 minutes, or until top springs back when touched in center. Serve warm, with whipped cream, if desired. YIELD: 16 pieces.

CHESTNUT CAKE WITH WHIPPED CREAM

✣ CHIOS

Tourta me Kastana

6 eggs separated
1¼ cups sugar
1 cup canned unsweetened chestnut
    purée
½ cup ground almonds, lightly toasted
1 teaspoon vanilla
Pinch of salt
1½ cups heavy cream, whipped
10 ounces glacéed chestnuts

A simplified version of a very popular—and delicious—Greek dessert.

Preheat oven to 325°F.

In a bowl beat the egg yolks and sugar with electric beater or a whisk until the mixture forms ribbons when the beater is lifted. Add the chestnut purée, ground almonds, and vanilla. Beat egg whites with salt until stiff. Add one-fourth of the whites to the yolk mixture and combine well. Gently fold the remaining whites into the yolk mixture. Pour the batter into two buttered and floured 9-inch cake pans and bake for 35 minutes. Let the layers cool in the pans for 15 minutes. Turn them out onto racks and cool completely. Fill and frost the layers with whipped heavy cream. Decorate with glacéed chestnuts, if desired. YIELD: 10–12 pieces.

FARINA CAKE

Ravani

1 pound sweet butter, at room
    temperature
2 cups sugar
12 eggs
2 cups sifted flour
2 tablespoons double-acting baking
    powder
1½ cups farina

SYRUP:

4 cups sugar
4 cups water
1 tablespoon vanilla

Preheat oven to 350°F.

In a large mixing bowl, beat the butter with an electric mixer until fluffy. Slowly add the sugar, continuing to beat. Add eggs, one at a time, beating well but at low speed after each addition. Sift flour and baking powder together, then add to mixture. Add farina and mix well until batter is fairly thick. Spread batter evenly in a greased 11- x 17-inch cake pan. Bake for 40 to 45 minutes. While *Ravani* is baking, prepare syrup. In saucepan, combine sugar, water, and vanilla. Bring to a boil, and simmer for 40 minutes. Once cake is done, ladle hot syrup over hot cake (keep cake in baking pan). Cover with aluminum foil and let cool. When cake is completely cool, cut into 1½-inch squares. YIELD: 48 pieces.

Note: Recipe may be successfully halved. This cake freezes well.

FARINA CAKE WITH CREAM SAUCE

Tourta Farina me Krema

¼ pound sweet butter, melted
1 cup milk
1 cup sugar
⅛ teaspoon baking soda
2 teaspoons double-acting baking
    powder
½ teaspoon ground cinnamon
½ teaspoon vanilla
3 eggs, separated
1 cup farina

SYRUP:

1½ cups water
1 cup sugar

CREAM SAUCE:

4 tablespoons butter
4 tablespoons flour
4 cups milk
⅛ teaspoon salt
6 tablespoons sugar
2 teaspoons vanilla

Preheat oven to 350°F.

In a large bowl, combine the butter, milk, sugar, soda, baking powder, cinnamon, and vanilla. Beat egg yolks and add to mixture, stirring well. Add farina and mix well. Beat egg whites until stiff but not dry. Fold into batter. Pour into a well-buttered 9- x 13-inch pan. Bake for 20 to 30 minutes, or until golden brown. Cool. While cake bakes make syrup by boiling the water and sugar together for 10 minutes. Pour hot syrup over cool cake. To prepare cream sauce melt the butter in a pan (do not brown). Remove from heat and stir in the flour until smooth. Add milk, salt, and sugar and return to the heat. Stir constantly until mixture boils and thickens. Allow to simmer slowly for 3 minutes. Remove from heat and add vanilla. Cool before pouring evenly over cake. YIELD: 24 pieces.

ALMOND-TOPPED *RAVANI*
Ravani me Amigdala

1 cup sweet butter
1 cup sugar
6 eggs, beaten
1 cup flour
1 teaspoon double-acting baking powder
1 cup farina
1 teaspoon vanilla
1 cup ground almonds or walnuts

SYRUP:

2 cups sugar
4 cups water

Preheat oven to 350°F.

Combine butter and sugar in mixing bowl; beat with mixer until smooth. Add eggs gradually, beating constantly. Sift together the flour, baking powder, and farina and stir into the butter-egg mixture. Add the vanilla. Turn into a greased 13- x 9- x 2-inch pan. Sprinkle with almonds. Bake for 30 minutes, or until a clean knife inserted in the center comes out clean. Meanwhile, combine syrup ingredients and boil for 10 minutes. Cool. Pour cooled syrup over hot cake. YIELD: 16–20 pieces.

COCONUT *RAVANI*
Ravani me Karida

SYRUP:

2 cups sugar
2 cups water
1 teaspoon vanilla

½ pound sweet butter
4 eggs
1 cup sugar
1½ cups flour
1 tablespoon double-acting baking
    powder
½ cup milk
1 (7-ounce) package coconut

✢ MYTILENE

Though coconut is a relatively new product in Greece and must be imported from afar, it is frequently used in various recipes.

To make the syrup bring the sugar and water to a boil and simmer for 10 minutes. Add vanilla. Set aside to cool.
Preheat oven to 350°F.
Melt the butter and let cool. Beat the eggs with the sugar until thick and lemon-colored. Add the butter and beat for 2 minutes. Sift the flour with the baking powder and add along with the milk and 1½ cups of the coconut to the egg-sugar mixture (reserve ½ cup coconut for topping). Bake in a buttered 9- x 13-inch pan for 30 minutes. Top with cold syrup and sprinkle remaining coconut over the top. YIELD: approximately 24 pieces.

CUSTARD CAKE
Yalatopeta

3 packages lady fingers
1½ quarts milk
1 cup sugar
½ cup farina
9 eggs
1 tablespoon vanilla

SYRUP:

1 cup sugar
1 cup water

Preheat oven to 350°F.
Line a 9- x 11- x 2-inch pan with the lady fingers. Combine the milk, sugar and ¼ cup of the farina in a large saucepan and cook over medium heat until it comes to a very slow boil. Remove from heat. In a large bowl, beat the eggs. Add the remaining ¼ cup farina and the warm milk mixture. Return custard to the saucepan and bring *just* to the simmer, stirring constantly. Don't overcook or eggs will curdle. Add the vanilla. Pour custard mixture into the pan and bake for 15 minutes. Remove from oven and cool. Meanwhile, to make the syrup bring the sugar and water to a boil and let simmer for 20 minutes. Pour hot syrup over cool cake. YIELD: 24 pieces.

COCONUT TORTE

Tourta me Karida

½ cup sweet butter, at room temperature
1 cup sugar
6 egg whites
1½ cups lightly packed coconut
1¾ cups sifted flour
½ teaspoon salt
2 teaspoons baking powder
¾ cup milk
1 teaspoon almond extract

SYRUP:

2 cups sugar
1½ cups water
Rind of ½ lemon, cut up
5 whole cloves
2 sticks cinnamon
1 cup honey
4 tablespoons lemon juice
2 tablespoons rum or brandy

Preheat oven to 350°F.

Cream together the butter and sugar. Add the unbeaten egg whites and continue to beat until creamy. Stir in the coconut. Sift together the flour and salt and add to the mixture, mixing well. Dissolve the baking powder in the milk and add to mixture, mixing for just 1 minute. Blend in the almond flavoring. Pour into a lightly greased 8- x 10- x 2-inch pan and bake for 40 minutes, or until a knife inserted in the center comes out clean. Cool for ½ hour. While the cake is baking prepare the syrup.

. Combine all the ingredients in a saucepan and simmer for 10 minutes. Cool while the cake is cooling. Strain and pour over the cake. Allow to stand 2 hours before cutting. Torte can be kept for a few days at room temperature. Do not refrigerate. YIELD: 12–16 pieces.

CORINTHIAN RAISIN CAKE

Tourta me Stafides Korinthou

¾ cup sweet butter, at room temperature
1¾ cups sugar
4 eggs
2 cups milk
3 teaspoons ground cinnamon
½ teaspoon ground cloves
1 teaspoon ground lemon peel
1 teaspoon grated orange peel
3½ cups flour
½ cup currants or raisins
3 teaspoons double-acting baking powder
½ cup confectioners' sugar

Preheat oven to 350°F.

Cream the butter and sugar for 5 minutes. Add the eggs, milk, 1 teaspoon cinnamon, the ground cloves, lemon and orange peel, and half of the flour. Combine currants, baking powder, and remaining flour and blend with the egg mixture until smooth. Pour into a greased loaf pan (which should be three quarters full). Bake for 40 minutes. Cool and turn cake onto a plate. Combine confectioners' sugar with cinnamon and dust top of cake. YIELD: 10–12 pieces.

GOLD AND WALNUT CAKE

Karidato Kozanis

FIRST LAYER:

4 eggs
1 cup sugar
3 cups cake flour
3 teaspoons double-acting baking
    powder
½ pound sweet butter

SECOND LAYER:

10 eggs
4 cups sugar
6 cups chopped walnuts
2 cups zwieback crumbs
1 teaspoon ground cinnamon
½ teaspoon ground cloves
¼ cup water
2 cups whipped cream (optional)

This unusual cake from Kozane consists of two layers baked one on top of the other.

Preheat oven to 350°F.

To prepare first layer beat the eggs, and gradually add the sugar, beating all the while. Sift flour with baking powder and add slowly to the mixture. Melt the butter and blend half of it with the batter. Pour the other half into a 10- x 15- x 3-inch baking pan. Pour the batter into the pan and bake for 15 to 20 minutes. While first layer bakes, beat second batch of eggs until creamy. Add the sugar slowly. Add the chopped nuts, zwieback crumbs, cinnamon, cloves, and water and beat until smooth. Remove first layer from oven, pour second batter on top and continue to bake for 25 minutes, or until knife comes out clean (do not overbake). When cool cut in diamonds and serve with whipped cream, if desired. YIELD: 36–40 pieces.

HALVA

Halvas tis Katsarolas

3 cups sugar
4 cups water
¾ cup sweet butter
2 cups simigdali (farina or cream of
    wheat)
½ cup almonds, blanched and quartered
Ground cinnamon

Most non-Greeks associate the word Halva with a very sweet sesame candy. In Greece, however, the term also applies to a popular dessert made with farina. Fast and easy to make, Greek Halva is an excellent last-minute dessert for unexpected guests.

Prepare a syrup by combining the sugar and water in a large saucepan. Bring to a boil and cook for 1 minute. Set aside. In another saucepan heat the butter. Add the farina and almonds and cook over medium heat until the mixture turns a light golden color. Pour the syrup into the farina and blend well. Cover and cook until it thickens. To test doneness, insert a clean knife in the mixture; if it comes out clean, the Halva is done. Transfer to a small mold and allow to cool. Unmold and sprinkle with cinnamon. Serves 12.

OVEN *HALVA*

Halvas tou Fournou

¾ cup sweet butter
1 cup sugar
4 eggs
2 cups farina
1 cup chopped almonds (or other nuts)
1 teaspoon ground cinnamon

SYRUP:

2 cups sugar
4 cups water

Preheat oven to 350°F.

Cream the butter and the sugar. Beat in the eggs, one at a time. Add farina, almonds, and cinnamon. Grease a 9- x 13- x 3-inch pan. Pour the batter into the pan and bake for 35 to 40 minutes. While the *Halva* bakes, combine the sugar and water in a large saucepan and boil for 10 minutes. Remove the *Halva* from the oven and pour the syrup over the hot *Halva*. Cool and cut in squares. YIELD: 24 pieces.

PAN *HALVA*

Halvas Fournou

5 eggs
2 cups sugar
½ pound sweet butter, melted
2 cups milk
1 teaspoon vanilla
1 (14-ounce) box farina
2 teaspoons double-acting baking powder
1¼ teaspoons baking soda
1 teaspoon ground cinnamon
1 cup chopped walnuts or slivered almonds

SYRUP:

2 cups sugar
2½ cups water
Juice of ½ lemon

Preheat oven to 325°F.

Beat the eggs in a medium mixing bowl. Gradually add the sugar, melted butter, milk, vanilla, and dry ingredients and mix well. Add the nuts. Pour into a 10- x 14- x 2-inch baking pan. Bake for 40 to 45 minutes. In the meantime, boil all the syrup ingredients for 15 minutes. Pour hot syrup over *Halva* while it is still hot. Cut in squares. YIELD: 24 pieces.

ORANGE *HALVA*

Halvas me Portokali

2 tablespoons sweet butter
1 cup farina
½ cup chopped almonds or walnuts
Juice of 1 large orange
1 cup honey
1 cup water
½ teaspoon ground cinnamon
1 cup heavy cream, whipped

Melt the butter in an iron skillet, add farina and brown over low heat, stirring constantly. Add nuts and orange juice, stir and remove from heat. In a saucepan, bring the honey and 1 cup water to a boil. Stir in farina mixture and cover. Simmer for 20 minutes. Stir, cover, and simmer for 20 minutes longer. Transfer to a serving dish and sprinkle with cinnamon. Serve with whipped cream. Serves 6–8.

NUT CAKE I

Karidopeta

½ pound sweet butter
1 cup sugar
7 eggs
2 teaspoons ground cinnamon
1 cup flour
2 teaspoons double-acting baking
    powder
½ pound walnuts, chopped

SYRUP:

1½ cups sugar
2 cups water

Preheat oven to 350°F.

Beat the butter with the sugar. Add the eggs one at a time. Add the cinnamon, flour, and baking powder and beat well. Mix in the walnuts. Spread in a greased 9- x 12-inch pan. Bake for 30 minutes. Meanwhile, prepare a syrup by boiling the sugar and water together for about 15 minutes. Cool. Cut the nut cake into diamond-shaped pieces while still warm. Pour the cooled syrup over the warm cake. YIELD: approximately 20–24 pieces.

NUT CAKE II

Karidopeta Horis Siropi

10 eggs
4 cups sugar
½ cup sweet butter, melted
3–4 cups chopped nuts (walnuts or
    almonds)
1 cup zwieback
1 teaspoon baking soda
Juice of ½ lemon
1 teaspoon ground cinnamon
1 teaspoon ground nutmeg

The traditional *Karidopeta* is served with a syrup; this delicious version is so rich that it is served without a syrup.

Preheat oven to 350°F.

Beat the eggs with the sugar. Beat in the butter and add the remaining ingredients. Grease well an 11- x 14-inch rectangular cake pan. Pour mixture into the pan and bake for 35 minutes. Cool completely. Cut into squares. May be served with whipped cream. YIELD: 24 pieces.

HONEY CAKE

Keik me Meli

5 eggs
1 cup sugar
1 cup vegetable oil
1 cup honey
1 cup lukewarm milk
1 teaspoon baking soda
2 teaspoons double-acting baking
    powder
3 cups flour
1 teaspoon ground cinnamon (optional)
½ cup chopped nuts (optional)

Preheat oven to 350°F.

Beat the eggs with the sugar at high speed until fluffy. Add the oil and beat at low speed. Continue beating, adding the honey, milk, baking soda, and baking powder. Add flour, a little at a time. If desired, add the cinnamon and nuts at this point. Pour mixture into greased 8- x 14-inch pan. Bake for 1 hour. Do not open oven door during the first half hour of baking time. Remove from oven and cool. YIELD: 20–24 pieces.

NOUGAT TORTE

Tourta Nougatina

CRUST:

3 cups almonds, blanched and finely
    chopped, or 3 cups walnuts, finely
    chopped
1¼ cups sugar
1 tablespoon ground cinnamon
8 egg whites, at room temperature
    (reserve yolks for filling)
4 tablespoons flour

FILLING:

3 tablespoons flour
3 tablespoons cornstarch
½ cup sugar
8 egg yolks
3 cups milk
1 teaspoon vanilla
¼ pound sweet butter

TOPPING:

3 tablespoons apricot preserves
½ pint heavy cream, whipped
½ cup toasted almonds, chopped
1 (1-pound) can sweet cherries

Preheat oven to 300°F.

In a bowl, mix the ground nuts, sugar, and cinnamon. Beat the egg whites until stiff. Fold the egg whites into nut mixture. Line the bottoms of three 8-inch round baking pans with wax paper and butter and flour them lightly. Pour one third of the mixture into each pan and flatten to form crusts. Bake for 15 minutes. Cool. To prepare filling, mix the flour, cornstarch, sugar, egg yolks, and about 1 cup of the milk in the top part of a double boiler. Mix well with wire beater. Set over simmering water, add the remaining milk and cook until the mixture thickens. Add the vanilla and butter. Put in refrigerator to cool.

To assemble, place one crust on a dish and cover well with half the filling. Top with another crust and the remaining filling. Spread the marmalade over the third crust and place on top of the filling. Cover the top and sides with whipped cream. Sprinkle the toasted almonds on top and decorate with sliced cherries. YIELD: 10–12 pieces.

ORANGE WALNUT SURPRISE

KITHIRA

Karidopeta me Marmelada

½ pound sweet butter, at room
    temperature
1 cup sugar
4 eggs
3 teaspoons double-acting baking
    powder
¼ cup cognac
2 teaspoons lemon peel
3 cups flour
1 (8-ounce) jar orange marmalade

FILLING:

10 eggs
3½ cups sugar
1 teaspoon ground cinnamon
1 cup bread crumbs
2 pounds shelled walnuts, chopped

Preheat oven to 350°F.

Cream the butter and sugar. Add the eggs, one at a time, and continue beating. Add the baking powder, cognac, and lemon peel and blend well. Add the flour, 1 cup at a time, to form a soft dough. Place this dough in a 12- x 15- x 2-inch baking pan. Spread the orange marmalade over dough and set aside. To prepare the filling, beat the 10 eggs and the sugar together in a mixing bowl for 5 minutes, or until thick and lemon-colored. Add the cinnamon, bread crumbs, and walnuts to this mixture. Blend well and pour over the marmalade-covered dough. Bake for 45 minutes. Cool and cut into squares. YIELD: 10–12 pieces.

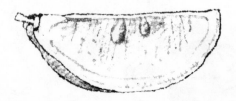

ORANGE RING CAKE
Tourta Portokali

1 cup sweet butter, at room temperature
1 cup sugar
3 eggs separated
1 cup yogurt
Grated rind of 1 orange
1¾ cups sifted flour
1 teaspoon double acting baking powder
1 teaspoon baking soda

ORANGE SYRUP:

juice of 2 oranges
Juice of 1 lemon
¾ cup sugar
dash of salt
¼ cup rum

Preheat oven to 325°F.

Cream the butter and sugar. Add egg yolks, yogurt, and orange rind and beat until light and fluffy. Sift together flour, baking powder, and baking soda and stir into first mixture. Beat the egg whites until stiff but not dry. Fold into the batter. Pour into a greased and floured 9-inch tube pan and bake for 50 to 60 minutes. Remove from oven and let stand for about 10 minutes. Loosen carefully around the edge and turn out onto a plate. To prepare syrup combine all ingredients and boil gently for 3 to 4 minutes. Pour hot orange syrup slowly over top of cake. YIELD: 10–12 pieces.

POLITIKO KADAIFE
Politiko Kadaife

3 packages yeast
1 teaspoon sugar
Pinch of salt
⅛ cup warm water
3–4 tablespoons flour
4 eggs
3 tablespoons sugar
1 teaspoon salt
1 cup milk, scalded and cooled
3¼ cups flour
¼ pound sweet butter, melted

SYRUP:

4 cups sugar
2 cups water
Peel of ½ lemon

TOPPING:

1 quart heavy cream
1½ teaspoons cornstarch
¼ cup milk

Greeks from Constantinople and Asia Minor are renowned for their cooking skill and inventiveness, to which this recipe attests. Though called *Kadaife*, the recipe employs a yeast dough in lieu of the traditional shredded-wheat-like *phyllo* that is the true *Kadaife*. The word *politiko* indicates the recipe's origin in Constantinople.

Mix the first five ingredients and set aside in a warm place for 10 to 15 minutes until a sponge forms.

Preheat oven to 350°F.

Beat the eggs. Add sugar, salt, milk, and the yeast mixture. Add half the flour, then the melted and cooled butter. Beat in the remaining flour until smooth and elastic. Cover bowl with wax paper and a damp towel. Set in warm place to rise, about 20 minutes. Place dough in a 10- x 15-inch pan and set in warm place to rise again. Bake for 30 to 40 minutes, or until golden brown. Meanwhile, prepare the syrup by combining the sugar, water, and lemon peel. Bring to a boil and simmer for 15 minutes. Remove cake from oven and slowly add syrup until all is absorbed. For the topping, scald the cream in a heavy pot. Dissolve the cornstarch in the milk and add to the cream. Stir over low heat until thickened. Cool in the refrigerator and then spread on cake. YIELD: 35 pieces.

Note: Whipped cream may be substituted for the topping.

"PARIS CAKE"
Pasta Pari

PASTRY:

1 cup sweet butter, at room temperature
½ cup sugar
1 egg, lightly beaten
3 tablespoons whiskey
1 teaspoon double-acting baking powder
2⅔ cups flour
1 cup apricot or cherry preserves

FILLING:

6 eggs, separated
1 cup confectioners' sugar
Rind of ½ lemon, grated
3 cups chopped unblanched almonds
½ teaspoon double-acting baking powder
3 tablespoons apricot brandy or whiskey,
    or 1 teaspoon almond extract

Preheat oven to 350°F.

Beat butter and sugar until smooth and creamy. Add egg, whiskey, and baking powder. Add flour to make a soft dough. Chill. Press chilled pastry against bottom and slightly up the sides of a greased 11- x 16-inch baking pan. Spread with preserves. Set aside. To prepare filling, beat egg yolks with sugar until light and fluffy. Add rind and almonds. Dissolve baking powder in whiskey and add to the egg mixture and blend well. Fold in stiffly beaten egg whites. Pour mixture over pastry and preserves, spreading evenly. Bake for 30 minutes, or until golden brown. Cool thoroughly. Cut in diamond-shaped pieces. Sprinkle with confectioners' sugar, if desired, before serving. YIELD: about 40 pieces.

Variation: For the filling, use 3 cups chopped walnuts and 1 teaspoon cinnamon, omitting the almond flavoring.

PUMPKIN CAKE
Keïk Kolokithas

✤ KASTORIA

3 cups flour
2 cups sugar
2 teaspoons double-acting baking
    powder
1 teaspoon baking soda
1 teaspoon salt
1 tablespoon ground cinnamon
1 cup finely chopped walnuts
1½ cups cooking oil
4 eggs, well beaten
2 cups cooked pumpkin purée (see note)
1 square unsweetened chocolate, melted
    and cooled
1 cup chopped raisins, soaked in ½ cup
    warm water, then drained

Preheat oven to 350°F.

Combine flour, sugar, baking powder, baking soda, salt, cinnamon, and walnuts in a large bowl and mix well. Make a well in the center of the dry ingredients and add the oil, eggs, and pumpkin purée mixed with the chocolate. Mix until ingredients are well blended. Fold in the raisins. Spread in a greased 9-inch round tube pan and bake for 60 to 70 minutes, or until an inserted knife comes out clean. Cool in pan. Wrap and store at room temperature for 24 hours before serving. (Cake may be refrigerated or frozen.) YIELD: 10–12 pieces.

Note: To purée pumpkin, peel and cut pumpkin into small cubes. Place in a pot with ½ cup water. Steam until tender, about 10 minutes. Drain and purée by hand or in a food processor. Leftover pumpkin may be frozen.

PASTA FLORA WITH QUINCE
Pasta Flora me Kidoni

3 cups flour
2 teaspoons double-acting baking
    powder
6 ounces sweet butter
4 eggs
3 tablespoons cognac
Grated lemon peel
1½ cups quince preserves

Preheat oven to 350°F.

Blend together the flour, baking powder, and butter. Add eggs, cognac, and a little grated lemon peel. Blend well. Pat three quarters of the dough in a 12-inch round pan. Cover with the quince preserves. Fashion the remaining dough into ropes and place them lattice-style on top of the pie. Beat remaining egg and brush pastry lattice. Bake for 20 to 30 minutes. Let cool. Cut into thin pieces. YIELD: about 30 pieces.

RUM TORTE
Tourta Methismeni

½ cup sweet butter, at room temperature
1 cup sugar
2 eggs, separated
1 teaspoon orange rind
½ cup orange juice
3 tablespoons white rum
¼ teaspoon almond extract
½ teaspoon vanilla
2 cups sifted flour
2 teaspoons double-acting baking
    powder
¼ teaspoon salt
¼ teaspoon baking soda

WHIPPED-CREAM FILLING:

2 teaspoons unflavored gelatin
2 tablespoons cold water
2 cups heavy cream
½ cup confectioners' sugar
⅛ cup white rum

CHOCOLATE FROSTING:

4 squares unsweetened chocolate
1 cup confectioners' sugar
2 tablespoons hot water
2 eggs
6 tablespoons sweet butter, softened

TOPPING:

6 tablespoons white rum
1½ cups chopped walnuts

Preheat oven to 350°F.

Cream the butter with ¾ cup of the sugar until soft and fluffy. Beat in egg yolks one at a time. Add the orange rind. Sift together the flour, baking powder, salt, and baking soda. Combine the orange juice with the rum and extracts. Add liquids to the sugar mixture alternately with the sifted dry ingredients, blending well. In a separate bowl, beat the egg whites until they form soft peaks, gradually adding ¼ cup sugar. Fold the batter into the egg whites. Pour into two greased 9-inch layer cake pans. Bake for 25 minutes, or until done. Cool.

To prepare whipped-cream filling, sprinkle the gelatin over the water and heat in a saucepan over a low flame until gelatin dissolves. Let cool. Whip the heavy cream with the sugar until thick. Gradually add the rum. Beat in the gelatin, beating just until stiff enough to hold its shape. Refrigerate.

Gently melt the chocolate for the frosting. Remove from the heat and add the sugar and water. Beat in the eggs one at a time. Add the butter and beat until smooth and light.

To assemble: Cut each cake layer in half horizontally to make four layers. Sprinkle one layer with 2 tablespoons of the rum, then spread some of the cream filling over it. Top with a second layer; sprinkle it with rum, and repeat the process. When the four layers are assembled, frost top and sides of cake with the chocolate frosting. Press the walnuts into the sides of cake. Refrigerate overnight. YIELD: 12 pieces.

SAINT FANOUREO CAKE
Fanouropita

1 cup orange juice
½ cup brandy
2 tablespoons sweet butter
2 cups golden raisins
¾ cup sugar
½ cup honey
½ teaspoon salt
1 tablespoon ground cinnamon
¼ teaspoon ground cloves
2 cups flour
2 teaspoons double-acting baking
    powder
½ teaspoon baking soda
2 tablespoons grated orange rind
½ cup sesame seeds (optional)
¼ cup brandy

Saint Fanoureo is the patron saint of the "lost and found." According to tradition, whenever a treasured possession is lost, the owner pledges to bake a fruit cake for Saint Fanoureo in the hope of finding it. When the article is found the owner makes good on his vow and presents the cake to his neighborhood church for blessing. Afterwards, it is distributed to the poor and needy.

Preheat oven to 325°F.

Combine orange juice, brandy, butter, raisins, sugar, honey, salt, cinnamon, and cloves in a large heavy-bottomed saucepan. Bring to a boil, reduce heat, and simmer for 10 minutes, or until thick and syrupy. Set pot in cold water to cool mixture completely. Sift flour, baking powder, and baking soda into cooled syrup. Beat vigorously for 8 to 10 minutes, or until batter is smooth and bubbly. Stir in grated rind. Turn into well-buttered 7-inch fluted tube pan or 8-inch loaf pan. Sprinkle with sesame seeds. Bake for 1 to 1½ hours, or until an inserted knife comes out clean. Sprinkle with brandy and cool cake in pan. YIELD: 12–16 pieces.

(Lenten)

SAMALI
Samali

3½ cups farina
1½ cups sugar
3 teaspoons double-acting baking
    powder
1½ cups water
Juice of ½ lemon
Grated rind of ½ lemon

SYRUP:

1½ cups sugar
1½ cups water
¾ cup honey
Grated lemon rind to taste

Preheat oven to 350°F.

Combine the farina, sugar, baking powder, water, lemon juice, and rind, and mix well. Pour the mixture into a buttered 8- x 8-inch pan; smooth surface with a wet spatula. Bake for 20 minutes. Remove from oven and cut into diamonds. Return to oven and bake for 30 minutes. Remove from oven and let cool. Prepare syrup by boiling the sugar and water for 10 minutes. Add honey and a little lemon rind. Pour hot syrup over cool *Samali*. YIELD: 16 pieces.

TIPSY TORTE

Tourta me Krema

3 eggs
1 cup sugar
1 tablespoon grated lemon rind
1 tablespoon lemon juice
1 cup sifted flour
¼ teaspoon salt
1½ teaspoons double-acting baking
    powder
6 tablespoons hot milk

¼ cup liqueur, such as brandy or rum
½ cup milk

FILLING:

1 cup heavy cream
½ cup confectioners' sugar
1 teaspoon vanilla
1 cup chopped walnuts

FILLING # 2:

1 cup sugar
1 tablespoon water or cognac
2 cups milk, scalded
3 eggs, well beaten
5 tablespoons flour
1 square unsweetened chocolate, melted
½ teaspoon vanilla
½ teaspoon almond extract
½ cup ground toasted almonds (or
    walnuts)
1 cup heavy cream, whipped

Preheat oven to 350°F.

Beat the eggs until thick and lemon-colored. Gradually add sugar and lemon rind, then add lemon juice. Sift flour, salt, and baking powder together and gently fold into the batter. Add the milk and mix quickly until smooth. Turn at once into a loaf pan lined with buttered wax paper. Bake for 35 to 40 minutes. Cool the cake. Remove from pan and slice into three horizontal layers. Dip each slice first in the liqueur and then in the milk until saturated, but not soggy; let stand on a paper towel for a few minutes. Whip the cream with the confectioners' sugar and vanilla. Cover each layer with whipped cream and sprinkle with chopped walnuts, then cover the entire cake with cream and nuts. Keep refrigerated. YIELD: 10–12 pieces.

Variation: Bake cake as directed above but use the following filling.

To make the filling, place ½ cup of sugar in a small shallow pan with 1 tablespoon water or cognac; cook over moderate heat until sugar dissolves and turns golden. Remove from heat and combine with scalded milk. In a mixing bowl, beat the eggs well. Add ½ cup sugar and the flour and mix. Slowly add the milk mixture, stirring constantly until thickened. Divide this cream filling in two parts. Add melted chocolate to one half, and add extracts and nuts to the other.

Place a layer of sponge cake on an oblong platter; cover with the chocolate filling. Place a second layer of cake over the filling and cover with the nut filling. Finish with a top layer of sponge cake. Chill in refrigerator for at least 3 hours, or overnight. Before serving, spread top and sides with whipped cream. YIELD: 10–12 pieces.

Note: Instead of covering cake with whipped cream, confectioners' sugar may be sprinkled over it.

(Lenten)

TAHINI CAKE
Tahinopita Nistisimi

1 cup *tahini* (sesame seed paste, available in Greek or Middle Eastern specialty shops)
1 cup sugar
2 tablespoons cognac
1 teaspoon baking soda
1½ to 2 cups flour
2 teaspoons ground cinnamon
2 cups chopped walnuts, white raisins, and glacéed fruit peel, mixed
1 cup orange juice
½ cup water, if necessary
Confectioners' sugar

Preheat oven to 350°F.

If *tahini* has separated, stir to blend. Beat *tahini* in a large bowl with an electric mixer and gradually add the sugar. Combine the cognac and baking soda and add to the mixture. Sift together 1½ cups of flour with the cinnamon and combine with the mixed nuts, raisins, and fruit peel. Add the flour mixture and orange juice alternately to the *tahini* batter, mixing thoroughly after each addition. (At this point beat by hand if you have been using an electric mixer.) Add water or more flour only if necessary to attain proper consistency—batter should be thicker than an average cake batter. Butter the bottom and sides of a 9- x 12- x 2-inch baking pan and line the bottom with buttered wax paper. Pour the batter into the pan and spread evenly. Bake for 45 minutes, or until cake is a deep chestnut color. Cool in pan. Dust with confectioners' sugar while cake is still warm. When cake is completely cool cut into bars or diamond shapes. YIELD: approximately 36 bars.

Note: 1 cup walnuts and 1 cup raisins, or 2 cups walnuts may be used instead of the mixture indicated.

(Lenten)

WALNUT CAKE
Karithopita Nistisimi

4 cups flour
1 tablespoon ground cloves
3 teaspoons baking powder
1 cup raisins
1 cup oil
1½ cups sugar
2 cups water
1 teaspoon double-acting baking soda
½ cup cognac
1 tablespoon grated lemon peel
1½ cups chopped walnuts
Confectioners' sugar
Ground cinnamon

Preheat oven to 350°F.

Sift the flour into a bowl with the cloves and the baking powder. Sprinkle a little of the flour mixture over the raisins. Add the oil to the flour and rub between the palms of your hands until well blended. Make a well in the center of the flour-oil mixture. Add the sugar, water, and baking soda dissolved in the cognac. Mix lightly. Add the lemon peel, raisins, and nuts. Mix well. Grease a 9- x 12-inch pan and pour in the batter. Bake for about 1 hour. Remove and sprinkle with confectioners' sugar and cinnamon. Cut into squares and serve cold. YIELD: 24 pieces.

WALNUT TORTE

Tourta Karidiou

9 eggs, separated
1 cup sugar
3 cups ground walnuts
½ cup dry bread crumbs
1 tablespoon grated orange rind
2 teaspoons grated lemon rind
1 teaspoon ground cinnamon
½ teaspoon ground cloves
½ teaspoon salt
2 teaspoons double-acting baking
    powder
1 teaspoon vanilla
½ cup water

BRANDY BUTTER CREAM:

½ cup sweet butter or margarine
⅛ teaspoon salt
1 (1-pound) package confectioners' sugar
1 egg
1 teaspoon vanilla
2 tablespoons brandy
⅔ cup coarsely broken walnuts

Preheat oven to 350°F.

Line the bottoms of three 8-inch layer cake pans with wax paper. In a medium bowl, beat the egg yolks with the sugar at high speed until very thick and lemon-colored. In another large bowl, stir together the ground walnuts, bread crumbs, orange rind, lemon rind, cinnamon, cloves, salt, and baking powder. Mix the vanilla and water with the egg yolks, then stir into walnut mixture. In a third large bowl, beat the egg whites until stiff but not dry. Fold gently into the walnut batter until thoroughly combined. Pour into the prepared pans. Bake for 30 minutes, or until cake tester, inserted in center, comes out clean. Invert the pans on racks to cool. Loosen each cake around the edges and turn out of pan; remove wax paper.

To prepare the brandy butter cream filling, beat the butter until creamy in a small bowl. Add the salt and sugar and blend well. Beat in the egg, vanilla, and brandy. Fill and frost the three layers with the cream. Lightly press the broken walnuts into the frosting on top of torte. YIELD: 10–12 pieces.

YOGURT CAKE I

Yiaourtopita

2 cups yogurt
3½ cups farina
1 teaspoon baking soda
2 teaspoons double-acting baking
    powder
2¼ cups sugar
¼ pound blanched almonds, coarsely
    chopped
2 tablespoons grated orange peel

SYRUP:

3½ cups sugar
3 cups water
1 lemon, grated peel only

Preheat oven to 350°F.

Put the yogurt into a bowl and beat it lightly with a fork. In another bowl, mix the farina with the baking soda and baking powder and add to the yogurt. Add the sugar, almonds, and orange peel and mix well for 2 or 3 minutes. Pour the batter into a well-greased 9-inch square baking pan and bake for 30 to 40 minutes. While the cake is baking make the syrup. Place the water and sugar in a saucepan and bring to a boil. Add the lemon peel. As soon as the cake is baked—while it is still hot—pour the syrup over the top. Allow it to cool. Serves 8—10.

YOGURT CAKE II

Yiaourtopeta

½ cup sweet butter, at room temperature
1 cup sugar
1 teaspoon grated lemon rind
4 eggs, separated
1 (8-ounce) container plain yogurt
¼ cup finely chopped almonds or
    walnuts
½ teaspoon vanilla
½ teaspoon baking soda
2 tablespoons brandy or rum
1½ cups sifted cake flour
1½ teaspoons double-acting baking
    powder
¼ teaspoon salt
¼ teaspoon almond extract

SYRUP:

½ cup sugar
⅛ cup water
½ teaspoon grated lemon rind
2 whole cloves
1 small stick cinnamon
¼ cup honey
1 tablespoon lemon juice
1½ teaspoons brandy or rum extract

Preheat oven to 325°F.

Beat the butter, sugar, and lemon rind in a large mixing bowl until fluffy. Add the egg yolks and mix well. Add the yogurt and continue to mix about 1 minute. Add the nuts and vanilla. In a small bowl, dissolve the baking soda in the brandy or rum. Sift together the flour, baking powder, and salt. Add the baking soda-brandy mixture and the sifted flour mixture to the batter, mixing well for a few minutes, scraping down the sides of the bowl to blend. In another bowl, beat the egg whites until stiff, but not totally dry. Gently fold the batter into the egg whites. Add the almond extract. Pour into a greased 9-inch tube pan. Bake for 35 to 40 minutes, or until cake tests done. Cool cake 5 minutes in pan, then turn out on a large cake plate to finish cooling. While the cake bakes make the syrup. Place the sugar, water, lemon rind, cloves, and cinnamon stick in a saucepan. Bring to a boil, stirring well, and continue cooking until syrup thickens. Remove from heat. Add honey, lemon juice, and brandy. Strain carefully over the still-warm cake. Allow to stand several hours at room temperature before serving. YIELD: 12–16 pieces.

APPLE DESSERT

Mylopeta

FILLING:

2 cups peeled, cored and sliced apples
¼ cup firmly packed brown sugar
½ cup sugar
1 tablespoon lemon juice
1 teaspoon ground cinnamon
½ teaspoon ground nutmeg

PASTRY:

2 cups flour
¼ teaspoon salt
¾ cups sugar
1½ teaspoons double-acting baking
    powder
½ cup sweet butter
2 egg yolks

TOPPING:

½ teaspoon grated lemon peel
2 tablespoons finely chopped walnuts
2 tablespoons butter, at room
    temperature

Preheat oven to 375°F.

Make the filling by combining all ingredients in a saucepan and mixing well. Bring to a boil and cook for 5 minutes over medium heat, stirring occasionally, until liquid is almost completely absorbed. Remove from heat and drain, reserving liquid. Cool.

To prepare the pastry, sift dry ingredients together and cut in the butter. Add egg yolks and blend thoroughly. Reserve 1 cup of mixture for topping. Press remaining pastry into bottom and sides of an 8- x 12-inch baking pan. Pour in the drained filling. For the topping, add the lemon peel and walnuts to reserved pastry mixture. Sprinkle over apple filling. Dot with soft butter and pour reserved apple syrup over top. Bake for 45 minutes, or until golden brown. YIELD: 24 pieces.

CHESTNUT PIE

Tourta Kastano

2 pounds chestnuts
1 (14-ounce) can sweetened condensed
    milk
2 tablespoons sweet butter
8 lady fingers (or more, if necessary)
¼ cup cognac
1 cup whipped cream for garnish

Chestnuts are very popular in Greece, where they are used frequently in pies and cakes, as well as eaten plain, boiled or roasted. One of the most popular snacks for school children, in fact, is a colander full of boiled chestnuts kept warm with a heavy terry cloth cover. The one drawback is that chestnuts are somewhat tedious to prepare. In this recipe two 8-ounce cans of chestnut purée may be substituted for the whole nuts.

Simmer shelled nuts in water for about 15 minutes, or until tender but not mushy. Purée with the milk and butter. Cook over low heat stirring constantly, until mixture comes to a boil. Add a little water if mixture is too thick. Remove from heat. Cover the bottom and sides of a 9-inch pie plate with the lady fingers. Sprinkle with cognac. Fill with the chestnut purée and decorate with whipped cream. YIELD: 10–12 pieces.

PREPARATION OF CHESTNUTS

To shell chestnuts cut an X on the flat side of each nut. Put in cold water, bring to a boil, cover, and boil for 1 to 2 minutes. Remove pan from heat but do not drain nuts. Scoop out 2 or 3 at a time, and remove hard outer shell and the inner brown skin.

HONEY PIE

✢ SIPHNOS

Melopeta

PIE SHELL:

2 cups flour
½ cup sugar
⅔ cup sweet butter, at room temperature
1 egg plus 1 egg yolk
2 tablespoons cognac

FILLING:

1 pound *mizithra* or ricotta cheese
3 eggs
⅓ cup sugar
½ cup honey
1 tablespoon grated lemon rind
3 tablespoons flour
Ground cinnamon

An Easter treat on the island of Siphnos, this delicious pie is made from a soft, unsalted ewe's milk cheese called *mizithra*. Since *mizithra* is not easily obtainable outside of Greece, ricotta cheese, which it closely resembles, can be substituted.

Preheat oven to 350°F.
To prepare the pie shell, mix the flour, sugar, and butter together. Add the eggs and cognac and blend well. Press half of mixture evenly in a 9-inch pie plate. Freeze the other half for another time or use as a crust for a second pie. Mix all filling ingredients except the cinnamon and pour into the unbaked shell. Sprinkle with cinnamon and bake for 1 hour. YIELD: 8–10 pieces.

SWEET RICE *PETA*

Glekia Rizopeta

CRUST:

3 cups flour
1 teaspoon salt
3 tablespoons olive oil
1 cup warm water
½ pound melted sweet butter
¼ cup sugar
Ground cinnamon

FILLING:

¾ cup raw rice, soaked in water for 4
   hours
½ cup warm water
1½ quarts milk
¼ pound sweet butter
1-cup sugar
½ teaspoon lemon rind (optional)
4 eggs

Another excellent recipe from Kastoria in northern Greece.

Preheat oven to 375°F.

To make the crust (while the rice for the filling soaks), sift the flour and salt into a bowl. Add the oil and water. Mix and knead for 15 minutes, using more flour if necessary to keep from sticking. Divide the dough in half. Cover one half with a damp towel and divide the other half into 10 balls. On a floured table, roll each ball out into a thin circle; brush each circle with butter and stack on a plate. Fold layers into a ball and refrigerate until butter hardens. Repeat this procedure with remaining dough.

For the filling, cook the rice, water, milk, butter, sugar, and lemon rind over low heat until thick. Cool to warm. Beat eggs well and add to rice mixture. Roll the first cold pastry ball out on a floured table to a size two inches larger all around than an 11- x 17- x 1-inch pan or equivalent. Butter the pan and lay pastry in it. Pour in the filling; roll out a second pastry ball like the first and place it on top of the filling. This top layer should be loose and wrinkly. Fold the edge of bottom crust over top; roll and seal by fluting. Brush with additional melted butter. Bake for 1 hour. Allow to cool before cutting. Sprinkle with cinnamon-sugar (¼ cup sugar plus 1 tablespoon cinnamon, or to taste) before serving. YIELD: 36 pieces.

COOKIES

ALMOND SQUARES

Tetragona Amigdalota

1 cup sweet butter, at room temperature
1 cup sugar
2 cups flour
1½ tablespoons ground cinnamon
1 egg yolk
2 egg whites, lightly beaten
½ cup sugar
1 cup chopped almonds

Preheat oven to 350°F.

Mix butter, sugar, flour, 1 tablespoon cinnamon, and egg yolk together and knead thoroughly. Press dough into a buttered 9- x 13-inch pan. Brush surface of the dough with the lightly beaten egg whites. Mix the sugar and remaining cinnamon together and sprinkle over the dough. Sprinkle the almonds on top. Bake for 20 to 25 minutes, or until golden. Cut into squares while still hot. YIELD: 16 pieces.

ALMOND COOKIES

Pastoules

¾ cup sweet butter, at room temperature
1 cup sugar
1 teaspoon double-acting baking powder
4 eggs, separated and at room temperature
3¼ cups flour
¾ pound almonds, shelled and chopped
1 (8-ounce) box confectioners' sugar
1 (8-ounce) jar orange or raspberry preserves

Preheat oven to 350°F.

Cream together the butter and sugar. Add the baking powder and the egg yolks, one at a time, to the batter. When the yolks are blended, add the flour, one cup at a time. Beat to form soft dough. Beat the egg whites in a bowl until fluffy, but not stiff. Shape the dough into round, flattened balls 1 inch in diameter. Dip each cookie individually into the egg-white mixture and then roll in the almonds. Make a groove in the center and place on a cookie sheet about 1 inch apart. Bake for 30 minutes. Allow to cool on the sheet and then dip in confectioners' sugar. Place ¼ teaspoon preserves in the center of each cookie. YIELD: 45–50 cookies.

ALMOND MERENGUES

Bezedes

4 egg whites at room temperature
1 cup sugar
1 teaspoon vanilla
1 teaspoon ground cinnamon
½ cup coarsely chopped blanched almonds

Preheat oven to 200°F.

Beat egg whites until stiff. While beating add sugar, a little at a time. Add vanilla, cinnamon, and almonds and continue beating. Place spoonfuls of mixture into a large baking pan lined with wax paper. Bake for 1 hour, or until golden. Serve cool as a cookie. YIELD: 36 pieces.

ANISE AND SESAME SEED COOKIES

Koulourakia me Glikaniso

¾ cup olive oil
1 tablespoon aniseed
1 tablespoon sesame seeds
1 cup sugar
½ cup lemon juice
1 teaspoon grated lemon peel
1 teaspoon grated orange peel
4½ cups sifted flour
1 tablespoon ground cinnamon
Sliced blanched almonds
Cinnamon sugar

Preheat oven to 375°F.

Heat the olive oil, anise-, and sesame seeds over medium heat for 5 minutes. Cool. Add sugar, lemon juice, lemon peel, and orange peel. Stir flour, 1 cup at a time, and cinnamon into the mixture. Work dough with hands until smooth. Cover and let stand for 30 minutes. Roll out dough on a lightly floured board to ¼-inch thickness. Cut with a 2-inch round cookie cutter and place on an ungreased cookie sheet. Decorate with almond slices, pressing so they adhere. Bake for 12 to 15 minutes, or until lightly brown. Sprinkle with cinnamon sugar and cool. YIELD: 8 dozen.

Note: This recipe can readily be cut in half.

CANDIED FRUIT TURNOVERS

Skalstounakia me Fruota

4 cups sifted flour
1 level teaspoon double-acting baking
    powder
3 tablespoons sugar
Dash of ground cinnamon
1 cup sweet butter
2 egg yolks, beaten
3 tablespoons apricot brandy
½ cup white raisins
½ cup finely chopped candied fruit
1 cup chopped nuts
1 cup apricot marmalade
Rosewater
Confectioners' sugar

Preheat oven to 375°F.

Sift together the flour, baking powder, sugar, and cinnamon. Cut in the butter and work with the fingers until well blended. Combine beaten egg yolks with the brandy. Add to mixture and knead slightly. Roll out portions of dough until thin. Cut in 4 to 5-inch rounds. Combine the raisins, fruit, nuts, and marmalade. Place 1 tablespoon of filling on each round of dough. Wet edges with water and fold over to form a half moon. Press edges with fork to seal in filling. Place on greased cookie sheets and bake for 20 minutes. Sprinkle turnovers with rosewater and roll in confectioners' sugar. YIELD: 3 dozen cookies.

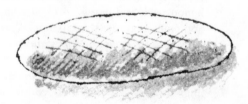

CHERRY DELIGHT

Pasta me Visino

6 eggs
2 cups sugar
4 cups milk, scalded and cooled
1 tablespoon vanilla
1 box zwieback crumbs
Visino preserves (see note) or
    maraschino cherries

Preheat oven to 375°F.

Beat the eggs with the sugar until light. Stir in the milk and vanilla. Blend in the zwieback crumbs and pour into a buttered 10- x 14-inch pan. Bake for 30 minutes. Remove from oven and cut into squares or diamond shapes. Decorate with cherry preserves or maraschino cherry halves. YIELD: 16 pieces.

Note: *Visino* is a Greek sour cherry preserve available in gourmet and Greek specialty shops.

CHESTNUT CUPCAKES

Kastanokekakia

2 eggs, separated
1 cup sugar
1 cup sifted flour
2 teaspoons double-acting baking
    powder
½ teaspoon ground cinnamon
¼ teaspoon ground allspice
3 tablespoons vegetable oil
¼ cup drained plain yogurt (see note) or
    sour cream
1 (15½-ounce) can, or 2 cups
    unsweetened chestnut purée
1 teaspoon vanilla

Preheat oven to 350°F.

Place egg yolks in mixing bowl and beat until light and lemon-colored. Add sugar slowly, continuing to beat until mixture is thick and fluffy. Sift dry ingredients together and add to the yolk mixture, along with the oil, yogurt, and chestnut purée. Blend well and add the vanilla. Beat the egg whites until stiff and fold gently into the mixture. Pour the batter into 12 greased and floured individual cupcake molds. Bake for 25 to 30 minutes. Cool in pans for 5 minutes before turning out on a rack to complete cooling. YIELD: 12 cupcakes.

Note: To drain yogurt, empty one container plain yogurt into a cheesecloth bag and allow excess liquid to drip out.

COCONUT COOKIES

Biscota Karydas

¼ pound sweet butter
¾ cup sugar
4 large eggs
1 teaspoon vanilla
16 ounces shredded coconut
Cognac
Confectioners' sugar

Preheat oven to 350°F.

Cream butter and sugar together until light. Add eggs, one at a time, beating well after each addition. Add the vanilla and the coconut and mix well. Dampen hands with cognac. Take 1 tablespoonful of the mixture at a time and roll into balls. Place balls 1 inch apart on cookie sheets. Bake for 15 minutes, or until a light golden color. Sift confectioners' sugar onto a sheet of wax paper. Carefully remove cookies from cookie sheets and place on the sugar. Sift additional sugar over cookies. Store in an airtight container immediately after cooling. YIELD: approximately 7 dozen small cookies.

FENIKIA WITH WINE

Fenikia Krasata

3 cups corn oil
1 cup sweet butter
1 cup sugar
1 teaspoon double-acting baking powder
1 cup white wine
3 tablespoons whiskey
9–10 cups flour
1 pound shelled walnuts
1 teaspoon ground cinnamon

SYRUP:

2 cups water
1 (1-pound) jar honey
2 cups sugar

Preheat oven to 350°F.

In a mixing bowl, combine the oil, butter, and sugar and blend well. Dilute the baking powder in the wine and add to batter. Add the whiskey and the flour, 1 cup at a time, to form a soft dough (the last cups will probably have to be worked in by hand). Shape the dough one tablespoon at a time into oblong, sausage-shaped cookies. Place on an ungreased cookie sheet. Bake for 30 minutes, or until golden brown. Meanwhile, chop the walnuts finely, add the cinnamon, and set aside. When the cookies are cool, prepare the syrup by placing the water, honey, and sugar in a heavy saucepan and boiling for 10 minutes. Reduce heat to low and dip each cookie in the syrup; roll in the walnut-cinnamon mixture. YIELD: 150 cookies.

FRUIT TARTS

Tartes me Frouta

1 cup sweet butter, at room temperature
¾ cup sugar
2 eggs
1 teaspoon grated lemon rind
1 teaspoon vanilla
2½ cups sifted flour
1 teaspoon baking soda
½ teaspoon salt
Apricot, peach, cherry, or strawberry
    jam

TOPPING:

4 eggs, separated
1 cup sugar
1 teaspoon grated lemon rind
1 tablespoon brandy or rum
1 cup ground almonds

Preheat oven to 350°F.

Cream the butter and sugar and blend in the eggs, lemon rind, and vanilla. Sift together the flour, baking soda, and salt and add to the batter, blending in well. Knead the dough until smooth. Using greased cupcake pans or miniature tart pans, line bottoms and sides with a layer of dough, pressing it evenly with the fingers. (This is enough dough for about 36 tartlets.) Fill each tart with 2 teaspoons of jam. To prepare topping beat the egg whites until stiff, then add the egg yolks, one at a time, continuing to beat. Add the sugar, lemon rind, and liquor and beat a little more. Add almonds and beat enough to blend. Put 2 to 3 teaspoonsful on each tart. Bake for 30 to 35 minutes. YIELD: 3 dozen tarts.

FLAOUNES
Flaounes

¾ cup corn oil
2 eggs
4 teaspoons sugar
3 pieces mastic flavoring, optional (See "A Greek Spice Rack" in the Appendix)
¼ cup milk, warmed
2½ cups flour
1 teaspoon double-acting baking powder
¼ teaspoon salt

FILLING:

2 cups ricotta cheese
1 cup grated *kefalotiri* (or romano) and *kasseri* cheese, mixed
2 eggs
2 tablespoons semolina
2 tablespoons finely crushed mint leaves
Sesame seeds

These are the traditional Easter cookies of Cyprus.

In a mixer, beat the corn oil with 1 egg until thick. Add 3 teaspoons of the sugar and beat. Pound the mastic with the remaining teaspoon of sugar and add to the batter and then add the warm milk. Blend well. In another bowl, sift the flour with baking powder and salt. Gradually add to the batter, mixing by hand when the dough becomes thick. Knead for 6 to 10 minutes, or until elastic and smooth. Cover and allow to rest for a few hours before rolling. In the meantime, prepare the filling by combining the ricotta, the grated cheeses, 2 eggs, the semolina, and the mint. The filling should be thick and flavorful.

Preheat oven to 350°F.

Break off sections of the dough and roll out as thin as possible. Using a round plate or pastry cutter, cut out 6-inch circles. Fill the center of each with 2 heaping table-spoons of the filling. Fold up the sides of the circle to form squares or triangles, or some of each, leaving cheese filling exposed in the center. Beat the remaining egg and use to brush the dough edges. Sprinkle the *Flaounes* with sesame seeds and bake for 20 to 25 minutes, or until dough is crisp and a golden chestnut color and the filling is firm. Serve warm. YIELD: 24–30 pieces.

Variations: Cinnamon may be substituted for mint, and ½ cup raisins may be added along with the cheese. Cottage or farmer cheese may be used instead of ricotta if you are counting calories. Also, instead of making the dough from scratch, you might want to use refrigerated butterflake dinner rolls. Separate and flatten the pieces and proceed as described above.

HONEY ORANGE COOKIES
Biscotakia me Meli

½ cup shortening
½ cup sugar
1 egg
1 teaspoon grated orange rind
½ cup honey
3 cups sifted flour
3 teaspoons double-acting baking powder
½ teaspoon salt
½ cup orange juice
½ cup chopped walnuts
½ cup raisins

Preheat oven to 375°F.

In a bowl, cream the shortening. Gradually beat in the sugar until light and fluffy. Add the egg and grated orange rind and beat thoroughly. Blend the honey into creamed mixture. Sift together the flour, baking powder, and salt, and add to batter alternately with the orange juice. Stir in nuts and raisins. Drop by rounded teaspoon-fuls onto lightly greased baking sheets. Bake for 12 to 15 minutes, or until golden brown. Place cookies on racks to cool before storing in airtight containers. YIELD: 7 dozen cookies.

ICED *KOURABIEDES*

Zaharomeni Kourabiedes

½ pound whipped sweet butter, at room
    temperature
½ cup superfine or confectioners' sugar
1 egg yolk
1½ tablespoons cognac
2½ cups flour (approximately)

ICING:

2 cups sifted confectioners' sugar
2 tablespoons hot milk
½ teaspoon almond flavoring

Preheat oven to 325°F.

In a mixing bowl, beat butter for about 5 minutes at medium speed. Gradually add sugar and beat 3 minutes more. Add egg yolk and beat another 3 minutes. Add cognac and beat another minute. Gradually add 2 cups flour and mix well at low speed until dough is soft and slightly sticky. (Add the additional ½ cup flour if the dough is too sticky.) Shape dough by hand into any cookie shape desired; cookies should be about ½ inch thick. Bake for 15 minutes, or until pale golden brown. Cool.

To make the icing blend the sugar, milk, and flavoring well. Ice the cooled *Kourabiedes*. YIELD: 2 dozen cookies.

KOURABIEDES WITH CINNAMON

Kourabiedes me Kanela

1 pound sweet butter
1 cup confectioners' sugar, plus
    additional sugar for sprinkling
    baked cookies
2 egg yolks
2 tablespoons cinnamon
2 teaspoons double-acting baking
    powder
2⅜ cups flour
1 jigger brandy
1 pound almonds, toasted with their
    skins and coarsely ground
Rosewater

Beat the butter in electric mixer until very light and fluffy. Slowly add 1 cup confectioners' sugar and beat again. Add egg yolks one at a time, beating well after each addition. Mix the cinnamon and baking powder with 1 cup flour. Slowly add flour mixture and brandy to butter mixture, beating well. Then slowly add more flour, approximately 1⅜ cups, working it in by hand to form a soft dough. Add almonds to the dough and refrigerate dough for about 1 hour.

Preheat oven to 325°F.

Shape dough into small "S" shapes about ½ inch thick and place on a cookie sheet. Bake for 25 to 30 minutes. Sprinkle with rosewater and cover with confectioners' sugar while still warm. YIELD: 5 dozen cookies.

NUT SQUARES

Tetragona Marenga

1 cup sweet butter, at room temperature
1½ cups sugar
2 cups flour
1½ tablespoons ground cinnamon
1 egg yolk
2 egg whites, slightly beaten
1 cup chopped nuts

Preheat oven to 350°F.

Mix together the butter, 1 cup sugar, flour, 1 tablespoon cinnamon, and the egg yolk and knead thoroughly. Press dough lightly in a buttered 9- x 13-inch baking pan. Brush surface with egg whites. Combine remaining ½ cup sugar, nuts, and ½ tablespoon cinnamon and sprinkle over egg whites. Bake for 20 to 25 minutes, until nicely browned. Cut into squares while hot; cool in pan. YIELD: 32 pieces.

NUT BARS

Karidata

6 eggs, separated
1¼ cups sugar
3½ cups finely ground walnut meats
3 teaspoons almond extract

Preheat oven to 325°F.

Line the bottom of a 9- x 9- x 2-inch pan with wax paper and grease the paper. Beat the egg yolks until thick and about tripled in volume. Slowly add sugar, beating until thick, about 10 minutes. Slowly fold in nuts and almond extract. Beat egg whites until stiff but not dry. Fold egg whites into yolk mixture and pour into pan. Bake for 1 hour. Cool 10 minutes, remove from pan, peel off paper, and cut into squares. May be stored in the refrigerator or in a plastic container. YIELD: about 20 squares.

PINE NUT CRESCENTS

Misofengara me Koukounaria

1 cup sweet butter, at room temperature
⅔ cup sugar
3 egg yolks
1 teaspoon grated orange peel
½ teaspoon vanilla
2¾ cups flour
⅓ cup pignolias (pine nuts)
3 tablespoons honey

Preheat oven to 325°F.

In a bowl beat together the butter and sugar until creamy. Beat in egg yolks, one at a time. Beat in orange peel and vanilla. Stir flour into butter mixture until well blended. Measure about 1 tablespoon of dough for each cookie and roll between lightly floured palms into ropes about 2½-inches long. Place cookies 2 inches apart on a greased cookie sheet. Shape each into a crescent. Scatter pine nuts over cookies and press in firmly to anchor. Heat honey over low heat until it liquefies and brush it liberally over cookies. Bake for 15 minutes, or until golden. Cool cookies on a rack. Store in airtight container. YIELD: about 3½ dozen cookies.

"LITTLE THIEVES"
Kleftika Koulourakia

1½ packages dry yeast
2½ cups plus 1 teaspoon sugar
¼ cup warm water (lukewarm for
    compressed yeast)
½ cup butter
1 teaspoon salt
¾ cup milk, scalded
4 cups sifted flour
3 eggs, beaten
1 cup sweet butter, melted
1½ cups finely chopped walnuts

Dissolve yeast and 1 teaspoon sugar in the water. Combine the butter, ½ cup sugar, and salt. Add scalded milk and stir until butter melts. Cool to lukewarm. Add dissolved yeast and mix well. Add 2 cups of the flour and beat until smooth. Beat in eggs. Gradually add remaining flour, beating after each addition to make a soft dough. Knead on a lightly floured surface until smooth. Place in a greased bowl, cover, and let rise in a warm place until double in bulk, about 1 hour. Divide dough into fourths. Shape each piece on a lightly floured surface into a 12-inch roll. Divide each roll into 12 pieces. Shape each piece into a 7-inch rope. Dip each into melted butter, then sugar, melted butter, and chopped nuts. Fold each rope in half; twist to make a braid. Place on a greased baking sheet and cover. Let rise in warm place until double in bulk, about 20 minutes. Preheat oven to 350°F. Bake for 15 to 20 minutes. YIELD: 4 dozen pastries.

SESAME TURNOVERS
                                                          ✣ CRETE
Cretika Patouthia

FILLING:
2 pounds walnuts, finely ground
1 pound almonds, finely ground
1 cup sesame seeds
1 teaspoon powdered mastic flavoring
    (see Appendix)
1½ teaspoons double-acting baking
    powder
Honey

PASTRY:
1½ cups olive oil
1 cup water
½ teaspoon powdered mastic flavoring
    (see Appendix)
½ teaspoon double-acting baking powder
¾ tablespoon salt
½ cup sugar
Juice of 1 lemon
½ cup orange juice
3 cups flour
Cornstarch

¼ cup rose water (optional)
2 tablespoons confectioners' sugar
    (optional)

Preheat oven to 300°F.

Mix together all filling ingredients except honey. Add enough honey to blend mixture well. Set aside and prepare pastry. Mix all pastry ingredients together except flour and cornstarch. Gradually add flour, forming a dough that will not be sticky. Roll dough out to a thickness of ⅛ inch on a board sprinkled with cornstarch. Cut dough into 6-inch circles. Place a tablespoon of the nut mixture in the center of each circle. Fold over as for turnovers, pressing edges of dough together. Place on a greased pan and bake for 15 minutes. Remove from oven and, if desired, dip into rosewater and sprinkle generously with confectioners' sugar. YIELD: 20–30 turnovers.

SKALTSOUNIA COOKIES

Skaltsounia

FILLING:

1 cup chopped walnuts
1 cup chopped almonds
½ cup sesame seeds, roasted and
    pounded in a mortar
¼ cup sugar
3 tablespoons cognac
1 teaspoon ground nutmeg
½ teaspoon ground cinnamon
Grated rind and juice of 2 tangerines (or
    1 large orange)
Confectioners' sugar

DOUGH:

¼ pound sweet butter
⅓ cup sugar
⅓ cup vegetable oil
⅓ cup fresh orange juice
⅛ teaspoon ground cinnamon
¼ teaspoon baking soda
1½ tablespoons brandy
½ teaspoon double-acting baking powder
2–3 cups flour

Preheat oven to 350°F.

Mix the nuts, sesame seeds, sugar, cognac, nutmeg, cinnamon, tangerine rind, and juice together in a bowl. Set aside. To make the dough, cream the butter until fluffy. Gradually beat in the sugar and oil; continue beating for about 5 minutes. Add the orange juice, cinnamon, and baking soda diluted in brandy. Sift the baking powder with 1 cup flour and add to the mixture. Slowly add enough additional flour to form a soft dough. Work well. Roll out dough, one rounded tablespoon at a time into 4- or 5-inch circles. Place a full teaspoon of the filling on one half of each circle. Fold the other half down to form a crescent shape. Press down with the fingers to seal the edges or use a pastry crimp. Bake for 15 to 20 minutes, or until a very light rosy color. Immediately sprinkle generously with confectioners' sugar. YIELD: approximately 40 crescents.

(Lenten)

SKALTSOUNIA II

Skaltsounia

DOUGH:

3 cups flour
1 teaspoon double-acting baking powder
1 cup *tahini*
½ cup warm water
2 tablespoons honey

FILLING:

½ cup chopped walnuts
½ cup chopped almonds
½ cup seedless raisins
½ cup orange marmalade
2 tablespoons honey

Rosewater
1½ cups confectioners' sugar

Preheat oven to 350°F.

Sift flour and baking powder together. Add the *tahini* and blend with fingers. Add water and honey. Roll dough out to a thickness of ⅛ inch and cut into 5-inch rounds. Combine the nuts, raisins, marmalade, and honey for the filling. Place 1 tablespoon of filling on each round of dough. Fold dough to form a half circle, press edges together and brush with a little water to seal. Bake for 30 minutes. Sprinkle with rosewater when hot and sift confectioners' sugar over the *Skaltsounia*. YIELD: 24–26 pieces.

Note: The dough used in this recipe makes a good *nistisimo* (Lenten) pie crust for any purpose.

SWEET BISCUITS
Paximadakia

¾ pound sweet butter
1 cup corn oil
2 cups sugar
2 eggs
¼ teaspoon baking soda
1 cup warm milk
3 pounds flour (approximate)
2 teaspoons double-acting baking
    powder

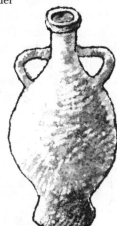

Preheat oven to 350°F.

Cream the butter and corn oil until light and fluffy. Gradually add the sugar. Beat in eggs one at a time and continue mixing. Dissolve the baking soda in the warm milk and add to the mixture. Mix 1 cup flour with the baking powder and add to the batter. Continue adding flour until you have a soft dough. Pat into narrow loaves about 1 inch high and 6 to 8 inches long. Place on a greased cookie sheet. Mark loaves into 1-inch slices, cutting halfway down. Bake for 20 to 25 minutes. Remove from oven and slice through while hot. Turn slices on their sides and return to oven. Bake for 10 to 15 minutes, or until golden brown. YIELD: 10–12 dozen biscuits.

WINE COOKIES
Tsourekakia

✣ KITHIRA

1¼ cups sugar
¾ pound sweet butter
½ cup vegetable oil
⅛ cup cognac
1 teaspoon double-acting baking powder
½ cup white wine
6–7 cups flour
1 egg, lightly beaten

Preheat oven to 350°F.

Cream the sugar and butter until well blended. Add the oil and beat well. Add the cognac. Dilute the baking powder in ¼ cup of the wine and add to the batter. When well blended, add the remaining ¼ cup of wine. Slowly add the flour, 1 cup at a time. Work the flour to form a soft dough, using your hands as the mixture thickens. To facilitate handling, divide the dough into chunks, knead each chunk several minutes and roll out to a thickness of ¼ inch. The traditional *Tsourekakia* is made by taking three 3-inch-long strips of dough, laying them next to each other and pinching them together at the ends. The rolled out dough may also be cut with any type of cookie cutter. Place on an ungreased cookie sheet. Using a pastry brush, brush each cookie with a little of the beaten egg. Bake for 30 minutes, or until golden. Cool completely before removing from cookie sheets. Store in airtight containers. YIELD: 75 cookies.

Note: Recipe may be doubled successfully.

YO-YO

Yioyio

1 pound sweet butter
½ cup confectioners' sugar
1 egg, beaten
1 cup finely chopped blanched almonds
5 tablespoons brandy
⅛ cup orange juice
1 teaspoon double-acting baking powder
4½–5 cups sifted flour
1 (1-pound) jar apricot preserves
Confectioners' sugar for topping

Preheat oven to 350°F.

Cream butter until very light. Beat in sugar, egg, almonds, brandy, and orange juice. Sift baking powder with flour and carefully blend into butter mixture. Shape into small round cookies the size of a quarter and about ¼-inch thick. Bake on ungreased baking pan for 15 minutes. Cool. Spread apricot marmalade over half the cookies and top with remaining half to form "sandwiches." Sprinkle a piece of wax paper with confectioners' sugar and place cookies on it. Sprinkle more confectioners' sugar on top to cover completely. Cool thoroughly before storing. YIELD: 3 dozen cookies.

PHYLLO DESSERTS

Despite the wide array of cakes, pies and cookies that appear on the preceding pages, to most people Greek desserts mean a *phyllo*-based pastry. We have encountered this extremely versatile, paper-thin dough in the appetizer and entrée sections of this book, but it is as a dessert that *phyllo* truly comes into its own. Who can resist that layered edifice of nuts, fruits, and melt-in-the-mouth dough known as *Baklava* or that shredded version of *phyllo* known as *Kadaife*? Diets are quickly forgotten in the presence of such honey-soaked delights as *Sourota* and *Galatoboureko*. Though *phyllo* is not difficult to work with, it does demand a certain amount of practice and we strongly recommend that you read the "How to Work with *Phyllo*" section of the Appendix before undertaking any of the following recipes.

ALMOND AND WALNUT TRIANGLES

Trigona me Amigdala ke Karidia

¾ pound walnuts, coarsely chopped
¾ pound almonds, coarsely chopped
2 cups sugar
5 eggs
1½ pounds *phyllo* pastry
1 pound melted sweet butter for
    brushing *phyllo*
Confectioners' sugar

Preheat oven to 350°F.

Combine the walnuts and almonds. Beat the eggs with the sugar until thick and lemon-colored. Add the nuts. Cut the *phyllo* sheets into thirds lengthwise. Butter the pastry strips, one at a time. (Keep remaining strips covered with plastic wrap.) Place a teaspoon of filling on the bottom of each strip and fold into a triangular shape. (Read How to Work with *Phyllo*, in Appendix.) Bake for 30 minutes, or until golden, When cool, sprinkle with confectioners' sugar. YIELD: 120 pieces.

Note: Triangles may be frozen, unbaked. When ready to use place unthawed in the oven and increase baking time by 15 minutes.

ALMOND PIE WITH *PHYLLO*

⚓ KITHIRA

Amigdalopeta

6 eggs separated
½ cup sugar
1 teaspoon double-acting baking powder
1 cup ground zwieback
2 cups shelled ground almonds
¼ teaspoon salt
1 pound *phyllo* pastry
¾ cup melted sweet butter for brushing
    phyllo

SYRUP:

2 cups sugar
1 cup water
Juice of ½ lemon

Preheat oven to 350°F.

Beat the egg yolks with the sugar until thick. Add the baking powder, zwieback crumbs, almonds, and salt and set aside. In another bowl, beat the egg whites until stiff but not dry. Fold into almond mixture. Grease a 9- x 13-inch pan. Butter half the *phyllo* sheets, one at a time, and overlap in the greased pan so as to cover the entire bottom and sides, with some overhang on all edges. (Keep unused sheets covered with plastic wrap or a damp cloth; see How to Work with *Phyllo*, in Appendix.) Pour almond mixture over the *phyllo* sheets. Fold over the overhanging *phyllo* and place the remaining sheets, brushed one at a time with butter, over the filling. After all the sheets have been used, score (but do not cut all the way through) the top layers of the pastry sheets with a sharp knife to make triangles. Bake for 35 to 45 minutes, until golden. Remove from oven and cool. While pastry cools, prepare syrup by combining sugar, water and lemon juice in a saucepan and boil for 15 minutes. Pour hot syrup over cooled pie. YIELD: 40–50 pieces.

ALMOND ROLLS

⚓ MYTILENE

Roula me Amigdala

1½ pounds sugar
1 cup water
2 teaspoons lemon juice
2 pounds shelled almonds, finely
    chopped
1 teaspoon vanilla
2 egg whites
2 pounds *phyllo* pastry
2 pounds melted sweet butter for
    brushing *phyllo*
Confectioners' sugar

Preheat oven to 350°F.

Place the sugar in a large saucepan. Add the water and lemon juice and bring to a boil to make a syrup. When mixture begins to thicken, immediately add the chopped almonds and vanilla and stir vigorously. When mixture is very thick remove from heat and let cool. Beat the egg whites, add to cooled mixture, and stir well. Cut each *phyllo* sheet into thirds lengthwise. Butter each strip, one at a time. Place 1 teaspoon of the filling at the bottom of each strip and roll up (see How to Work with *Phyllo* in the Appendix). Place rolls, seam side down, in a baking pan and bake for 25 to 30 minutes until golden. Cool and serve sprinkled with confectioners' sugar. YIELD: 160 pieces.

Note: These rolls may be prepared and frozen, unbaked. When ready to use, place unthawed in the oven and increase baking time by 15 minutes.

BAKLAVA WITH PISTACHIO NUTS

Baklava me Fistikia Aeginas

1 recipe Basic Sweet Syrup (see below)
1 pound shelled pistachio nuts, ground
2 teaspoons sugar
½ teaspoon rosewater
1 pound *phyllo* pastry
1 pound melted sweet butter for
    brushing *phyllo*

This and the following recipes are variations on the traditional basic *Baklava* recipes which appear on pages 173–174 of *The Art of Greek Cookery*.

Prepare Basic Sweet Syrup recipe and set aside to cool. Preheat oven to 350°F.

Mix the nuts, sugar, and rosewater together. Lightly grease a 9- x 13- x 2½-inch baking pan. Divide whole *phyllo* sheets in half and cover with plastic wrap or a damp towel until ready to use to prevent pastry sheets from drying out (see How to Work With *Phyllo*, in the Appendix). Butter the half sheets of *phyllo* one at a time and place in the baking pan until one half of the *phyllo* sheets are used. (Spread out and overlap sheets so as to cover entire bottom of pan.) Pour nut mixture over the *phyllo* and distribute evenly. Cover nut mixture with remaining *phyllo* sheets in the same manner as before, brushing each half-sheet individually with melted butter. With a sharp knife, mark diamond shapes on the *phyllo*, cutting only three quarters of the way through, not to the bottom of the pan. Bake until golden brown, about 1 hour. Remove from oven and immediately pour cold syrup over hot pastry. YIELD: 40–50 pieces.

Note: *Baklava* may be prepared and frozen, unbaked. When ready to use place unthawed in the oven and increase baking time by 20 minutes.

BASIC SWEET SYRUP

2 cups sugar
1 cup water
1 tablespoon lemon juice
Stick cinnamon
2 tablespoons honey

Boil together sugar, water, lemon juice, and cinnamon for 20 minutes. Remove from heat and add honey. Return syrup to low heat and simmer for 2 minutes. Makes 2 cups.

BAKLAVA ROLLS

Sourota

SYRUP:

2 cups sugar
2 cups water
1 tablespoon lemon juice
1 stick cinnamon
⅛ cup honey

PASTRY:

1 pound *phyllo* pastry
½ cup zwieback, finely chopped (in blender)
½ pound walnuts, finely chopped (in blender)
1 teaspoon ground cinnamon
¼ cup sugar
¾ pound melted sweet butter for brushing *phyllo*

To prepare the syrup, combine the sugar, water, lemon juice, and cinnamon in a saucepan and simmer for 40 minutes. Remove from heat and stir in honey. Set aside to cool.

Preheat oven to 350°F.

Cut the *phyllo* sheets into thirds; cover with plastic wrap or a damp cloth until ready to use. (See How to Work with *Phyllo* in Appendix.) Combine the zwieback, walnuts, cinnamon, and sugar. Take one sheet of *phyllo* at a time, brush with butter and keep the rest covered. Fold the long edges of the *phyllo* about ¼ inch in toward the middle. Spread 1 teaspoon of the mixture across the *phyllo* sheet about ¼ inch in from one of the unfolded narrow edges. Fold pastry up over the mixture. Place a dowel or pencil on the bottom edge of the *phyllo* (see diagram) and use to roll pastry into a cylinder. Push in the rolled *phyllo* from both sides, toward the center, to gather. Hold the pastry with left hand and pull out dowel with right hand. Place on a cookie sheet. Repeat procedure until all the *phyllo* and nut mixture are used up. Butter top of each *Sourota* well. Bake until golden, about 15 minutes. Dip hot pastry in cold syrup; place on dish. Do not cover. YIELD: approximately 75 pieces.

Note: Baked and dipped *Sourota* keep well almost indefinitely in the freezer. To serve, thaw at room temperature for about 1 hour.

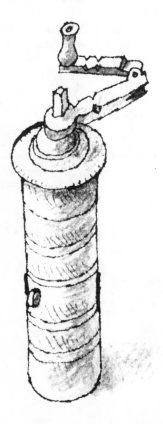

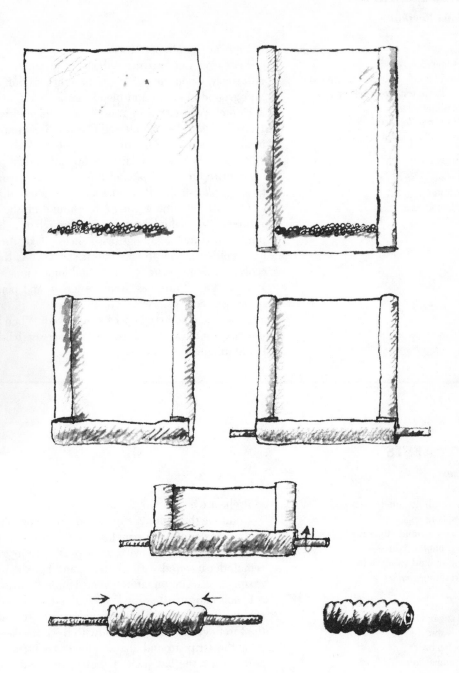

APRICOT *BAKLAVA*

Baklava Verikoko

12 eggs
1 cup sugar
1½ pound blanched almonds, ground
1½ pounds melted sweet butter for
 brushing *phyllo*
1½ pounds *phyllo* pastry
1 (1-pound) jar apricot preserves

SYRUP:

4 cups sugar
3 cups water
1 slice lemon

Preheat oven to 350°F.

Beat eggs until creamy, about 10 minutes. Gradually add sugar. Continue beating until light and fluffy. Slowly add ground almonds and blend thoroughly. Grease a 10- x 15-inch pan with 1 or 2 tablespoons of melted butter. Place 7 *phyllo* sheets, buttered one at a time, in pan. Pour in half the almond mixture. Arrange 6 or 7 *phyllo* sheets buttered as before over mixture. Spread apricot preserves over entire surface of *phyllo*. Cover with 6 or 7 more buttered *phyllo* sheets. Pour in remaining almond mixture. Cover with remaining *phyllo*, brushing each sheet one at a time with melted butter. Cut through top layers of *phyllo*, marking off lengthwise slices. Bake for 1 hour until golden. Allow to cool before cutting. As the pastry cools combine the sugar, water, and lemon in a saucepan and boil for 10 minutes. Remove lemon and pour warm syrup over cold pastry. YIELD: 48 pieces.

Note: Baklava may be frozen unbaked. When ready to use place unthawed in the oven and increase baking time by 20 minutes.

BIRDS' NESTS

↯ SAMOS

Folitses

1 pound walnuts, finely chopped
4 tablespoons sugar
½ teaspoon ground cinnamon
1 pound *phyllo* pastry
1 pound melted sweet butter for
 brushing *phyllo*

SYRUP:

4 cups sugar
2 cups water
2 slices lemon
1 stick cinnamon
1 teaspoon almond extract

TOPPING:

¼ pound pistachio nuts, finely chopped
1 cup apricot marmalade

Preheat oven to 350°F.

Combine the walnuts, sugar, and cinnamon. Cut *phyllo* pastry sheets into five equal strips. Brush each strip with melted butter (work with 1 strip at a time and keep remainder covered with plastic wrap). Spread 1 heaping teaspoon of walnut mixture over each *phyllo* strip, leaving a 1-inch margin all around. Fold all edges in toward the middle. Press down firmly on one end of the strip with the forefinger of one hand andwith the other keep wrapping the strip around the forefinger to form a "bird's nest." Tuck the last inch of pastry strip under the nest. Brush top of each roll with additional melted butter. Place on baking sheet and bake for 15 minutes, or until golden brown. Prepare the syrup by combining all syrup ingredients in a saucepan. Bring to a boil and simmer for 15 minutes. Keep the syrup over low heat. Dip nests gently in the syrup and allow excess to drain off. Sprinkle with chopped pistachio nuts and decorate each center with a scant teaspoon of apricot marmalade. YIELD: 80 pieces.

NUT ROLL

Baklavas Roulo

1 cup pistachios, finely chopped
1 cup walnuts, finely chopped
1 cup almonds, finely chopped
¼ cup sugar
½ teaspoon ground cloves
¼ teaspoon ground cinnamon
½ pound *phyllo* pastry
1 pound melted sweet butter for
    brushing *phyllo*

SYRUP:

1 cup water
1 cup honey
1 teaspoon fresh lemon juice

Preheat oven to 350°F.

Combine the nuts, sugar, cloves, and cinnamon and set aside. Brush 2 sheets of *phyllo* (one at a time) with melted butter and arrange one sheet atop the other. (Keep remainder covered in plastic wrap.) Sprinkle with 2 tablespoons of the nut mixture. Repeat this procedure until there are three layers of *phyllo* with nuts (six sheets). Roll lengthwise, jellyroll-style and place on a greased cookie sheet, seam side down. Slice the top of each roll into 1-inch pieces on a diagonal (do not cut all the way through). Prepare four more rolls in the same fashion. Brush nut rolls generously with butter. Bake for 20 minutes, or until golden brown. While pastry bakes, bring the water to a boil, add first the honey and then the lemon juice. Stir to blend, remove from heat and cool. Using a pastry brush, brush cooled syrup on hot pastry rolls. Cut slices through and cool. YIELD: 60 pieces.

Note: Any combination of nuts may be used in this recipe.

KATEMERIA

Katemeria

6 eggs
1 teaspoon baking powder
1 pound large curd cottage cheese
¾ pound melted sweet butter
1 pound *phyllo* pastry
Confectioners' sugar
Ground cinnamon

This is an ideal brunch dish or late evening dessert.

Preheat oven to 350°F.

Beat the eggs. Add the baking powder and cottage cheese and blend well. Butter one sheet of *phyllo* at a time (keep unused *phyllo* covered with plastic wrap or damp towel). Spread a large tablespoon of filling across one of the narrow edges of the sheet, covering about one third of the *phyllo*. Fold in each of the long edges, then fold up narrow edges, envelope style. Place on a greased baking pan. Repeat until *phyllo* is all used up. Bake for 20 to 30 minutes, until brown. Serve at once, with powdered sugar and cinnamon. YIELD: 25 pieces.

Note: Katemeria may be frozen prior to baking. Place unthawed in the oven and increase baking time by 30 minutes. *Katemeria* can be prepared the night before, refrigerated and baked in the morning.

CUSTARD SWIRLS

Yirista Galatoboureka

SYRUP:

2 cups sugar
2 cups water
juice of 1 lemon

FILLING:

6 egg yolks
1 cup sugar
1 cup farina
6 cups scalded milk
2 tablespoons vanilla

1 pound *phyllo*
1 pound melted sweet butter for
   brushing *phyllo*

Preheat oven to 350°F.

Combine the syrup ingredients, bring to a boil, and simmer for 15 minutes, or until syrup thickens. Set aside to cool. Prepare filling by beating egg yolks and sugar until thickened. Add farina and mix well. Slowly stir in the scalded milk. Add the vanilla. Cook over medium heat, stirring constantly, until mixture thickens. Let cool. Brush one sheet of *phyllo* with butter and fold in half width-wise. Place filling across one wide edge of the folded *phyllo* sheet by either spooning it across the width of the *phyllo* sheet, or piping it across. Fold the narrow edges in about 1 inch; roll the *phyllo* up into a long cylinder. Carefully take one end of the *phyllo* rolls and turn to form a spiral shape. Continue making spirals until all filling and *phyllo* is used. Place on an ungreased pan. Brush top of each swirl with additional butter. Bake approximately 45 minutes, or until golden. Remove from oven and cool for 5 minutes. Carefully ladle a spoonful of cooled syrup over each swirl. YIELD: 25 swirls.

CUSTARD TRIANGLES

Galatoboureko Trigona

1 quart milk
1 cup cream of rice
1 cup sugar
Pinch of salt
4 eggs, separated
¾ pound sweet butter, melted
1 pound *phyllo* pastry

SYRUP:

2 cups sugar
2 cups water
¼ lemon wedge

Preheat oven to 350°F.

Scald the milk. Gradually add the cream of rice, sugar, and salt. Cook, stirring constantly, until firm. In a large bowl beat the egg yolks; gradually add the rice mixture, taking care not to add the mixture too quickly. Stir constantly to prevent mixture from getting lumpy. Fold in stiffly beaten egg whites. Brush a *phyllo* sheet with butter and fold into thirds lengthwise. Brush again with butter. (Keep unused *phyllo* covered with plastic wrap or a damp towel.) Place a large spoonful of the custard mixture at one end; fold pastry into triangles (see How to Work with *Phyllo*, diagram 2, in the Appendix). Place on a baking sheet and bake for 30 minutes, or until golden brown. Cool. To make the syrup, combine the sugar, water, and lemon. Boil for 15 minutes. Just before serving dip, each triangle into the hot syrup. (Your guests will think you just baked these mouthwatering sweets.) YIELD: 30 pieces.

ORANGE *GALATOBOUREKO*

Galatoboureko me Portokali

4 cups milk
¼ cup sweet butter
⅛ cup sugar
½ cup farina
4 eggs
3 tablespoons orange juice concentrate,
    undiluted
1 teaspoon vanilla
1 pound *phyllo* pastry
½ cup melted sweet butter for brushing
    phyllo

ORANGE SYRUP:

1½ cups sugar
1 cup water
1 cinnamon stick
2 whole cloves
2 teaspoons grated orange peel

Preheat oven to 400°F.

To make the filling, scald the milk in a large saucepan and stir in ¼ cup butter and the sugar. Gradually add the farina, stirring constantly, and bring mixture slowly to a boil. Remove from heat. Beat the eggs in a bowl until they are frothy and lemon-colored. Slowly stir in the hot farina mixture. Add orange juice concentrate and vanilla. Let custard filling cool. Line a 9- x 12-inch baking pan with 1 sheet of *phyllo* (some of which will hang over the pan) and brush with butter. Layer 3 more sheets of buttered *phyllo* in the pan so that bottom and sides are completely covered with some overhang on all edges. Pour in the cooled custard. Cover with 1 sheet of *phyllo*; cut to fit the top of the pan and brush with butter. Layer 5 more individually buttered sheets of *phyllo* on top, and fold in the overhang. With a sharp knife, slice through top layers of *phyllo*, marking off 2¼-inch squares or diamond shapes. Bake for 10 minutes; reduce oven temperature to 350°F. and bake for 45 minutes. While pastry bakes, combine syrup ingredients in a large saucepan, bring to a boil, and simmer for 8 minutes. Let syrup cool. Place pastry pan on a rack and cool for 5 minutes. Pour cooled orange syrup over *Galatoboureko*. Cut all the way through and serve at room temperature. YIELD: 24 pieces.

ROLLED *GALATOBOUREKO*

Galatoboureko Roula

↝ KITHIRA

6 eggs
2 cups sugar
1 quart milk
½ cup farina
1 teaspoon lemon peel, grated
1 pound *phyllo* pastry
¾ pound melted sweet butter for
    brushing *phyllo*

Preheat oven to 350°F.

Combine the eggs and sugar and blend well. Put the milk in a saucepan, add the eggs, and heat gently to just below the boiling point (otherwise eggs will set). Add the farina slowly through a strainer, until mixture barely boils. Stir continuously to avoid burning. When mixture thickens remove from heat immediately and cool. Add the lemon peel. Cut each *phyllo* sheet in thirds and butter them, one at a time (keep unused *phyllo* covered with plastic wrap or damp towel (see How to Work with *Phyllo*, in Appendix). Put 1 teaspoon of filling about ¼ inch away from one of the narrow ends of a strip and roll. Continue until all of the *phyllo* is used. Place rolls on a lightly greased pan. Brush with butter. Bake for 25 to 30 minutes. Let cool for 10 minutes and serve lukewarm. YIELD: 60 pieces.

Note: Prior to serving, you may sprinkle rolls with confectioners' sugar.

FLAT *KADAIFE*

Kadaife Tapsiou

SYRUP:

4 cups sugar
6 cups water
1 stick cinnamon
2 teaspoons lemon juice
1 lemon rind

2 cups chopped walnuts
2 cups chopped almonds
¼ cup sugar
1 tablespoon ground cinnamon
1 pound *Kadaife*
¾ pound melted sweet butter

Similar in appearance to shredded wheat, *Kadaife* is packaged like *phyllo*. When unrolled, the dough is stringy and tightly packed together. Before you use it, gently pull the strands apart to air.

Preheat oven to 350°F.

Combine all syrup ingredients and bring to a boil; boil for 40 minutes, then set aside to cool. Meanwhile, combine the walnuts, almonds, sugar, and cinnamon and mix well. Arrange half the *Kadaife* in a greased 9- x 13- x 2-inch pan. Pour half the melted butter over the *Kadaife*. Sprinkle the nut mixture over the *Kadaife*. Arrange the remaining *Kadaife* over the mixture and pour the remaining melted butter over all. Bake for 30 to 40 minutes. Remove *Kadaife* from oven and immediately pour cool syrup over hot *Kadaife*. Cover with a towel and with another pan; let stand until cool. Cut into 2-inch squares. YIELD: 28–35 pieces.

Note: This recipe may be frozen with the syrup. To serve, thaw several hours at room temperature.

CUSTARD *KADAIFE*

Kadaife me Krema

4 cups milk
1 cup farina
3 tablespoons butter
1½ cups sugar
2 tablespoons vanilla
8 eggs
1 tablespoon grated orange or lemon
    rind
1 pound *Kadaife*
1 pound melted sweet butter

SYRUP:

4 cups sugar
3 cups water
2 tablespoons lemon juice
10 cloves
1 stick cinnamon

Preheat oven to 350°F.

Bring the milk to a boil in a large saucepan, add farina and butter, stir thoroughly, and remove from heat. Combine sugar, vanilla, eggs, and grated rind and blend thoroughly. Add to milk and farina mixture; return to heat. Cook over medium heat, stirring continuously until thickened and smooth. Allow it to cool. Spread half the *Kadaife* in a 12- x 15- x 3-inch pan. Pour half the melted butter over it. Spread the cream mixture evenly over the *Kadaife*. Add the rest of the *Kadaife* and the melted butter. Bake for about 1 hour until golden. While pastry bakes, combine syrup ingredients in a saucepan, bring to a boil and simmer for 10 minutes. Set aside to cool. Pour cool syrup over hot *Kadaife*; cover with a towel and let cool before serving. YIELD: 36–40 pieces.

KADAIFE ROLLS

Kadaife Roula

SYRUP:

4 cups sugar

2½ cups water

½ lemon (juice of lemon and grated rind)

1 cinnamon stick

2 cups chopped walnuts (or a mixture of almonds and walnuts

¼ cup ground zwieback

¼ cup sugar

1 teaspoon ground cinnamon

⅛ teaspoon ground clove

1 ounce cognac

1 pound *Kadaife*

¾ pound melted sweet butter

Preheat oven to 350°F.

Combine all syrup ingredients and bring to a boil. Simmer for 20 minutes then set aside to cool. Prepare the filling by combining the walnuts, zwieback, sugar, cinnamon, clove, and cognac. Separate the strands of the *Kadaife* and shape into 24 rectangular sections 10 to 12 inches long and three inches wide. Place 1 heaping tablespoon of filling at one narrow end of the *Kadaife*. Roll, jelly-roll fashion, squeeze to make the roll tight and place on a baking pan. Continue, until all the *Kadaife* is used up. Pour one tablespoon butter over each *Kadaife* roll. Bake until golden brown, about 25 to 30 minutes. Pour cold syrup over the hot *Kadaife*. Cover and let it stand until all the syrup is absorbed. YIELD: 24 pieces.

Note: These rolls can be baked and frozen. When ready to serve, thaw at room temperature for about 1 hour.

NUT CHOCOLATE "CIGARS"

Poura

SYRUP:

2 cups sugar
2 cups water
Lemon peel

3 egg yolks
1 cup sugar
¾ pound nuts, chopped
1 ounce sweet chocolate, melted
¼ teaspoon ground cinnamon
1 pound *phyllo* pastry
1 pound melted sweet butter for
    brushing *phyllo*

Preheat oven to 350°F.

Combine the ingredients for the syrup and bring to a boil. Cook for 25 minutes and then cool. Beat egg yolks until lemon-colored. Add sugar, nuts, melted chocolate, and cinnamon. Mix until well blended. Cut *phyllo* into thirds width-wise. (See How to Work with *Phyllo* in the Appendix.) Cover with plastic wrap to keep from drying out. Butter one strip of *phyllo* at a time and place a heaping teaspoon of filling at a narrow edge. Fold in long edges of *phyllo* and roll up from the edge with the filling. Place rolls seam side down on a cookie sheet. Brush with butter. Bake until *phyllo* is golden brown, about 20 minutes. Dip hot rolls into cool syrup. YIELD: 60 pieces.

Note: This recipe may be frozen prior to baking. When ready to use, place in oven, unthawed, and increase baking time by 10 minutes.

PHYLLO ROLLS WITH *LOUKOUMI*

Bourekia me Loukoumi

1 (10-ounce) bag shelled walnuts,
    chopped
1½ tablespoons ground cinnamon
¼ cup sugar
1½ pounds *loukoumi* (Greek jellied
    candy, sold in specialty shops)
½ pound melted sweet butter for
    brushing *phyllo*
1 pound *phyllo* pastry
Confectioners' sugar

Preheat oven to 350°F.

Prepare filling by combining the walnuts, cinnamon, and sugar. Cut each *loukoumi* lengthwise in three pieces. Cut the *phyllo* crosswise into thirds. (Read How to Work with *Phyllo*, in the Appendix). Butter the *phyllo* one strip at a time (keep remaining *phyllo* covered with plastic wrap or damp towel). Put 1 teaspoon of nut mixture ¼-inch in from one of the narrow ends of the *phyllo* strip. Place a piece of *loukoumi* on top of nut mixture. Fold in the long edges and roll up from the narrow end with the filling. Place seam side down on ungreased cookie sheet. Butter the top of the rolls. Bake for 30 minutes, or until golden brown. Cool thoroughly. Sprinkle with confectioners' sugar before serving. These rolls will keep well stored in airtight containers. YIELD: about 80–90 pieces.

BOUGATSA

Bougatsa

6 cups milk
1 cup sugar
2 eggs, beaten
1 cup farina
1 pound sweet butter
1 pound *phyllo* pastry
Ground cinnamon
Confectioners' sugar

Slices of *Bougatsa* are sold in street stands throughout Greece as a quick snack. It is served warm, sprinkled with confectioners' sugar.

Preheat oven to 300°F.

Place the milk, sugar, eggs, and farina in a pot and bring to a boil over medium heat, stirring constantly to prevent mixture from burning. When mixture bubbles and thickens remove from heat immediately. Melt the butter and add one quarter of it to the farina. Butter two pans, measuring 14- x 18-inches, with a little of the remaining butter. Butter ¼ of the *phyllo* sheets, one at a time (see How to Work with *Phyllo* in the Appendix), and overlap them in one pan so as to cover the entire bottom and sides, with some overhang on all edges. Repeat this procedure with the second pan, using ¼ of the *phyllo* and buttering and overlapping each sheet. (Keep unused *phyllo* covered with plastic wrap or a damp cloth.) Pour half the farina mixture over the *phyllo* in each pan. Cover each with the remaining *phyllo* sheets, buttering each sheet and overlapping them as before. When this is done, fold over the overhanging *phyllo* from the bottom crust and seal with the top. Prick the top with a fork in several places. Bake for 25 minutes, or until brown. Remove from oven and allow to cool. (For best results allow pastry to set overnight). Prior to serving reheat and cut into squares. Sprinkle cinnamon and confectioners' sugar over each piece. YIELD: 12–16 pieces.

Note: This dessert keeps, unrefrigerated, for a few days. It can also be baked, cooled, and leftover pieces may be frozen for later use. When ready to use place in 300°F. oven for about 20 minutes, until defrosted and warm.

PUMPKIN PIE WITH *PHYLLO*

Kolokethopeta

2½ pounds butternut squash
8 ounces *Anthotyro* cheese (see The
    Cheeses of Greece, page 120) or 1
    (8-ounce) package cream cheese
¼ pound sweet butter, at room
    temperature
1 cup brown sugar
1 teaspoon ground nutmeg
2 eggs plus 2 yolks
14 sheets *phyllo* pastry
½ cup melted sweet butter for brushing
    phyllo

Preheat oven to 375°F.

Place squash in a pan and bake for 1½ to 2 hours, until very soft. Add a little water to the pan as the juice of the squash seeps out. Peel and mash the squash. Reduce oven temperature to 325°F. Add the cheese, butter, brown sugar, and nutmeg to the squash. Add the eggs and blend well. Place 8 overlapping individually buttered sheets of *phyllo* in an 8 or 10-inch deep pie plate so as to cover the entire plate (a deep quiche dish or oblong baking dish may also be used). Pour in filling and spread evenly. Top with 6 additional sheets of *phyllo*, again individually buttered and fitted carefully around the pan. Score top layers of *phyllo* into 8 or 10 wedges and bake for ½ hour. Reduce oven temperature to 275°F. and bake for 1 hour longer. YIELD: 8–10 pieces.

VILLAGER PUMPKIN *PETA*

Horiatiki Kolokethopita

1 (3–4 pound) fresh pumpkin

SYRUP:

3 cups sugar
3 cups water
1 stick cinnamon

1 cup white raisins
1–2 cups walnuts
1 teaspoon ground cinnamon
½ teaspoon ground cloves
2 cups brown sugar
½ teaspoon salt
½ pound melted sweet butter for
    brushing *phyllo*
½ pound *phyllo* pastry

Split the pumpkin and remove the seeds. Divide the pumpkin into small pieces for easier handling. With a sharp knife, remove the outer skin. Coarsely grate the peeled pumpkin pieces. Allow the pumpkin to drain overnight in a colander.

Preheat oven to 350°F.

The next day, prepare the syrup by combining the sugar, water, and cinnamon in a large saucepan. Bring to a boil and simmer for 30 minutes. Set aside to cool. In the meantime, squeeze out as much water from the pumpkin as possible. Mix pumpkin meat with raisins, nuts, cinnamon, cloves, brown sugar, and salt. Butter 5 or 6 sheets of *phyllo* (one at a time) and layer in an 11- x 14-inch pan (see How to Work with *Phyllo*, in Appendix). Pour the pumpkin mixture over *phyllo*. Cover with remaining *phyllo* sheets, buttered and layered one at a time. Score top layers of *phyllo* into triangles and bake until crispy and light brown, about 45 minutes. Pour cool syrup over hot pie. YIELD: 20 pieces.

OTHER DESSERTS

ISLANDER PUFFS
Loukoumades

✦ CORFU

2 eggs
1 cup cake flour
1 cup fresh *mizithra* or ricotta cheese
2 tablespoons sugar
Oil for frying

SYRUP:

1 cup honey
1 cup water
2 cups sugar
Cinnamon

Tradition has it that to make *Loukoumades* when a child is born will ensure good luck throughout its life. It also doesn't hurt to prepare them on the child's first day of school. This recipe is a variation of the traditional *Loukoumades* recipes that appear on pages 185–187 of *The Art of Greek Cookery*.

In a bowl beat the eggs lightly. Add the flour, cheese, and sugar. Let stand in the refrigerator for 1 hour. Drop the batter one tablespoon at a time into a deep pot of hot oil (375°F.) and fry until brown on all sides. Remove from oil and drain on paper towels. To prepare syrup, combine the honey, water, and sugar in a saucepan and boil for 10 minutes. Dip *Loukoumades* in hot syrup and place on racks to drain. Sprinkle with cinnamon. YIELD: 2 dozen.

RICH SWEET PUFFS
Lalangites

2 eggs
⅛ cup sugar
1 cup milk
1 package yeast
¼ cup lukewarm water
½ teaspoon salt
3½ cups sifted flour
2 cups vegetable oil

SYRUP:

1 cup sugar
1 cup water
1 tablespoon lemon juice
1 stick cinnamon
⅛ cup honey

COATING:

½ cup ground walnuts
½ cup confectioners' sugar
½ tablespoon ground cinnamon

These deep-fried, sugar-coated pastries are served by Macedonians to celebrate the birth of a baby.

Beat eggs well with electric beater. Gradually add sugar, continuing to beat. Pour in the milk, a little at a time, while beating at low speed. Dissolve the yeast in the lukewarm water, then stir into the mixture. Combine salt and flour and add to the mixture, blending thoroughly. Cover bowl with a cloth and put in a warm place to rise for 2 hours, or until double in bulk. In the meantime, prepare the syrup by combining the sugar, water, lemon, and cinnamon in a large saucepan. Bring to a boil and simmer for 20 minutes. Add the honey, stir, and cool.

In a deep, heavy saucepan or deep fryer, heat the oil to sizzling. Drop dough one teaspoonful at a time into the hot oil. Fry for a few minutes, or until the dough puffs up and turns golden brown. Drain on paper towels. Mix together the ground walnuts, confectioners' sugar, and cinnamon. While still warm, dip the puffs in the cold syrup and roll in the nut mixture to coat well. YIELD: about 6 dozen puffs.

BATTER PUFFS

Svinghi

1 cup boiling water
4 tablespoons butter or margarine
¼ teaspoon salt
1 tablespoon sugar
½ teaspoon grated orange rind
1 cup flour
1 teaspoon double-acting baking powder
4 eggs
2 cups vegetable oil for frying
Ground cinnamon

SYRUP (see note):

2 cups sugar
1 cup water
2 teaspoons lemon juice

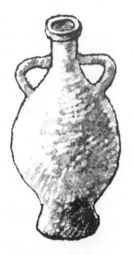

Sometimes referred to as Greek doughnuts, *Svinghi* are similar to *Loukoumades* (see page 201) but less filling. They make a great snack!

In a medium-size saucepan, combine the boiling water, butter, salt, sugar, and orange rind and bring to a boil. Meanwhile, sift together the flour and baking powder. Add the dry ingredients all at once to the hot mixture in the saucepan, beating hard with a wooden spoon over medium heat until the mixture forms a compact mass and leaves the sides of the pan. Remove from heat and let cool 1 minute. Add the eggs, one at a time, beating hard after each addition. The mixture should be smooth, glossy and thick. Heat the oil in a deep pot almost to the smoking point, then drop the batter into the oil one tablespoon at a time, without crowding. The batter will at first sink and then rise as puffs. When they do so, turn them to fry on all sides, using tongs. When completely golden remove puffs from oil and let drain on paper towels. Place on a warm platter and keep warm. To make syrup, boil the syrup ingredients for 5 minutes, and spoon over the puffs. Sprinkle with cinnamon and serve hot. YIELDS: 28–30 3-inch puffs.

Note: Warm honey may be substituted for the syrup.

CREAMY RICE PUDDING

Rizogalo

½ cup raw rice
8 cups milk
1 tablespoon flour
1 cup sugar
2 eggs, beaten
1 teaspoon vanilla
Ground cinnamon

✧ SPARTA

Gently simmer the rice and 6 cups of the milk in a heavy-bottomed aluminum saucepan, stirring often to prevent rice from sticking on the bottom of the pan. Cook for 20 minutes, or until rice is tender. In a mixing bowl, mix together the flour and sugar. Add the beaten eggs, remaining 2 cups milk, and vanilla and blend thoroughly together. Slowly add this mixture to the rice mixture and gently simmer until thickened, about 35 minutes (the rice will rise to the top when done). Do not overcook. Cool. Sprinkle with cinnamon and refrigerate after pudding has thoroughly cooled. Serves 8–10.

GRAPE PUDDING
Moustalevria

10 cups *mousto* (10–12 pounds purple
    grapes, squeezed)
1 slice bread
1 cup flour
½ cup cornstarch
Ground cinnamon
Sesame seeds
Chopped nuts

This unusual pudding is a popular dessert throughout Greece at grape harvest time. Fresh grapes must be squeezed either by hand or in a juice extractor to collect the *mousto* or grape juice that is the main ingredient of the pudding.

Boil *mousto* for 5 minutes with the bread. Cool and remove bread. Strain through a cheesecloth. Measure out 8 cups of clear *mousto*. Mix 2 cups of it with the flour and cornstarch and bring the other 6 cups to a boil. Add the flour mixture to the boiling *mousto* a little at a time, stirring constantly unil the mixture thickens. Pour into small dishes and sprinkle with cinnamon, sesame seeds, and nuts. Serve cold. Serves 16–20.

AMBROSIA WITH *OUZO*
Ambrosia me Ouzo

Fresh oranges, grapefruit, tangerines,
    and grapes to total 4 cups fresh fruit
½ cup sugar
½ cup coconut
½ cup *ouzo* or cognac
Juice of ½ lemon or lime

    With a sharp knife, section oranges, grapefruit, and tangerines, and remove membranes and seeds. Arrange fruit in layers, sprinkling each with sugar and coconut. Pour *ouzo* and citrus juice over fruit. Chill before serving. Serves 4–6.

(Lenten)
CHESTNUT COMPOTE
Komposta Kastana

1½ pounds chestnuts, shelled and peeled
    (see page 175 for Preparation of
    Chestnuts)
Water as needed
1½ cups sugar
1 lemon rind
1½ cups water
1 teaspoon vanilla

    Place chestnuts in a large pot, add cold water to cover, and boil until tender but not mushy, about 20 minutes. Drain. In another pot, boil together the sugar, lemon rind, and 1½ cups water until the syrup thickens slightly. Add the chestnuts and simmer for 8 minutes. Remove the chestnuts to a compote dish with a slotted spoon. Add the vanilla to the syrup and boil a few minutes longer to thicken further. Cool the syrup and pour over the chestnuts. Serves 4–6.

CHESTNUT NESTS
Kastana Folia

1½ cups milk
1 pound chestnuts, shelled and peeled
    (see page 175 for Preparation of
    Chestnuts), or 1 (1-pound) can
    chestnut purée
3 tablespoons sugar
Dash of salt
1¼ cups heavy cream
1 teaspoon vanilla
6 maraschino cherries

Heat the milk until warm. Add the chestnuts, 2 table-spoons of the sugar, and the salt and simmer until all the milk is absorbed, about 30 minutes. Remove from heat and cool. Grind chestnuts in food grinder and add ¼ cup cream and the vanilla. Mash until very smooth. With a pastry tube shape the chestnut mixture into nests on dessert plates (start with round layer of the mixture and continue building up rings around the perimeter until you have a "cup" of chestnut purée). Whip the remaining cup of cream along with the remaining tablespoon of sugar. Fill the nests with whipped cream and top with a cherry. Chill in refrigerator for 1 hour before serving. Serves 6.

(Lenten)
DRIED FRUIT COMPOTE
Housafi

1 cup black raisins
½ cup light raisins
½ cup dried prunes
½ cup dried apples
½ cup dried pears
3 cups water

Boil the dried fruits in the water for 20 to 30 minutes. Serve hot or cold. YIELD: about 10 half-cup servings.

Variation: Add dried figs or any other dried fruit desired. When boiling, cinnamon sticks may be added for flavor.

QUINCE COMPOTE
Kidoni Komposta

6 large quinces
3 cups water
2 cups sugar
1 stick cinnamon
2 whole cloves
1 tablespoon lemon juice

Pare, quarter, and core the quinces. Cut each quarter into 3 slices. Add the remaining ingredients and simmer gently for 1 hour, or until the fruit is tender and has turned an orange color. Cool and serve. This is also a good accompaniment for roast poultry and meats. Serves 8.

CANDIES

ALMOND BALLS
Troufes Amegthalotes

1 pound blanched almonds, ground
1 cup confectioners' sugar plus enough
    sugar to coat balls
4 tablespoons light cream

These are popular for name days and weddings.

Combine the almonds, 1 cup sugar, and cream and knead with the hands until very well blended. Shape into small balls and roll in confectioners' sugar. YIELD: 2 dozen.

BRANDY BALLS
Balitses Cognac

1 cup finely chopped almonds
1 cup finely chopped walnuts
1 (6-ounce) chocolate bar, grated
1 tablespoon cocoa powder
¼ cup sugar
½ cup finely ground vanilla wafers
¼ cup fresh orange juice
Rind of 1 orange
3 tablespoons brandy
Confectioners' sugar or colored sugar

Combine almonds and walnuts in a saucepan. Add the remaining ingredients, except the confectioners' sugar. Place over medium heat and, stirring continuously, simmer until liquids evaporate. Place saucepan in refrigerator for 1 hour. Shape mixture into balls approximately 1 inch in diameter and roll in confectioners' sugar. Store for at least 10 days in a cool place before serving. YIELD: about 2 dozen.

CHOCOLATE BALLS
Troufes Sokolata

4 cups sweet milk chocolate (32 ounces)
4 cups ground walnuts
2 cups ground pecans
1 cup ground almonds
2 cups confectioners' sugar
3 tablespoons warm cream
2 tablespoons rum extract
Blanched almonds

This candy recipe is an old favorite throughout Greece.

Break up chocolate and place in a large bowl over hot water to melt. When the chocolate is a soft, smooth consistency add the nuts, sugar, cream, and flavoring. If the mixture is too stiff to work, add a little more warm cream. Shape the mixture one tablespoon at a time into balls. Top each with half a blanched almond. YIELD: 12 dozen balls.

CINNAMON BALLS

Balitses me Kanela

1 cup butter, at room temperature
⅓ cup sugar
2 teaspoons vanilla
3 tablespoons cognac
2 cups sifted cake flour
1 teaspoon ground cinnamon
¾ cup zwieback crumbs
1 cup finely chopped walnuts
Confectioners' sugar

Preheat oven to 350°F.

In a large bowl, blend the butter, sugar, and vanilla and add the cognac. Sift together the flour and cinnamon and add to sugar mixture. Add crumbs and nuts and mix very well. Shape into small balls about 1½ inches in diameter. Place on greased baking sheets. Bake for 20 to 25 minutes. Roll immediately in confectioners' sugar. YIELD: about 5 dozen balls.

FRUIT BALLS

Fruta Zaharota

1 (8-ounce) can almond paste
1 cup confectioners' sugar
2 tablespoons water
½ cup dried chopped apricots
½ cup chopped raisins
1½ teaspoons rum extract
½ teaspoon vanilla

FROSTING:
1 egg white
1 cup confectioners' sugar
1 tablespoon white vinegar
1 teaspoon vanilla
Food coloring (optional)

Mix all but the frosting ingredients thoroughly in a bowl. Form into balls. Beat the frosting ingredients until the mixture is the consistency of icing. Roll the balls in the frosting and put on a rack to drain for 24 hours. Store in airtight containers. Yield varies according to size of ball; approximately 2 dozen balls.

JELLIED GRAPEFRUIT SQUARES AND TRIANGLES

Kitron Glyko

Grapefruits
Sugar
Juice of ½ lemon
Water

Grate outer surface of thick-skinned grapefruits. Carefully remove the pulp, peel in sections, and scrape off white inner skins. Cut the peel into squares and triangles. Cover with water and soak overnight. Drain, cover with fresh water, and bring to a boil. Simmer until rind is transparent, adding more water if necessary. Measure fruit and liquid and add equal amount of sugar and simmer until jelly state is reached (about 220° on a candy thermometer). Add the lemon juice and simmer for 5 minutes. Pour into sterilized jars and seal properly for storing.

Note: Thick-skinned oranges can be prepared in the same way.

SESAME BARS
Pastele

2 cups sesame seeds
1¼ cups honey

Preheat oven to 400°F.

Toast the sesame seeds in the oven for 10 minutes (be careful not to let them burn). Combine the toasted seeds and honey in a heavy saucepan. Bring slowly to the very firm ball stage (250° to 256° on a candy thermometer); this should take 6 to 8 minutes and the mixture should be golden brown. Pour the hot mixture onto a marble slab or a large tray. Spread with a wooden spoon to a thickness of about ⅛ inch. Cut into bars about 2 x 4 inches and wrap individually in wax paper or plastic wrap. Store in an airtight container. YIELD: 15–18 bars.

NUT AND SESAME SEED CANDY
ANDROS

Pasteli me Karydia

4 cups coarsely chopped walnuts
⅓ cup zwieback or toasted bread crumbs
1½ cups honey
1 cup granulated sugar
Orange blossom water
1½ cups sesame seeds

In a large bowl, combine the walnuts and crumbs and set aside. In a heavy saucepan, combine the honey and sugar. Bring to a boil over medium heat, stirring constantly. Continue to boil, uncovered, until the syrup reaches the very firm ball stage (250° to 256° on a candy thermometer; see note) then remove from the heat. Add the syrup to the walnut-crumb mixture, stirring with a heavy wooden spoon. Meanwhile, have ready a marble slab or tray lightly moistened with orange blossom water and sprinkled generously with sesame seeds (a 12- x 18-inch surface will be sufficient). With a spatula and fingers moistened with orange blossom water spread the walnut-syrup mixture to a thickness of ½ inch onto the sesame-covered surface. Sprinkle liberally with sesame seeds. Cool and cut into diamond shapes. Store indefinitely in covered containers. (The flavor improves after a few days.) YIELD: about 70 1- x 2-inch candies.

Note: If a candy thermometer is unavailable, the hard ball stage may be determined by dropping a spoonful of the candy on a dish; if it hardens immediately, proceed with the recipe.

NUT STUFFED FIGS

Sika Gemista

1 (12-ounce) package dried whole figs (24)
1 cup orange juice
1 tablespoon grated lemon peel
1 tablespoon lemon juice
3 tablespoons sugar
24 pecan halves or walnuts
Granulated sugar

Remove stem end from figs and put figs in a saucepan, along with the orange juice, lemon peel, lemon juice, and sugar. Heat to boiling and simmer, covered, until fruit is tender, about 45 minutes. Drain well and cool. Insert knife in the stem end of each fig to form a pocket. Fill each pocket with a pecan half. Roll figs in sugar until well coated. Let dry overnight. YIELD: 24 pieces.

APPENDIX

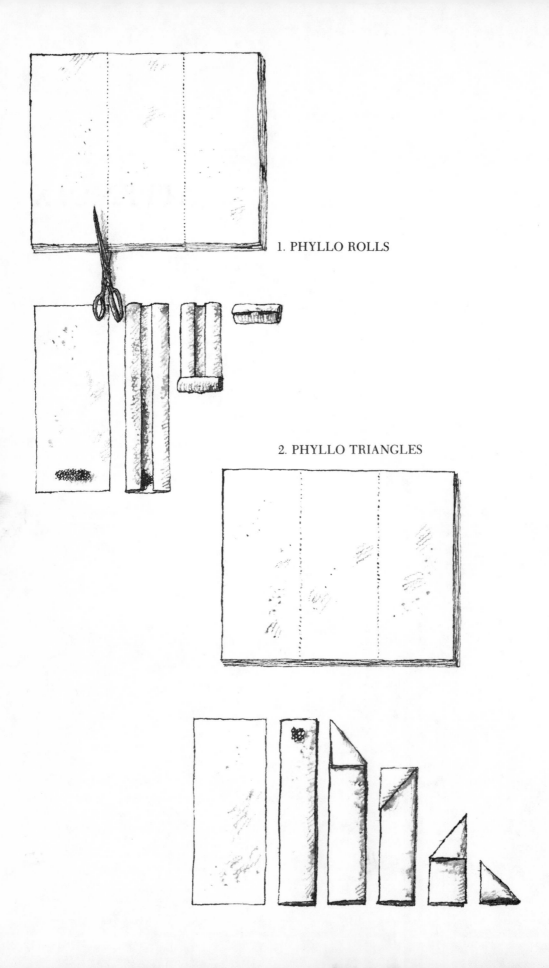

1. PHYLLO ROLLS

2. PHYLLO TRIANGLES

How To Work With Phyllo

A unique, paper-thin, extremely versatile pastry dough, *phyllo*† is ubiquitous in Greek cooking. From appetizers to desserts, there are thousands of uses for this remarkable product, which, fortunately for Grecophiles, is now readily available in gourmet and specialty food shops and even in many supermarkets across the country.

Phyllo is sold commercially in 1-pound boxes, each containing 24 to 30 rolled sheets of pastry. An unopened box of *phyllo* will keep in the refrigerator for several weeks, and almost indefinitely in the freezer. To defrost, simply leave the unopened package in the refrigerator overnight and the *phyllo* will be ready to use the next day (do not thaw at room temperature).

One of the difficulties in working with *phyllo* is that it tends to dry out very quickly once exposed to air. Thus speed is of the essence. Before unrolling the *phyllo*, make sure you have a large cleared area to work on and that all your ingredients and utensils (especially baking pans, a feather or pastry brush, the filling and, most important the melted, but not browned, butter that will be used to soak each individual sheet) are at hand. If you are going to bake the *phyllo* pastry immediately, your oven should be preheated.

Once you have unrolled the *phyllo*, work with one sheet or a portion of a sheet at a time, and keep the remainder covered with plastic wrap or a damp cloth (the former is preferable because easier to handle) to prevent it from drying out. Using a feather or pastry brush, spread an ample amount of butter on the sheet or part of a sheet you are working on, beginning at the edges and working inward. Use broad strokes and learn to work fast to prevent the sheets from drying out. (Note: Sweet or lightly salted butter may be used, depending on the particular recipe; margarine, but *not* oil, may be substituted for the butter.)

Phyllo appetizers, such as *Bourekakia*, generally call for the individual sheets to be cut into thirds lengthwise, filled with various ingredients such as spinach, cheese or crab meat, and shaped into triangles or rolls (see diagrams 1 and 2). *Phyllo* sheets for entrées, such as Baked Chicken Breasts°, are usually left whole and amply buttered. The filling is placed on the sheet, which is then folded envelope-style and placed seam-side down on a baking pan. For desserts like *Baklava*°, whole, individually buttered sheets are used. Layer half the amount of *phyllo* called for (one at a time) in a deep baking pan, spread nut (or whatever) filling on top, and add remaining *phyllo* to cover. When baking *phyllo* in a pan, it is best to score the top sheets with a sharp knife (a triangular or diamond design is traditional) to facilitate later cutting; do not, however, cut all the way through the sheets. To ensure a crisp pas-

†Variously spelled as *phyllo*, *filo*, or *fylo*; the correct pronunciation is FEEL-o.

try, sprinkle the top layer of *phyllo* with cold water before baking; this will also prevent the sheets from breaking.

One of the great advantages of *phyllo* is that it freezes extremely well, either baked or unbaked (the latter is preferable). To cook frozen *phyllo* pastries or dishes, place directly (without prior thawing) in a preheated oven and increase cooking time according to directions in the individual recipes. Previously baked and frozen *phyllo* dishes may be reheated in a 350°F. oven until piping hot.

Do not be afraid of working with *phyllo*. Once you get the hang of it, it is actually very simple. Organization, speed and, especially, practice are the only prerequisites. And the results are certainly worth the effort.

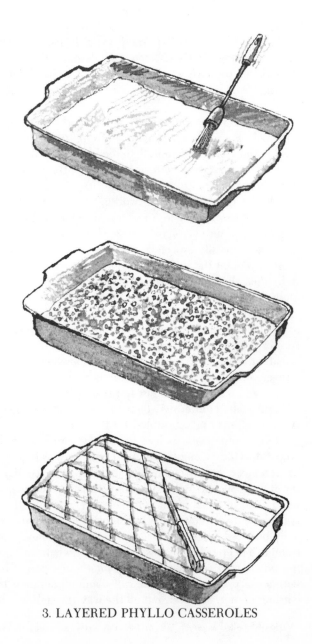

3. LAYERED PHYLLO CASSEROLES

Suggested Menus

The following menus cover a wide variety of dining possibilities, from formal dinner parties to low-cost buffets. All of the recipes mentioned appear in this book and italicized items lend themselves to advance preparation and freezing.

BRUNCH

Bougatsa or *Katemeria*
Greek Sausage
Orange Swirl Bread
Flaounes
Anise and Sesame Seed Cookies

LUNCHEON

Crabmeat Puffs
Feta Cheese Bourekakia
Manti
Stuffed Tomatoes
Country-style Salad
Gold and Walnut Cake
Cinnamon Kourabiedes

COCKTAIL PARTY

Chicken Liver Pâté
Cocktail Shish-kebab
Feta Cheese Puffs
Assorted Bourekakia
(Cheese, Mushroom, Shrimp, Crabmeat)
Taramasalata
Feta and Kasseri Cheeses
Marinated Vegetables
Pastitsio Turnovers
Dolmades
Salt Sticks
Apricot Baklava
Almond Cookies
Chestnut Cake with Whipped Cream

BUFFET DINNER

APPETIZERS
Taramasalata
Lamb Rolls
Feta Mold

MAIN COURSES
Shrimp Scorpio
Moussaka with Artichokes
Lamb Chunks in Phyllo
Pilafi
Greek Salad

DESSERT
Orange Galatoboureko
Pastoules
Nougat Torte

BUDGET BUFFET

APPETIZERS
Cocktail Meatballs with Cheese Centers
Taramasalata
Triple Cheese Bars
Marinated Celery

MAIN COURSES
Pastitsio
Islander Chicken
Salt Sticks

DESSERT
Ravani
Butter Cookies with Wine
Nut Chocolate Cigars

FAMILY DINNER

Yogurt Soup with Barley
Beef with Orzo
Black-eyed Beans with Fennel
Country-style Salad
Sesame Seed Rolls
Honey Pie

DINNER PARTY

APPETIZERS
Cumin Sticks
Marinated Mussels

MAIN COURSES
Molded Spinach Ring
Chicken Breasts in Phyllo
Pilafi with Artichokes
Salad with Yogurt Dressing

DESSERT
Pasta Flora with Quince
Karidopeta

SEAFOOD DINNER

APPETIZERS
Seafood Bourekakia (bite-size)
Mussels with Mustard Sauce
Feta Cheese Rounds

MAIN COURSES
Baked Fish with Vegetables
Artichoke Tomato Salad
Round Loaves

DESSERT
Ambrosia with Ouzo
Apricot Almond Cake

SUMMER DINNER

APPETIZERS
Marinated Artichokes
Assortment of Greek Cheeses and Olives
Cocktail Shish-kebab

MAIN COURSES
Lobster Tails with Feta Cheese
Lentils and Rice Pilaf
Summer Salad
Olive Muffins

DESSERT
Rum Torte
Almond Meringues with Fresh Fruit

AN INFORMAL SUMMER DINNER

APPETIZERS
Cucumber and Yogurt Dip
Garlic Sauce with Fresh Vegetables
Assorted Cheeses

MAIN COURSES
Molded Spinach Peta
Shrimp with Feta
Cracked Wheat Salad

DESSERT
Melon Balls with Ouzo
Yogurt Cake

ENTERTAINING FOR A CROWD

APPETIZERS
Feta Dip
Mushroom Triangles
Onion Puffs
Marinated Shrimps
Marinated Olives
Meatless Stuffed Grape Leaves

MAIN COURSES
Pastitsio with Phyllo
Lamb Cubes with Minted Yogurt Sauce
Tipsy Rice
Squash Cretan Style
Islander Bread

DESSERT
Cinnamon Nut Ring
Baklava Rolls

LENTEN DINNER

APPETIZERS
Chick-Pea and Tahini Dip
Marinated Olives, Celery, and Mushrooms

MAIN COURSES
Mussels Yiahni
Baked Rice
Cauliflower Kapama

DESSERT
Walnut Pie
Skaltsounia II

EASTER DINNER

APPETIZERS
Feta Mold
Dolmades
Chicken Phyllo Rolls

MAIN COURSES
Baked Lamb with Olives and Cheese
Artichoke Moussaka
Molded Spinach Peta
Spring Salad
Easter Bread

DESSERT
Kadaife Rolls
Tipsy Torte
Wine Cookies

HOLIDAY BUFFET

APPETIZERS
Artichoke Puffs
Walnut Spread
Stuffed Mushrooms

MAIN COURSES
Stuffed Leg of Lamb with Feta Cheese
Leek Pie in Phyllo
Rice with Chestnuts
Christmas Bread

DESSERTS
Custard Kadaife
Finikia
Iced Kourabiedes
Baklava with Pistachio Nuts

Common Greek Cooking Terms and Ingredients

AMIGTHALA   Almonds

ANGINARES   Artichokes

ARNI   Lamb

AVGOLEMONO   An egg and lemon mixture generally used as a sauce or soup base.

BAKLAVA   The most famous dessert of Greece, made of layers of *phyllo* pastry interspersed with chopped nuts and topped with a honey-flavored syrup.

BOUREKI or **BOUREKAKIA**   *Phyllo* puffs (made with a variety of fillings)

DOLMADES   Grape leaves (sometimes cabbage leaves) stuffed with meat and rice

ELLIES   Olives

FETA   The classic white goat cheese of Greece

FILO (also **PHYLLO**)   The paper-thin pastry dough essential to Greek cuisine

GARIDES   Shrimp

GIOUVETSI   Greek for "casserole" or "baked in the oven"

GOUDI   A brass or wooden mortar

KAFES   Coffee

KEFALOTIRI   A hard, salty cheese, excellent for grating

KEFTEDES   Meat balls

KOURABIEDES   Butter cookies topped with confectioners' sugar

KRITHARAKI   Tiny oblong-shaped pasta

LADOLEMONO   Oil and lemon juice dressing

MASTICHI   The sap drawn from the *mastichodenro* bush (grown only on the island of Chios), Mastichi is a basic ingredient of chewing gum, as well as a flavoring for liqueurs, breads, and cookies.

MOSHARAKI   Veal

MOUSSAKA   A layered casserole usually made with eggplant and chopped meat, topped with a cream sauce. One of the classic Greek recipes.

ORZO   Tiny almond-shaped pasta

OUZO   A colorless alcoholic drink, flavored with anise. Like Pernod and other anise-based liqueurs, *ouzo* turns milky-white when combined with water or poured over ice.

PASTITSIO   A layered casserole of macaroni and chopped meat, topped with a cream sauce

PILAFI   Rice boiled in broth with onions and other flavorings

RETSINA   White or rosé wine flavored with pine resin

SKORDALIA   Garlic sauce

SPANAKOPITA   *Phyllo* puffs stuffed with spinach

TAHINI   Crushed sesame seed paste

TARAMA   Fish roe

TARAMOSALATA   Fish roe spread

TIROPETES   *Phyllo* puffs stuffed with cheese

TSAKISTES   Cracked olives marinated in oil and vinegar

VOTHINO   Beef

YIAHNI   Stew

YIAOURTI   Yogurt

Basil

Mint

Bay

Oregano

Rosemary

Thyme

A Greek Herb and Spice Rack

ANITHO   Dill

BAHARI   Allspice

BASILIKOS   Basil (rare in Greek cuisine because of its religious significance)

DAPHNE   Bay Leaf (The distinctive flavor of bay or laurel enhances many Greek stews, meat, and fish dishes. In ancient times a wreath of laurel leaves was awarded to the victor of the Olympic Games.)

GARIFALO   Cloves

GLIKANISO   Anise (This is the source of *Ouzo's* licorice flavor.)

HAMOMILO   Chamomile (The flowers of this herb are brewed as a tea renowned for its medicinal properties.)

KANELLA   Cinnamon

KARDAMO   Cardamom

KIMINO   Cumin

MAHLEPI   Cherry-flavored seeds used in a variety of Greek cakes and breads.

MAINTANOS   Parsley

MARATHO   Fennel (Another source of licorice flavor, commonly used in soups, to process olives, and to pickle vegetables.)

MATZOURANA   Marjoram (Used for flavoring stews and fish dishes, marjoram is also brewed as a medicinal tea.)

MOSHOKARIDO   Nutmeg

PIPERI   Pepper

RIGANI   Oregano (The indispensable herb of Greece, oregano grows everywhere and is used in countless dishes.)

SKORTHO   Garlic

THENTHROLEVANO   Rosemary

THIOSMOS   Spearmint

THYMARI   Thyme (This aromatic herb is commonly used to flavor fish and meat dishes and is also the predominant flavor of Greece's most famous honey, that produced on Mount Hymettus near Athens.)

Retail Sources for Greek Products

ALABAMA

Hamilton Foods Co. Inc.
3607 1st Ave. So.
Birmingham 32501

Milton Grocery
1531 S. 13 Place
Birmingham 32501

Lignos Grocery
160 Government Street
Mobile 33602

Penny Profit Supermarket
837 S. Hull St.
Montgomery 36104

ARIZONA

Mercury Sales
3303 W. Osborn St.
Phoenix 85013

Niccolis Grocery
623 W. Pierson Ave.
Phoenix 85013

Southwestern Grocery
127/131 East Toole Ave.
Tucson 85711

The Gourmet
4128 North Oracle Rd.
Tucson 85702

ARKANSAS

Capitol Distributing Co.
1111 Autumn Rd.
Little Rock 72211

CALIFORNIA

C & K Importing Co.
2771 West Pico Blvd.
Los Angeles 93336

Gourmet Specialties
2550 McKinnon Ave.
San Francisco 94103

Greek American Food
  Specialty
223 Valencia St.
San Francisco 94103

Apollo Baklava
198 Guerraro St.
San Francisco 94103

Greek Village
800 Alhambra Blvd.
Sacramento 95816

A & G Market
1807 Robinson Ave.
San Diego 92103

CONNECTICUT

Manos Meat Market
2804 Fairfield Ave.
Bridgeport 06605

Milano's Deli
North Street Shopping Center
Danbury 06810

Conn. Macaroni Co.
1098 Main St.
East Hartford 06108

Gourmet Galley
100 Greenwich Ave.
Greenwich 06830

Spiros Farmington
246 Farmington Ave.
Hartford 06105

North Street Market
96 North St.
New Britain 06051

Naha's Grocery
89 Willets Ave.
New London 06320

Crown Supermarket
1168 Whalley Ave.
New Haven 06515

Steve's Market
157 Washington St.
Norwalk 06854

The Colonial Inn
220 Sound Beach Ave.
Old Greenwich 06870

Cheese Shops
Thruway Shopping Center
Riverside 06878

Fitzgerald's Super Market
710 Hopemeadow St.
Simsbury 06070

Farmer's Corner
1132 Main St.
Stamford 06902

Fairlawn Food Center
1132 Main St.
Stamford 06902

Appleton Co.
995 Farmington Ave.
West Hartford 06107

Gourmet Galley
261 East State St.
Westport 06880

DELAWARE

Say Cheese
14 Polly Drummond
Newark 19711

Calavrita Importing Co.
12 East 4 St.
Wilmington 19801

DISTRICT OF COLUMBIA

Hellas Greek Imports
1245 20 St. NW 20036

Marjack Co.
1816 Half St. SW 20036

FLORIDA

Mediterranean Deli
1001 West Oakland Pk. Blvd.
Ft. Lauderdale 33311

Fara Imported Foods
705 McDuff Ave.
Jacksonville 32205

Leonard's Wine
253 Commercial Blvd.
Lauderdale-by-the-Sea 33311

Greek American Grocery
2690 Coral Way
Miami 33145

Cacciatore Bros.
2301 West Buffalo Ave.
Tampa 33607

Barbers Imported Foods
613 N. Pinellas Ave.
Tarpon Springs 33589

Greek Islands Deli
501 Dedecanes Blvd.
Tarpon Springs 33589

Middle East Bakery
327 5th St.
West Palm Beach 33401

GEORGIA

Happy Herman's
2293 Cheshire Bridge Rd. NE
Atlanta 30324

IDAHO

University Bakery & Grocery
408 S. 4 St.
Pocatello 83201

ILLINOIS

Astro Grocery & Meat Market
309 S. Holstead St.
Chicago 66607

Athens Grocery
811 W. Jackson Blvd.
Chicago 66607

Koutavas Enterprises, Inc.
1651 Rand Rd.
Des Plaines 60016

INDIANA

Nicks Wholesale & Retail
   Produce
3844 Broadway
Gary 46408

Quality Foods Inc.
1830 Wayne Trace
Ft. Wayne 46803

Velona Italian Foods
103 City Market
Indianapolis 46219

IOWA

Graziano Bros.
1601 S. Union St.
Des Moines 50315

KENTUCKY

A. Thomas & Sons Meat
   Market
309 E. Jefferson
Louisville 40202

LOUISIANA

Central Grocery Co.
923 Decatur St.
New Orleans 70116

Sigmund's Inc.
5238 Florida Blvd.
Baton Rouge 70815

Gourmet World
2316 Clearle Ave.
Metairie 70002

MAINE

Commercial Fruit Store
47 India St.
Portland 04106

MARYLAND

Parthenon Foods
5414 S. Old Town St.
Baltimore 21224

Basil Bros. Food Market
6228 Eastern Ave.
Baltimore 21224

Chevy Chase Supermarkets,
   Ltd.
8531 Connecticut Ave.
Chevy Chase 20015

Aloupis Co.
5006 E. Buchanan St.
Hyattville 20781

Bloomingdale's
White Flint Mall
Kensington 20795

Mediterranean
558 Randolf Rd.
Rockville 20852

Thomas Market
2650 W. University Blvd.
Wheaton 20902

MASSACHUSETTS

Tripolis Grocery
133 Harvard Ave.
Allerton 02045

Pougarides Market
458 Massachusetts
Arlington 02174

Fami's Market
145 Malvery Rd.
Auburn 01501

Samas Importing
346 Tremont St.
Boston 02116

Anthony Greek Market
10 Central Sq.
Cambridge 02139

Milano Importing Co.
988 Main St.
Springfield 01103

Reliable Market
174 Chandler St.
Worcester 01609

George Fragakis
1420 Centre St.
Roslindale 02131

MICHIGAN

Athens Grocery
527 Monroe Ave.
Detroit 48226

Greek Town Market
571 E. Lafayette
Detroit 48204

Martorelli Imported Foods
726 S. Port Hwy.
Flint 48503

Roma Bakery & Import Foods
432 Cedar St.
Lansing 48912

G. B. Russo & Sons
1935 Eastern Ave. SE
Grand Rapids 43507

Mediterranean Foods
19822 Kelly Rd.
Harper Woods 48225

MINNESOTA

Morellis Supermarket
533 Collins St.
St. Paul 55101

International House
75 W. Island Ave.
Minneapolis 55401

MISSOURI

ABC Specialty Foods
5541 Fenton Dr.
Hazelwood 63044

La Rocca Grocery
815 E. 5 St.
Kansas City 64104

MISSISSIPPI

McCarm Holman
453 Mills St.
Jackson 39203

Delta Meat Co.
P.O. Box 149
Leland 38756

NEBRASKA

A. Marino Grocery
1716 S. 13 St.
Omaha 38756

NEW HAMPSHIRE

Co Op Food Store
43 S. Park St.
Hanover 03755

Hellenic Agora
110 Spruce St.
Manchester 03103

Superior Market
20½ South State St.
Concord 03301

NEW JERSEY

Cheese & Things
103 W. Allendale Ave.
Allendale 07401

Acropolis Grocery
1004 Main St.
Asbury Park 07712

Andrews Deli
305 Sewall Ave.
Asbury Park 07712

Jackson Super Market
4712 Ventnor Ave.
Atlantic City 08401

The Store Rest
55 S. Finley Ave.
Bay Head 08742

Bergenfield Farm
49 Main St.
Bergenfield 07621

Cheese Shop
641 Shunpike Rd.
Chatham 07928

Woodcock's Gourmet
60 E. Main St.
Chester 07930

Parthenon Gift Shop
344 Clifton Ave.
Clifton 07011

International Deli
272 Closter Dock Rd.
Closter 07624

Dick's Bakery
Rt. 46
Dover 07801

Olympos Food
Wood & Oaktree Rd.
Edison 08840

Gourmet Cheese
1413 Plaza Rd.
Fair Lawn 07410

Hiza Co., Inc.
95 Anderson Ave.
Fairview 07022

Fort Lee Cheese
1369 16th St.
Fort Lee 07024

Maria's Deli
1576 Anderson Ave.
Fort Lee 07024

Lambiro Grocery
26 South St.
Freehold 07728

Greek American Deli
257 South Ave.
Garwood 07027

Central Food
63 Main St.
Hackensack 07601

G & A Grocery
640 Holmdel Rd.
Hazlet 07730

Cheese & Things
Brook Plaza
Jackson 08527

P & M Food Center
317 Baldwin
Jersey City 07036

Royal Deli
730 Bergen Ave.
Jersey City 07036

Acropolis Gift Shop
220 Stuyvesant Ave.
Lyndhurst 07071

Henry's Deli
50½ Main St.
Madison 07940

Pantree Gourmet Shop
200 Franklin Ave.
Middle Park 07032

Cheeses & Spices
32 Essex St.
Milburn 07041

Cheese Shop
590 Valley Rd.
Montclair 07043

Cheese Shop
Moorestown Mall
Moorestown 08057

Gourmet Cheese
Main St.
Oldwick 08858

Orange Deli
357 Main St.
Orange 07050

Five Continents
Paramus Park Mall
Paramus 07652

Belmonte Import.
16-18 Fair St.
Paterson 07501

Fattal Syrian Bakery
977 Main St.
Paterson 07501

Famile Food Shop
153 Belmont Ave.
Paterson 07501

George's Meat
368 Getty Ave.
Paterson 07501

Cheese Junction
5 W. Ridgwood Ave.
Ridgewood 07450

Marvel's Gift Shop
41 E. Ridgewood Ave.
Ridgewood 07450

Olympia Foods
906 Kinderkamack Rd.
River Edge 07661

Bloomingdale's
Short Hills Mall
Short Hills 07078

Jugtown Smoke House
The Mall
Short Hills 07078

South Orange Gourmet
312 Irvington Ave.
South Orange 07079

Cheese & Gourmet Food
75 Union Place
Summit 07901

Cheese Gourmet
500 Cedar Lane
Teaneck 07666

Cedars Bakery
951 Teaneck Rd.
Teaneck 07666

Cheese Shop
31 Washington Ave.
Tenafly 07670

Gristede's Bros.
21 Washington Ave.
Tenafly 07670

Karen Food
393 Minnisink Rd.
Totowa 07512

Carmen Armenti's
13 N. Warren St.
Trenton 08608

California Market
74 E. Church St.
Washington 07882

Preakness Gourmet
Preakness Shop. Ctr.
Wayne 07470

Caldwell Cheese
758 Bloomfield Ave.
W. Caldwell 07006

Cheese Shop
149 Woodbridge Mall
Woodbridge 07095

Village Cheese Shop
397 Franklin Ave.
Wyckoff 07481

NEW YORK

Albany Frozen Foods
P.O. Box 5327
Albany 12205

M. Pellegrino Imp.
1117 Central Ave.
Albany 12205

Gourmet's Delights
1111 Main St.
Cold Spring Harbor 11724

The Bari Imp. Co.
146 Main St.
Cortland 13045

Cortland Food Store
154 Main St.
Cortland 13045

Freeport Deli
52 W. Merrick Rd.
Freeport 11520

Hellenic Gift Shop
25 N. Franklin St.
Hempstead 11550

Alpen Cheese Shop
Westchester Mall
Lake Mohegan 10547

The Cheese Shop
20 Chatsworth Ave.
Larchmont 10538

Cheese Villa
219 Sunrise Mall
Massapequa 11758

Mediterranean Deli
84 Merrick Ave.
Merrick 11566

Ardito Deli
160 Jericho Tpke.
Mineola 11501

Laraia's Imports
134 E. Rt. 59
Nanuet 10954

Anoula's Donut Shop
Mid Valley Mall
Newburgh 12550

Euro Continental
110 S. 2nd St.
New Hyde Park 11040

International Fine Foods
658 South Rd.
Poughkeepsie 12601

John Lembesis
26 Strait Ave.
Poughkeepsie 12603

The Cheese Shop
33 Purchase St.
Rye 10580

Cheese Shop
66 B Garth Rd.
Scarsdale 10583

Scarsdale Central Deli
656 Central Ave.
Scarsdale 10583

The Farm
415 Nottingham Rd.
Syracuse 13201

Phaedra Imports
109 Congress St.
Troy 12180

Jack Murad & Sons
241 James St.
Utica 13501

Mediterranean Pastries
361 S. Broadway
Yonkers 10705

NEW YORK CITY

BROOKLYN

Beirut Grocery
199 Atlantic Ave.
11201

Bay Ridge Fruit
477 60th St.
11220

Damascus Bakery
195 Atlantic Ave.
11201

Ellas American Imports
8704 4th Ave.
11209

Five Continents
King's Plaza Shop Ctr.
11234

Greek American Deli
2115 Avenue U
11229

Herschey Deli
548 Flatbush Ave.
11225

Jerusalem Grocery
517 Kings Hwy.
11223

Jimmy's Inter.
4910 20th Ave.
11204

Khasky Oriental Groc.
429 Avenue U
11223

Lucky Athens
7911 5th Ave.
11209

Malko Bros.
197 Atlantic Ave.
11201

Malko Importing
182 Atlantic Ave.
11201

Malko Grocery
150 Atlantic Ave.
11201

Near East Bakery
185 Atlantic Ave.
11201

Oriental American
5015 18th Ave.
11204

Setton Oriental Groc.
509 Kings Hwy.
11223

Sandy Grocery
6819 3rd Ave.
11220

7815 Food Market
7815 5th Ave.
11209

T & C Pork Store
1406 Avenue U
11220

Tripolis Grocery
5923 4th Ave.
11220

Tucillo Market
84-16 5th Ave.
11209

BRONX

Bissal Corp.
24-38 Jerome Ave.
10468

Cheese Shop
3536 Johnson Ave.
10463

Fordham Fruit Exch.
25 W. Fordham Rd.
10468

Cheese Shop
5910 Riverdale Ave.
10471

Riverdale Market
229 W. 231 St.
10463

S & D Pork Store
1720 Grosby Ave.
10461

MANHATTAN

A & K Deli
200 W. 50th St.
10020

Bloomingdale's
59th & Lexington Ave.
10022

Central Grocery
2843 Broadway
10025

Friendly Grocery
1420 St. Nicholas
10033

Garden of Delights
1192 Lexington Ave.
10028

International Market
529 9th Ave.
10018

Ideal Cheese
1205 2nd Ave.
10021

Java Coffee Corp.
1537 St. Nicholas Ave.
10033

Kassas Bros.
570 9th Ave.
10036

Kornig Tashjan Groc.
380 3rd Ave.
10016

Margarite's Grocery
390 8th Ave.
10001

Moschahlades Bros.
28-30 Moore St.
10004

Narlian Oriental Foods
1530 St. Nicholas Ave.
10033

P & G Deli
383 3rd Ave.
10016

Dan Olympos Food
302 W. 40th St.
10018

New International Market
517 9th Ave.
10018

Paradise Grocery
1480 St. Nicholas
10033

Shop Best
1451 St. Nicholas
10033

Tragos Deli
71 Sherman Ave.
10040

QUEENS

Apo & Artan Oriental
4203 Queens Blvd.
11104

Associated Foods
3715 31st Ave.
11103

Andom's Deli
2137 31st St.
11105

Armen Food
42-20 43rd Ave.
11104

California Fruit Market
3915 Bell Blvd.
11361

Corona Park Deli
1446 College Point
11356

Domand Deli
3808 Broadway
11103

Five Continents
9015 Queens Blvd.
11373

Florida Fruit Market
205-02 Hillside Ave.
11423

Flushing Market
159-27 Northern Blvd.
11358

Frind's Food Store
35-02 Ditmars Blvd.
11105

Gourmet Deli
7705 37th Ave.
11372

Greek American Deli
122-26 116th St.
11356

Herbert Cheese Co.
22-42 31st St.
11106

Hye Grocery
96-15 Metropolitan Ave.
11374

Ikaros Grocery
69-06 Woodside Ave.
11377

International Grocery
46-15 Queens Blvd.
11104

John's Deli
8303 37th Ave.
11372

John & Angelo
2903 Broadway
11106

Kalamata Import
38-01 Ditmars Blvd.
11105

Kyriakos Grocery
29-29 23rd Ave.
11105

Mediterranean Imp.
3320 30th Ave.
11103

Mediterranean Deli
85-02 Parsons Blvd.
11432

Merritt Farms
86-11 Rockaway Blvd.
11416

M & M Market
4101 National St.'
11368

Oriental Knishes
6379 Saunder St. & 63rd Dr.
11374

Pangi Deli
8334 Parsons Blvd.
11432

Panellinion Deli
3703 28th Ave.
11101

Perista Enterprises
122-26 Beach 116 St.
11420

Roumania Grocery
112-20 Queens Blvd.
11375

Superette
88-32 Sutphin Blvd.
11435

Sarkis
39-52 Queens Blvd.
11104

147 Blvd. Market
147-16 Northern Blvd.
11354

STATEN ISLAND

Hellenic Import Co.
81-83 Prospect St.
10304

NORTH CAROLINA

Stop & Shop
135 Haywood St.
Asheville 28801

Fowler's Food Store
306 W. Franklin St.
Chapel Hill 27514

East Trade Grocery
402 E. Trade St.
Charlotte 28202

Garden of Eden
423 Woodbern Rd.
Raleigh 27605

College Beverage
102 Radford St.
Winston-Salem 28801

NORTH DAKOTA

Mar-Son
9th Ave. & 21st St.
Minot 58701

OHIO

Bison's Inc.
2695 W. Market St.
Akron 44313

Canton Importing Co.
1136 Wertz N.W.
Canton 44708

La Rosa, Inc.
2411 Boudinot Ave.
Cincinnati 45238

Athens Pastries
2545 Lorain Ave.
Cleveland 44113

Athens Pastries & Frozen
   Foods
2097 Columbus Rd.
Cleveland 44113

Easy Living Cheese & Wine
   Shop
4016 E. Broad St.
Columbus 43213

OKLAHOMA

Nayphe's International Foods
7519 N. May Ave.
Oklahoma City 73116

American Pacific Co.
2320 N.W. 21st St.
Portland 97208

Portland Wholesale Grocery
3929 S.E. 26th Ave.
Portland 96202

PENNSYLVANIA

Stravino's
438 Washington St.
Allentown 18102

Nick Tatalias
1101 Linden Ave.
Allentown 18102

Giacomo Italian Specialty
1212 Washington St.
Easton 18042

Mandros Grocery
351 N. Charlotte St.
Lancaster 17603

Michael's Greek Grocery
930 Locust St.
Philadelphia 19147

Napoli Bella
924 S. 9th St.
Philadelphia 19147

Salino Importing Co.
925 Elm St.
Reading 19601

Thriftway Inc.
101 S. 69th St.
Upper Darby 19082

RHODE ISLAND

Athenian Market
999 Oaklawn Ave.
Cranston 02912

Near East Market
602 Reservoir Ave.
Cranston 02912

The Cheese Shoppe
176 Bellvue Ave.
Newport 02840

Bond Foods Inc.
10 Gary St.
Providence 02903

SOUTH CAROLINA

Five Points Deli
611 Harden St.
Columbia 29205

Murray Bros. Inc.
1649 Cox St.
Columbia 29202

Johnson's Greek Products
4630 D Vine St.
Columbia 29202

Cheros Food Products
201 Donington Dr.
Greenville 29615

Ankie's Continental Gourmet
404 McCrady Dr.
Spartanburg 29303

TENNESSEE

Shapiro's Inc.
723 Cherry St.
Chattanooga 37402

A & B Distributors
107 Randolph St.
Knoxville 37915

Barzizza Bros. Inc.
351 S. Front St.
Memphis 38101

TEXAS

Centennial Food Imports
2932 Guadeloupe St.
Austin 78701

The Common Market
304 W. 13th St.
Austin 78701

J. J. Cohen Sale Co.
318 Cadiz St.
Dallas 75231

Al's Food Store
8209 Park Cove
Dallas 75231

Antone Imp. Co.
807 Taft St.
Houston 77006

Sahadi Importing Co.
708 N. 10th St.
McAllen 78501

Cliff's Convenience Foods, Inc.
110 Blues Star St.
San Antonio 78204

UTAH

Broadway Shopping Center
24 E. Broadway
Salt Lake City 84111

Granato Imported Delicassies
758 S. 200 W.
Salt Lake City 84110

Mediterranean Market
3942 S. State
Salt Lake City 84107

VIRGINIA

Aphrodite Greek Import
5886 Leesburg Pike
Falls Church 22041

Excel Market
3230 Tidewater Rd.
Norfolk 23509

Nick's Produce
504 E. Marshall St.
Richmond 23219

Safeway Stores
3507 W. Cary St.
Richmond 23221

The New Yorker Deli
2802 Williamson Rd. N.W.
Roanoke 24012

WASHINGTON

De Laurenti Italian &
  International Food
1435 First Ave.
Seattle 98101

Gino's World Food Market
126 N. Washington St.
Spokane 99201

WEST VIRGINIA

Ellis Supermarket
917 Bridge Rd.
Charleston 25314

Mansour's Food Market
12th St. & 11th Ave.
Huntington 25701

Zack's Market
3840 Boone St.
Whitesville 25209

INDEX

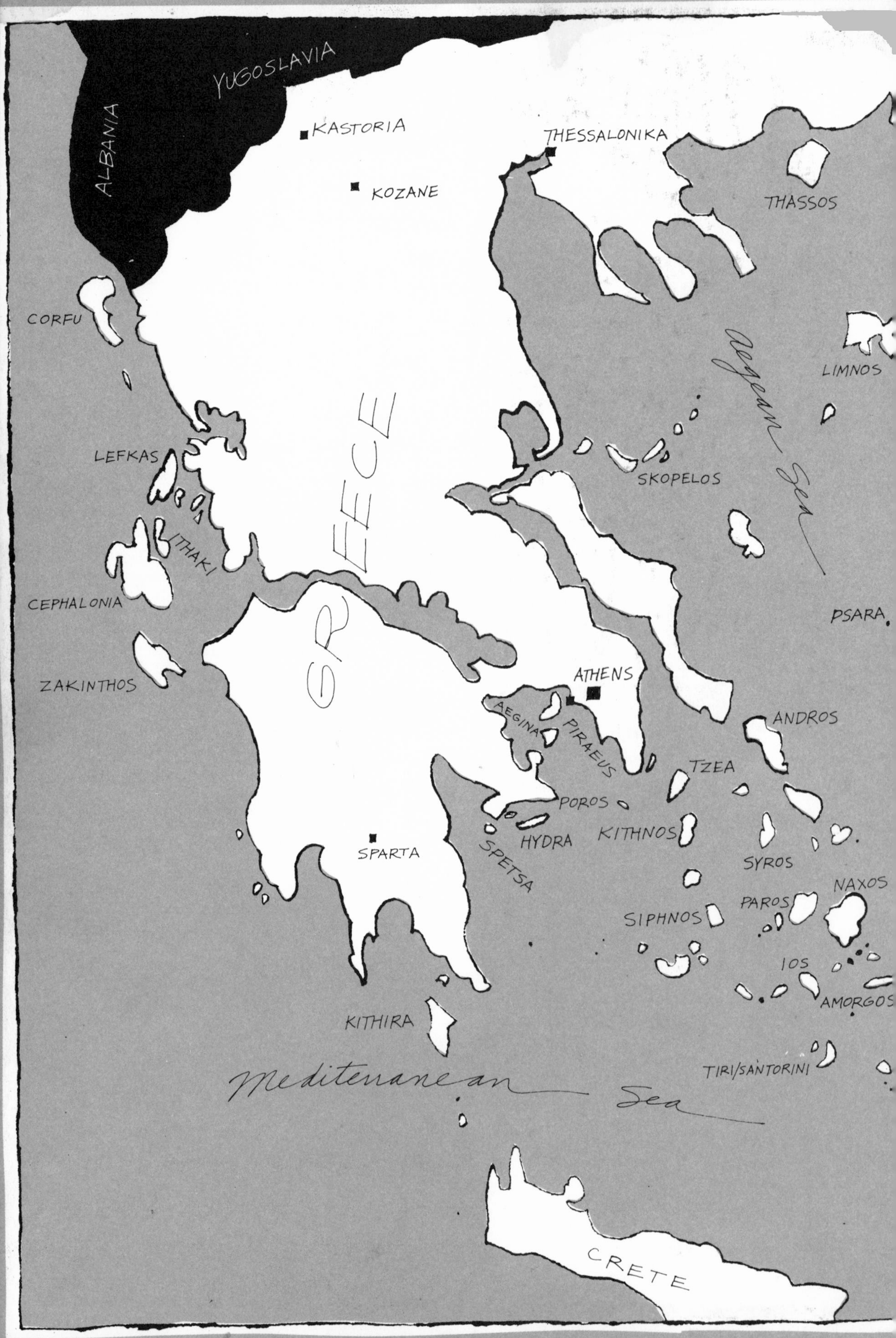
YUGOSLAVIA
ALBANIA
KASTORIA
THESSALONIKA
KOZANE
THASSOS
CORFU
LIMNOS
Aegean Sea
GREECE
LEFKAS
SKOPELOS
ITHAKI
CEPHALONIA
PSARA
ZAKINTHOS
ATHENS
AEGINA
PIRAEUS
ANDROS
TZEA
POROS
HYDRA
KITHNOS
SPETSA
SPARTA
SYROS
NAXOS
PAROS
SIPHNOS
IOS
AMORGOS
KITHIRA
TIRI/SANTORINI
Mediterranean Sea
CRETE